Internationalizing the Writing Center

Second Language Writing
Series Editor: Paul Kei Matsuda

Second language writing emerged in the late twentieth century as an interdisciplinary field of inquiry, and an increasing number of researchers from various related fields—including applied linguistics, communication, composition studies, and education—have come to identify themselves as second language writing specialists. The Second Language Writing series aims to facilitate the advancement of knowledge in the field of second language writing by publishing scholarly and research-based monographs and edited collections that provide significant new insights into central topics and issues in the field.

Books in the Series

Internationalizing the Writing Center: A Guide for Developing a Multilingual Writing Center by Noreen Groover Lape (2020)

Professionalizing Second Language Writing, edited by Paul Kei Matsuda, Sarah Elizabeth Snyder, and Katherine Daily O'Meara (2018)

Graduate Studies in Second Language Writing, edited by Kyle McIntosh, Carolina Pelaez-Morales, and Tony Silva (2015)

Scientific Writing in a Second Language by David Ian Hanauer and Karen Englander (2013)

Foreign Language Writing Instruction: Principles and Practices, edited by Tony Cimasko and Melinda Reichelt (2011)

Practicing Theory in Second Language Writing, edited by Tony Silva and Paul Kei Matsuda (2010)

Building Genre Knowledge by Christine M. Tardy (2009)

The Politics of Second Language Writing: In Search of the Promised Land, edited by Paul Kei Matsuda, Christina Ortmeier-Hooper, and Xiaoye You (2006)

INTERNATIONALIZING THE WRITING CENTER

A GUIDE FOR DEVELOPING A MULTILINGUAL WRITING CENTER

Noreen Groover Lape

Parlor Press
Anderson, South Carolina
www.parlorpress.com

Parlor Press LLC, Anderson, South Carolina, USA

© 2020 by Parlor Press
All rights reserved.
Printed in the United States of America
S A N: 2 5 4 - 8 8 7 9

Library of Congress Cataloging-in-Publication Data on File

1 2 3 4 5

Second Language Writing
Series Editor: Paul Kei Matsuda

Cover design by Paul Kei Matsuda and David Blakesley
Printed on acid-free paper.

Parlor Press, LLC is an independent publisher of scholarly and trade titles in print and multimedia formats. This book is available in paper, cloth and eBook formats from Parlor Press on the World Wide Web at http://www.parlorpress.com or through online and brick-and-mortar bookstores. For submission information or to find out about Parlor Press publications, write to Parlor Press, 3015 Brackenberry Drive, Anderson, South Carolina, 29621, or email editor@parlorpress.com.

Contents

Preface	*vii*
Introduction	*3*
1 Multilingual Writing Centers in Context	*14*
2 Holistic Tutoring Practices: Toggling Between the Parts and the Whole	*34*
3 Holistic Tutoring Practices: Creating a Supportive Learning Environment	*61*
4 Helping Writers Understand Writing Culture Shock and Develop Intercultural Competence	*77*
5 Working with Stakeholders to Develop and Administer a Multilingual Writing Center	*100*
6 Developing an MWC with Foreign Language Faculty	*125*
Appendix A: The Arc of a Tutoring Session	*147*
Appendix B: Directive and Nondirective Tutoring Techniques	*150*
Appendix C: Tutoring for Language Acquisition	*152*
Appendix D: Google Translate Exercise	*156*
Appendix E: Creating a Positive Learning Environment by Sharing Second Language Learning Experiences	*165*
Appendix F: Practicing Intercultural Competence in a Writing Center Session	*166*
Appendix G: What Would You Do? Holistic Tutoring Scenarios	*168*

Appendix H: Holly and Leila: A Problem-Based Learning Exercise	*171*
Appendix I: One-Day Tutor Training Agenda and Monthly Staff Training Schedule	*185*
Notes	*187*
Works Cited	*193*
About the Author	*207*
Index	*209*

Preface

The main character of this book, so to speak, is the Norman M. Eberly Multilingual Writing Center (MWC), which I direct. The MWC has a feature that is unique among writing centers: peer writing tutoring in eleven languages. Established as an English writing center in 1978, the MWC grew to include foreign language (FL) writing tutoring in 2009. Currently, writing tutors assist writers in Arabic, Chinese, English, French, German, Hebrew, Italian, Japanese, Portuguese, Russian, and Spanish. In the first year of operation, FL writing tutors facilitated 819 sessions; in the last seven years, the MWC has averaged approximately 1550 sessions per year in languages other than English.

It is becoming more common to hear about writing centers that provide tutoring in languages other than English. Members of the WCENTER listserv regularly post queries about FL writing tutoring though, it seems, many centers are in the pilot stage, offering language assistance only when their English writing tutors happen to be multilingual. As Pam Bromley, a writing center administrator (WCA) in the US, shared:

> We do consultations with students in languages other than English—what languages depends on what languages the current staff have. Always French and Spanish, often Korean, Russian, and Chinese. We match students with an appropriate tutor by hand–I'd say we do at least 50 of these consultations a year. We underscore that the assistance we offer is geared towards HOCs [higher order concerns]—coming up with a thesis, restructuring the paper. If students want help with their grammar or sentence construction, we refer them to our language lab. It is a bit of an awkward division, but it has worked well enough for us.

Beyond such anecdotal reports, it is difficult to find models of FL writing tutoring practice. Foreign languages are rarely mentioned on US writing center websites. (Conversely, as I will examine in chapter one, the majority of writing centers outside the US support English). Yet every few months a WCA seeks information on WCENTER about FL writing tutoring practices. For example, Ann Gardiner, who directs a writing center in Switzerland, wrote:

> I am new to this list and really appreciate the many conversations taking place here! These conversations have helped tremendously as the Writing and Learning Center where I work in Switzerland takes on new responsibilities. One of these new developments is a language tutoring program, similar to our writing tutor program. My colleague and I are having difficulty finding training materials specifically aimed at language tutoring. The tutors work closely with professors in 100-level Italian, French, and German languages, the languages of Switzerland.
>
> Does anyone have any ideas about resources for training language tutors? We do continuous training at the moment and are borrowing much from well-known works for writing tutors. Any ideas would be much appreciated.

Gardiner's request for help "finding training materials specifically aimed at language tutoring" no doubt arises from her awareness that "borrowing much from well-known works for writing tutors," presumably of English, has its limits. Bromley hints at the limitations when she mentions the "awkward division" between the writing center, which assists with higher-order concerns, and the language lab, which handles, to use English writing center lingo, lower- or later-order concerns. Queries, like these, for information about FL writing tutor training have generated frequent conversation despite the lack of literature on the subject.

As I built the MWC, I decided to make it my own research laboratory where I could study FL writing tutoring from the perspectives of writers, tutors, and faculty and perhaps even propose a model that draws on writing center scholarship while acknowledging the singularities of FL learning. I read widely in writing center, second language acquisition, and FL writing studies and attended regional and national conferences. My goal was to create an MWC model that was not only theorized but also sustainable—that is, financially supported and not limited to the multilingual abilities of a constantly changing English writing staff (more on that in chapter five). As word got out, WCAs and tutors interested in incorporating FL writing tutoring into their centers began to contact me from places like Fairfield University, Jackson State University, University of Iowa, Muhlenberg College, Penn State, Dartmouth College, DePauw University, and UCLA, among others. In fact, this project grew out of my many conversations with WCAs, tutors, and FL faculty from across the country who wanted to know how the MWC developed. Their questions served as heuristics as I wrote this book:

- How many hours of FL writing tutoring do you provide per week?
- How many FL writing tutors do you employ, and what are their language backgrounds?
- How does the MWC work structurally? How are the English and FL writing center staffs integrated?
- How are the FL professors involved in the MWC?
- Do you offer separate training for monolingual English and FL writing tutors?
- Is the training for each language individualized, or are all FL writing tutors trained together?
- How do FL writing tutors assist with error correction without helping too much?
- How does the MWC now make you think about multilingualism, translingualism, and the intercultural experience?

After several conversations that followed a similar script, it occurred to me that I was continually reproducing an oral text that disappeared into the ether when the call ended or the talk concluded. Perhaps—I thought to myself—I should write this down. In crafting this book project, I have tried to address the thoughtful questions of my interlocutors.

When the MWC was in its earliest stages, I was anxious about being asked one question in particular: as director of the MWC, what was my language background? In fact, I am not bilingual, although for several years I was a second and even third language learner, which enabled me to experience the language acquisition process. Throughout my schooling, I studied Spanish and French and passed reading exams in both languages as a requirement for the PhD. Still, I never actually achieved proficiency, and so I was nervous about undertaking the MWC project. Not having mastered a second language, I wondered if I could be effective, specifically when training FL writing tutors. Despite my reservations, I took on the project because, as I detail in chapter five, the idea came from a FL faculty member, and several of her FL colleagues believed it would address a need in the writing culture. What's more, my institution is a leader in global education, and the MWC complemented our global education strategic goals.

I can now speak to the fact that WCAs need not be bilingual—just collaborative—to build a successful MWC. To echo what we WCAs tell our writing center staffs, just as writing tutors do not have to be experts in all disciplines to assist writers, administrators do not need to be experts in all areas—second language acquisition, FL pedagogy, intercultural competence, sociocultural knowledge—to create the MWC model. There is no one person who could speak all eleven languages, know all the cultures, and master all the research surrounding this topic. Instead, the work of creating an MWC draws on core writing center values: collaboration and teamwork. To fill in the gaps when it comes to issues of FL pedagogy and second language acquisition, WCAs can rely on their FL colleagues. To consider the dynamics of a FL writing session, they can listen to the insights of the writing tutors. In turn, WCAs trained in English-centric writing center pedagogy can contribute their knowledge of writing centers, tutor training, writing studies, and second language acquisition. Through the collaborative and inclusive work that forms the core of our ethos, WCAs can create and sustain an MWC.

Acknowledgments

Speaking of collaboration, this book exemplifies how writing is a social act. The idea for the MWC came about in a meeting with FL departments in 2009; later, the plan to write a book grew out of the many emails, phone calls, and face-to-face encounters that I had with WCAs and writing tutors across the country. In establishing (and now sustaining) the MWC at Dickinson, I work with an amazing and committed group of colleagues, most of them in the foreign languages, who value second language writing, believe in the benefits of cross-disciplinary collaboration, and support the MWC at every turn. In alphabetical order, I thank Mark Aldrich, Elise Bartosik-Velez, Alex Bates, Samantha

Brandauer, Carolina Castellanos, Alyssa DeBlasio, Lucile Duperron, Margaret Frohlich, Nitsa Kann, Luca Lanzilotta, Junjie Luo, Nan Ma, Nicoletta Marini-Maio, Sarah McGaughey, Akiko Meguro, Mariana Past, Sonja Paulson, Antje Pfannkuchen, Magda Siekert, Luca Trazzi, and Lisa Wolff. We would not have been able to get the MWC off the ground without the generous support of Dickinson College, and for that I am particularly obliged to Neil Weissman, Provost and Dean of the College. I would be remiss if I did not acknowledge the generosity of the MWC's patrons, Joseph and Shirley Eberly, who have been "paying it forward" to generations of Dickinson students on behalf of Joseph's father, Norman M. Eberly, class of 1924.

Equally important, I am grateful to my writing center team at Dickinson: Carol Wetzel and John Katunich. Carol's top-notch skills as a coordinator and her rapport with the writing tutors makes our MWC a productive and positive environment. John's knowledge of multilingual writers and thoughtful mentoring style enable him to provide strong support for the staff and a vision for future growth.

Needless to say, the talented, multilingual FL writing tutors who built the MWC—too numerous to name—receive my deepest gratitude. Many offered crucial feedback as we worked out the kinks and theorized our mission and training. Some had more of a direct influence on this book, contributing to its key insights: Ellen Aldin, Rinaldys Castillo, Anna Ciriani-Dean, Kathleen Getaz, Leigh Harlow, Julien Herpers, Gabrielle Kushlan, Diane Lee, Elizabeth Pineo, Audrey Schlimm, Orli Segal, Sagun Sharma, Christina Socci, Mackenzie Stricklin, Kat Swantak, Nadia Tivvis, Tram Ton, Katherine Welch, and A.J. Wildey. Besides these dedicated Dickinson students, the MWC benefitted from the work of exchange students, otherwise known as Overseas Assistants. There were several who took my 2018 course "Working with Writers: Theory and Practice" (FL writing version) and allowed me to try out parts of the book on them: Federico Corradini, Gaston Dorigutti, Maksim Gaetskii, Manuela Hernandez, Eléa Kayiranga Lionnet, and Renato Santos de Medeiros.

The International Writing Center Association supported this project with a timely research grant, making it possible for me to hire a transcriber. (For anyone looking for a good transcriber, I recommend Karen Myers.) In addition, the Dickinson College Research and Development committee provided funds to hire an indexer. I appreciate the energetic encouragement of Mickey Harris who published my early work on the MWC, "Going Global, Becoming Translingual: The Development of a Multilingual Writing Center," in *Writing Lab Newsletter*. Mickey later nominated the article, and it was ultimately included in *The Best of the Independent Rhetoric and Composition Journals 2014*. As I worked on that article, I received insightful feedback from Janet Auten, then co-editor of *WLN*. Also, pieces of "The Worth of the Writing Center: Numbers, Value, Culture, and the Rhetoric of Budget Proposals," published in *Praxis: A Writing Center Journal*, made their way into the book. I thank the anonymous readers of that manuscript for their feedback. Carol Severino read some early drafts, suggested scholarly articles, and shared insights that helped me revise. She piloted chapter two, "Holistic Tutoring Practices: Toggling between the Parts and the Whole," in her tutor training course at the University of Iowa. Her student Emilia Illana Mahiques also read that chapter and offered a very helpful critique.

As the manuscript started to take shape, I benefitted from the input of my writing group at Dickinson College: Liz Lewis, Sherry Ritchie, and Sarah Kersh. Although we were from different disciplines, we formed an accountability group, helping each other stay focused on our research agendas and motivated to write. In one of our meetings when I was sharing my jumbled thoughts about translating, Sherry Ritchie's questions came with a whoosh of insight that knocked my argument into place. I was lucky to find a peer review partner like Sarah Kersh, who offered the most thoughtful feedback on every chapter. A kind and attentive reader, she showed me how imagining a receptive audience, as she was to me, can motivate a writer. In the final stages of the writing process, I was lucky to have the expert assistance of David Blakesley, editor of Parlor Press; Paul Kei Matsuda, editor of the series on Second Language Writing; and Ben Rafoth, a thoughtful and incisive peer reviewer.

At last, I want to thank my family for their encouragement and care. Dale, Miranda, and Noah—you are the best, the intellectual and emotional support for my writing life. Noah, I promised I would dedicate this one to you, so there it is Bucko.

INTERNATIONALIZING THE WRITING CENTER

Introduction

In an increasingly internationalized world and, correspondingly, an increasingly internationalized academia, writing centers are always already multilingual. For several decades, US writing center scholars have been studying international students, bilinguals, and/or heritage speakers who bring different languages, cultures, and rhetorics into their *English* tutoring sessions. This book is about the other multilingual writers—those who are becoming writers in languages other than English. Of the 470 colleges and universities that responded to the most recent National Census of Writing, 30 percent reported that their writing centers offer assistance with writing in languages other than English. This book puts forth a rationale, a pedagogical plan, and an administrative method to maximize the potential of our writing centers' nascent multilinguality.

Entering the Conversation

When I was planning the MWC with my language faculty colleagues, I expected to find at least a few articles on FL writing tutoring in the scholarly literature. In fact, I found none–not in writing center, or second language, or FL writing studies. While there is quite a body of scholarship on tutoring second language writers in English, I could not locate any published research on tutoring writers in languages other than English–at least not research written in English. As yet, there have been no published discussions in US academic journals about the ways "native" English, multilingual English, and FL writing tutor training overlap and vary from each other. I hoped to begin that conversation with my 2013 article "Going Global, Becoming Translingual: The Development of a Multilingual Writing Center" in the *Writing Lab Newsletter*.

My aim has been to expand on that piece and create a book that would be useful to WCAs, scholars, and writing tutors; and US and non-US-based FL administrators and teachers. With its unique focus on FL writing tutoring, this book extends the work on second language tutoring of multilingual writers of English. Books like Shanti Bruce's and Ben Rafoth's *ESL Writers: A Guide for Writing Center Tutors*, which was updated in 2016 and renamed *Tutoring Second Language Writers*, and Dudley W. Reynolds's *One on One with Second Language Writers: A Guide for Writing Tutors, Teachers, and Consultants* provide practical suggestions for working with multilingual writers whose target language is English. More recently, Ben Rafoth's *Multilingual Writers and Writing Centers* draws on second language acquisition research as it prepares monolingual students to work with multilingual writers in English-centric writing centers. Following these models, this book converses with second language acquisition theorists (most notably, second language writing and foreign language writing) to tease out FL writing tutoring practices—all in an effort to appeal to WCAs who wish to include other languages or may already be doing so in their writing centers.

This book would also be useful to scholars and practitioners in FL writing, a subfield of second language acquisition. Melinda Reichelt points out that there are relatively few works about FL writing—with the notable exception of research in English as a foreign language ("Toward"). However, the FL writing community continues to grow and produce more work (Reichelt et al.). Two recent edited collections are central to this book: *Foreign Language Writing Instruction* by Tony Cimasko and Melinda Reichelt, and *Handbook of Second and Foreign Language Writing* by Rosa M. Manchon and Paul Kei Matsuda. *Internationalizing the Writing Center* contributes to the burgeoning field of FL writing and would be of interest to those seeking to develop curriculum and support student learning.

GIVING VOICE TO WRITING TUTORS

The book also seeks to draw attention to the productive contributions of multilingual writers and tutors who actively shape the writing center community. In my MWC, those tutors can be both native and nonnative speakers, including domestic students (some of whom are heritage speakers or bilinguals), matriculated international students, and foreign exchange students. Among this group, there are international nonnative English speakers who are English writing tutors; US nonnative speakers of foreign languages who are writing tutors in their target languages; and both matriculated international students and foreign exchange students who tutor writing in their native languages and, in some cases, their second or even third languages. Because the MWC is conceived of as an inclusive space that employs a wide variety of language users, it openly flouts the privileging of "native" and the concomitant delegitimizing and marginalizing of "nonnative" speakers (Higgins 616-17). The MWC vitiates "native speakers' power and sense of superiority over those who feel othered by it" (Rafoth 44-45). In fact, native speaker privilege undermines the mission of the MWC when it causes students to avoid learning other languages for fear that they will never be able to speak (or write) correctly (i.e., like a native). Native speaker privilege is potentially reified in the MWC if writers disesteem tutors who are not native speakers (Rafoth 44-45). Neither a problem nor a liability nor the manifestation of linguistic deficiency, multilinguality is, instead, a solution, a capability, and a strength that makes possible a pedagogy that internationalizes the writing center.

Not only do these multilingual writing tutors create an inclusive learning environment, but they also shape MWC pedagogy. This book spotlights and celebrates their contributions. Sue Dinitz and Jean Kiedaisch note how early "theoretical constructions of writing centers" had "largely left out . . . tutor voices" (63). This book embodies a "listening tour," as it is populated with the voices of FL writing tutors (and, in the last chapter, faculty) from surveys, interviews, and session logs. I privilege tutor narratives over direct observations of tutoring sessions because I have chosen to position writing tutors as the producers of knowledge as opposed to the objects of knowledge (Boquet 18). As Beth Bouquet observes, when tutors are "objectified and essentialized in the literature devoted to them," they "are disallowed a voice in the literature that pertains most directly to them" (18). In this book, I aim to faithfully represent not only the insights I derived from their work but also the insights they generously shared with me as we collectively sought to build an effective MWC.

A Rationale for the MWC

Chapter one speaks to WCAs who are intrigued by the idea of an MWC but wonder why they would want to disrupt the traditional English-centered model. Examining three key political positions on language, the chapter challenges the language politics of English-centric writing centers and theorizes a justification and rationale for MWCs. First, globalization has resulted in the establishment of English as the lingua franca of scholarship and commerce, thus the prevalence of English-centric writing centers throughout the world. An analysis of websites from the International Writing Center Association directory reveals that MWCs are atypical, and English-centric writing centers ubiquitous even in countries in which English is not the official language. Second, writing studies scholars who identify themselves as translingualists embrace linguistic and discursive hybridity, privileging "heterogeneous, fluid, and negotiable" language and a "more tolerant and accommodating" view of error (Horner, Lu, Royster, and Trimbur 305, 306). Although a translingual approach can go awry when it conflicts with individual writers' learning outcomes, translingualism provides a useful lens for viewing the FL writing process. Third, entities within the US government and the European Union resist a common language and argue that linguistic diversity is central to understanding foreign cultures in the era of globalization. While English-centric writing centers enable the vision of a common language and translingualist pedagogy inculcates linguistic hybridity, MWCs support linguistic diversity by countering monolingualism in global (the writing center community) and local (the individual session) contexts.

A Pedagogy for the MWC

For WCAs who are planning to support or are already including FL writing tutoring in their centers, chapters two, three, and four address tutor training vis a vis the concept of holistic tutoring. Like a traditional writing center, an MWC is not focused solely on proofreading, editing, or linguistic correctness. While holistic FL writing tutors do not shy away from assisting with grammatical correctness, they are trained to consider the complexities of learning to write in a foreign language. Thus, these chapters theorize the practice of holistic tutoring by exploring how holistic writing tutors interrelate (rather than hierarchize) global and sentence-level concerns; evaluate the functionality of the writer's process and its impact on linguistic output; fashion a positive learning environment; and explore the relationship between writing and culture. Along with the appendices, these chapters include practical tips and exercises that WCAs can use in tutor training.

Chapter two rests on the assumptions that best practices for FL writing tutors differ from those of "native" language writing tutors because many FL writers are simultaneously acquiring a language and learning to write. The traditional strategy of offering feedback to native language writers is hierarchical—first higher-order concerns and then lower-order/late-order concerns. This chapter questions the effectiveness of that binary with FL writers and poses, as an alternative, the first aspect of holistic tutoring: the toggling between higher-order concerns and lower-order concerns with an awareness of their interconnection. It discusses how FL writing tutors can engage in holistic practices through techniques like noticing, hypothesis testing, metalinguistic awareness, and negotiated interaction. The chapter then discusses the holistic interplay between form, meaning, and writing process. While some FL writers truncate the writing process into two steps (composing and editing) or three (composing in the first language, translating into the second language, and then editing), holistic writing tutors enlarge writers' repertoires of process skills. Tutors can assist writers who draft in the first language and then translate into the target language by distinguishing between translating and composing—that is, thinking not in terms of literal words but in terms of meaning. By tracing problems with the written product back to the writer's process and exploring the interplay between language acquisition and writing, FL writing tutors can help writers make connections between the parts and the whole.

Chapter three extends the discussion of "holistic" tutoring to the whole person by focusing on how to create a positive learning environment so as to prevent or buffer the very real phenomenon of FL anxiety. Because a learning environment either exacerbates or soothes anxiety, FL writing tutors can intentionally build a foundation upon which language learning flourishes. Foreign language writing tutors can be trained proactively to create a supportive relationship with writers rather than reactively respond to "difficult" writers, especially given the fact that anxious writers are not always easy to spot from mere observation. Such an approach focuses tutors on what they can control (learning environment) rather than on what they cannot control (emotional writers). This chapter will explain the obstacles FL anxiety creates for language learners and then offer tips for creating a supportive learning environment that attenuates anxiety. The chapter ends with four case studies that can be used in tutor training from FL writing tutors who created different kinds of supportive learning environments in response to writers with different emotional needs.

Chapter four considers yet another dimension of holistic tutoring—the connection between the writer and the target culture. Foreign language writing assignments tend to task writers with acquiring cultural knowledge, addressing cultural audiences, and/or understanding intercultural rhetoric. In an MWC that seeks to be truly internationalized, FL writing tutors, particularly those who have studied abroad, may need to mediate "writing culture shock." First, drawing on interviews with students who have studied abroad in a foreign language, I analyze the conditions that create writing culture shock—namely, culture-specific academic genres and conventions, absence of support for the writing process, and conflicting definitions of "good writing." Then I suggest ways tutors can help writers develop the intercultural competence that will enable them to reframe their shock and navigate a new writing culture.

To complement the various pedagogical discussions in these chapters, this book also contains an FL writing tutor training guide that parses out the ways in which foreign language differs from other forms of writing tutor training. While the middle chapters are replete with tutoring tips and illustrative case studies, the appendices contain a variety of training exercises. The exercises are composed in English so that they can be used when training multilingual tutors who share English as a common language. Appendices A and B introduce FL writing tutors to tutoring fundamentals. Appendix A, "The Arc of a Tutoring Session," provides a script and a procedure to help new tutors navigate the beginning, middle, and end of a writing tutoring session. For example, the arc begins:

Before the session, read the appointment form on WCONLINE.

- Why is it important to know what the writer will bring to the session and what the writer wants to work on?
- Why is it important to know how long after the scheduled session the assignment is due?
- Why is it important to know if the writer's goals for learning the target language go beyond meeting the graduation requirement?

WCONLINE is subscription software that many writing centers use for online scheduling of appointments and for record keeping. When a writer makes an appointment, WCONLINE provides an appointment form that WCAs can customize to collect information for tutors. At the MWC I direct, we ask writers the typical questions about what they will bring to the session, what they want to work on, and the length of time until the due date; we also ask about their long-term plans, if any, for learning the language. During training, we discuss how a writer's answers to these questions can affect the writer's performance and the tutor's approach to the session. As we review the rest of the "Arc of the Tutoring Session," we discuss the purpose of each stage and the rationale for the associated techniques.

Appendix B, "Directive and Nondirective Tutoring Techniques," makes FL writing tutors think about their conversational technique. In line with current best practices, the exercise does not favor one technique over the other; instead, it is designed to make tutors apprehend the strategic use of both techniques. As Carol Severino and Jane Cogie have shown, the directive and nondirective debate has been "redefined by writing center discussion of language acquisition theory (459)." They conclude that second language writing tutors would benefit from determining "what combination of [directive and nondirective] styles most fosters the tutor's role as cultural and language informant and helps L2 students progress as language learners and writers" (459). They also point out that directive feedback given to maximize "comprehensibility and effectiveness" can also be potentially "face threatening" to writers from some cultures (461). In Exercise I, tutors revise a series of directive feedback statements—first nondirectively, and then directively but with attention to politeness and comprehensibility. Exercise II presents two authentic scenarios and asks FL writing tutors to identify the underlying problem and posit an approach using directive, nondirective, or a combination of techniques.

The exercises in Appendices C and D seek to operationalize tutors' use of second language acquisition techniques. In Appendix C, "Tutoring for Language Acquisition," Scenarios A and B focus on the FL writing tutor cases analyzed in chapter two. In both scenarios, the tutors explain through examples their practice of "holistic tutoring." The exercise prompts tutors-in-training to apply the concepts of holistic tutoring, noticing, hypothesis testing, and metalinguistic awareness to the examples. Scenario C provokes discussion on the most effective role of an FL writing tutor and how the strategic use of the aforementioned second language acquisition techniques can be a means to constructing that role. In Scenario D, a brief essay on world religion written by a second language writer, tutors examine how they might use negotiated interaction to begin a discussion with the writer.

Given the argument in chapter three that Google Translate presents an obstacle to the development of a functional FL writing process, the exercise in Appendix D aims to make FL writing tutors aware of when a piece of writing has been Google translated. The exercise is particularly powerful when the multilingual tutors discuss together the Google translate output of the same English passage, noting the evidence of Google Translator across languages as well as the evidence that is unique to languages or language groups. Once FL writing tutors are aware of essays that have been Google translated, chapter two offers strategies for helping writers develop a more functional writing process.

Appendices E and F coincide with chapters three and four respectively. Appendix E, "Creating a Positive Learning Environment: Sharing Second Language Learning Experiences," is an exercise in metacognitive reflection—a series of heuristic questions that prompt tutors to reflect on the hurdles they encountered when learning a second language. In *How Humans Learn,* Joshua R. Eyler makes a compelling case rooted in evolutionary science for the power of social pedagogies, like "peer instruction." Synthesizing research from multiple disciplines, he concludes that "crucial to students' educational experiences is their sense of social belonging" (84). As the tutors fashion their own narratives of struggle and resilience and practice them with each other, they discover the empathy that enables them to form connections with writers and invite them into the community of language learners. Appendix F, "Practicing Intercultural Competence in a Writing Center Session," contains two exercises that challenge tutors to investigate the connection between academic writing and culture. Focusing on a writing center session transcript, Exercise I asks tutors to identify the "critical event" and the cultural context, and then to formulate a new interpretation. Exercise II, another example of metacognitive reflection, encourages tutors to reflect on a piece of writing produced in colleges/universities in different countries, analyze how standards of "good" writing differ (or not) across cultures, and consider how those differences affect FL writing tutoring practices.

The final two appendices, G and H, present broad scenarios that challenge tutors to think holistically about the tips and techniques discussed throughout the book. The scenarios in both appendices are examples of problem-based learning in that they are drawn from authentic FL writing tutor experiences and are "ill-structured problems." Ill-structured problems are "open to interpretation" because they "possess an indefinite number of solution paths" (Jonassen and Hung 13, 15). Thus, these scenarios aim to provoke discussion and creative problem-solving. Appendix G, "What Would You Do? Holistic Tutoring Scenarios," is a collection of short vignettes, as told by FL writing tutors, that are organized by theme: sentence-level, essay-level, and FL writing anxiety. Tutors could reflect on different vignettes in writing, discuss them in small or large groups, and/or use them as prompts for mock tutoring. Appendix H, "Holly and Leila: A Problem-Based Learning Exercise," includes the transcript of an authentic session between a US writing tutor and a French exchange student. The transcript is in five sections: reading out loud, cultural differences in writing, holistic tutoring, negotiating meaning, re-assuring the writer, and articulating a revision plan. Since problem-based learning is a student-centered technique, prior to a large group discussion facilitated by the WCA, small groups of tutors can read the transcript one section at a time and then pause to discuss the question that appears at each section break.

An Administrative Approach to the MWC

For WCAs ready to move beyond piloting FL writing tutoring and build an administrative framework, chapter five offers guidance on how to expand an English-centric writing center into an MWC by securing stakeholders—namely, senior academic administrators and FL faculty. To persuade senior administrators, the chapter addresses three types of appeals: the *quantitative appeal*, which employs descriptive statistics; the *value-added quantitative appeal*, based on assessment data that measures ways in which the writing center adds value to students' learning experiences; and the *value-added cultural appeal*, which uses qualitative evidence grounded in an understanding of the writing culture and the mission of the institution to (re)imagine the worth of the writing center. To examine how the value-added qualitative appeal works, this chapter details how to conduct an ethnographic assessment of the writing culture in order to craft proposals and enter budget talks strategically and persuasively. In building relationships with FL faculty, the chapter discusses the importance of constructing a sustainable infrastructure through the creation of a faculty advisory committee composed of members from the FL departments, the writing program, and other relevant offices (like global education). As the MWC comes to fruition, the purpose of the committee evolves from planning to advising. Ultimately, to sustain the MWC, the committee ideally becomes a community of practice that not only deliberates about administrative issues but also participates in faculty development—in this case, by engaging in conversations that interrogate the interplay between writing center pedagogy, classroom practice, and the development of writing ability.

For WCAs who wish to start by broaching the subject of an MWC with FL colleagues, chapter six can serve as a conversation prompt. Based on interviews with six experienced FL faculty, the final chapter analyzes how the MWC can support and even enhance the goals of communicative language teaching, the predominant FL pedagogy since the mid-twentieth century. Communicative language teaching stresses communication (as opposed to grammar instruction) and views speaking, listening, reading, and writing as interrelated. The chapter appeals to the community of practice and urges WCAs and FL faculty to be open to a reciprocal relationship. On the one hand, WCAs will need to learn about mainstream FL pedagogy and allow for the presence of FL writers to modify writing center practices. On the other hand, FL faculty will need to learn how to improve the ways they teach writing—an area in which many have not been trained. The final chapter, then, examines how faculty shape the MWC and how the MWC, in turn, shapes the culture of writing in FL courses.

While writing this book, I came across these words from the International Writing Center Association's 2010 "Position Statement on Racism, Anti-Immigration, and Linguistic Intolerance": "As institutions committed to the democratization of education on university campuses, writing centers are invested in promoting social justice." Throughout our collective history, writing centers have been concerned with social justice. According to Paul Gillespie and Neal Lerner, "a powerful influence on the development of writing centers" was "the presence of students underprepared for higher education" (143). The writing center community's social justice commitment broadened from addressing under-preparedness to combating racism, sexism, homophobia, and ableism, among others. I write this book at a time when blatant acts of linguicism in US culture are undergirded by angrily flagrant discourses of nationalism, isolationism, and xenophobia. I hope to appeal to those WCAs, writing tutors, and FL faculty who believe in the power of languages to shape our lives, individually and collectively, and see in their writing centers the promise of "thinking globally, acting locally."

1 Multilingual Writing Centers in Context

Internationalizing the Writing Center: A Guide for Developing a Multilingual Writing Center theorizes a sustainable plan for a new type of writing center that is internationalized and multilingual. I intentionally used the word "internationalizing" to emphasize the difference between globalized/English-centric and internationalized/multilingual writing centers (MWCs). Globalized writing centers exist in colleges and universities throughout the world to help writers master English and North American academic writing. Internationalized MWCs, which are much less common, support writers who wish to become literate in languages and discourses besides English. Economist Herman E. Daly uses a colorful metaphor to define globalization: "The disintegration of the national egg is necessary to integrate the global omelette" (32). Internationalized MWCs keep the "national eggs" intact.

Another key term in the title is "multilingual." In writing center research, "multilingual" describes writers proficient in more than one language who write in English-centric contexts. While there are numerous examples, consider two recent ones: a 2015 book and a 2016 article. In *Multilingual Writers and Writing Centers,* Ben Rafoth addresses "directors and tutors" who "work with international multilingual students in the United States, or in any context where English is the dominant language" (1). Similarly, Liliana M. Naydan considers multilingual writers who are Generation 1.5—that is, domestic students studying in US institutions but whose home language is not English. Both critique the social and political inequities inherent in monolingualism as they make their case for new pedagogies that address the growing number of multilingual writers. Rafoth questions the assumption that English monolingualism is normative, asserting that it "grows among racial and cultural stereotypes on the hard clay of ignorance and isolation" (16). Naydan argues for rethinking the "master narrative" of "monolingual hegemony" that values tutors who speak English over writers who "need to learn English." Naydan calls for the creation of a "new narrative" for tutors and writers—one that recognizes "complex and hybridized" linguistic selves, "multiliteracies," and "liminal ways of thinking and working in the world" (29, 33). She theorizes a "translingual" writing center practice, specifically suited for "an ever-globalizing twenty-first century" in which writers and tutors move between multiple languages (33). Rafoth and Naydan revalue multilingual writers, specifically within writing centers in which the target language is English.

Although the writing center community, according to Rafoth, has "made progress" by "welcom[ing] other languages and cultures to the writing center," he envisions "next steps" in which writing centers "open the doors wider" (16). This book argues for the benefits of building writing centers whose doors are open so widely that the centers themselves—and not just the writers who inhabit them—are multilingual. In a globalized world, Rafoth and Naydan (among many others) do the important work of challenging monolingualism and creating theory and pedagogy geared toward multilingual writers. Yet writing center scholars need also to examine the implications of English monolingualism within writing centers across the globe. As I will show in this chapter, English-centric writing centers are prevalent in international universities because language politics in the era of globalization hinder the development of MWCs. I argue for the expansion of English-centric into multilingual writing centers because MWCs counteract "monolingual hegemony" while reinforcing the best FL writing and student-centered, translingual practices.

GLOBALIZATION AND ENGLISH-CENTRIC WRITING CENTERS

"Open doors" is an apt metaphor for higher education in the era of globalization. Throughout the world, a growing number of colleges and universities are seeking to diversify their student bodies, internationalize the curriculum, increase international student enrollments, and offer dynamic study abroad programs. Like many other colleges and universities, Dickinson College, which houses the MWC that I direct, offers a global education program with a tri-fold emphasis on regional studies, the interdisciplinary analysis of globalization, and foreign language learning ("Global"). The college offers fifty programs across six continents and in countries such as Australia, Cameroon, China, England, France, Germany, Italy, Japan, Korea, Russia, Spain, Argentina, and Brazil, among others. Roughly two-thirds of students study abroad, and many choose to immerse themselves in a foreign language ("Quick"). In addition, knowledge of a foreign language through the intermediate level is a graduation requirement.

To support the college's global education mission, the Writing Center, established in 1978 for writers working in English, became an MWC in 2010. By MWC, I mean a writing center that offers consistent and ongoing writing tutoring in multiple languages and that provides tutor training grounded in theories that address the needs of native, nonnative, and FL writers. Dickinson's Norman M. Eberly Multilingual Writing Center provides tutors for students writing not only in English but also in Arabic, Chinese, Hebrew, Japanese, French, German, Italian, Portuguese, Russian, and Spanish. Many students are able to realize their goals of studying abroad in a language other than English because they have access to an MWC to support their learning. The MWC, then, exists within a college with a clear global mission and a strong commitment to foreign language learning ("About").

Such global education initiatives are omnipresent throughout US higher education. According to the Association of American Colleges and Universities' recent survey of chief academic officers, ninety percent of these high-ranking administrators value "knowledge of world cultures as one of their topmost, desired learning outcomes," and seventy percent of their institutions have incorporated global courses into their general education requirements ("Ascent"). Yet despite the fact that understanding world cultures is a ubiquitous student learning outcome in academia, and FL learning is intrinsic to that outcome, MWCs appear to be a rare breed in the US. In the meantime, writing centers are spreading across the world, though most are English-centric, a fact that can be gleaned from examining the International Writing Center Association (IWCA) directory of writing centers. The IWCA directory lists the contact information for member writing centers from sixty-six countries. Seeking to identify writing centers that serve languages other than English, I reviewed writing center websites except for those in countries in which English is the official or dominant (as in the case of the US) language: Australia, Canada (except Quebec), Fiji, New Zealand, Singapore, South Africa, the United Kingdom, and the United States.[1] I omitted writing centers from English-dominant countries for two reasons. First, the lack of scholarship on FL writing tutoring in English-language writing center publications—*Writing Lab Newsletter; Writing Center Journal;* and *Praxis: A Writing Center Journal*—presupposes that MWCs have not been theorized and formalized in these countries.[2] Second, the preponderance of English-centric writing centers in English-dominant countries would skew the data. Instead, I focused on writing centers in countries whose official language(s) is not English. In examining the websites, I categorized ninety-five writing centers from thirty-seven countries using the following categories that emerged from the data: multilingual (offering writing tutoring in foreign languages in addition to English and/or the official language), English-only, both English and the official language, or the official language-only (see figure 1).

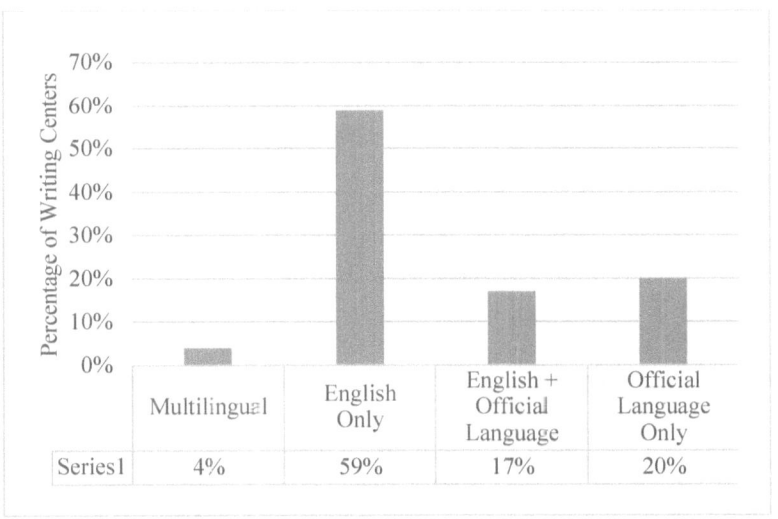

Figure 1: Writing centers in countries in which English is not the official/dominant language.

The results show that only 4 percent of writing centers are multilingual.[3] Instead, the majority offer English writing tutoring—with 59 percent offering only English[4] and 17 percent English plus the official language of the country.[5] The remaining 20 percent provide writing tutoring only in the official language of the country.[6] In short, 80 percent of the ninety-five worldwide writing centers in this sample provide support for writers of English.

The language politics associated with globalization account for the proliferation of English-centric writing centers throughout the world. English is the lingua franca, "the universal language of the intellect in the contemporary world" (Canagarajah, *Geopolitics* 41; Kirkpatrick). In *The Great Brain Race, How Global Universities Are Reshaping the World,* Ben Wildavsky states that English is the "universal language of scholarship." For every one native speaker, there are three nonnative speakers of English (43). Further, in the "new borderless world" where prospective students act "like consumers in a worldwide marketplace," these student-consumers, according to Wildavsky, seek institutions that prepare them for careers in which they will be "taking part in a global conversation of ideas and a global exchange of scholars" (20, 155, 157). As a case in point, he cites the Institut d'Etudes Politiques or Sciences Po, a "beacon of excellence" in France, which in 1996 became "globalized with a vengeance" (84). At Sciences Po, forty percent of matriculants were international students. Three hundred international universities participated in the exchange program, and students could choose to study from among fifteen foreign languages. Yet Richard Descoings, then-president of Sciences Po, explained, "English is not a foreign language—it is *the* international language . . . We have to stop saying that English is *one* of the languages. It is *the* language of international exchange: commercial, military, and also intellectual and scientific" (qtd. in Wildavsky 84). Given the primacy of English in business and academia, it is no wonder that English-centric writing centers are proliferating in countries in which English is not the official language.

Not only is English the dominant scholarly language, but rhetoric and composition, notes Suresh Canagarajah, is "very much a North American enterprise." In his analysis of mainstream versus periphery (or third-world) scholarly writing, Canagarajah explains, "In Europe, Asia, South America, and Africa the teaching of academic writing is not done in a systematic or institutionalized manner" (*Geopolitics* 44). Since 2002 when Canagarajah made that claim, the international academic community has begun to engage with writing studies. In 2008, Charles Bazerman organized the first Writing Research Across Borders conference, which resulted in the establishment of the International Society for the Advancement of Writing Research, whose mission is to advance "the development of interdisciplinary research into the many dimensions of writing and learning" ("ISAWR"). Bazerman has edited several anthologies that highlight the work of international writing researchers: *Traditions of Writing Research; International Advances in Writing Research: Cultures, Places, Measures;* and *Genre in a Changing World.* Christopher Thaiss led the *International WAC/WID Mapping Project.* As a follow-up to that project, he and colleagues Gerard Breuer and Paula Carlino invited several writing programs to contribute to *Writing Programs Worldwide: Profiles of Academic Writing in Many Places*, a collection of essays that examine writing programs in forty countries outside the United States. Terry Myers Zawacki, Magnus Gustaffson, Joan Mullin, and Federico Navarro edit International Exchanges on the Study of Writing, a book series that focuses on "worldwide perspectives on writing, writers, teaching with writing, and scholarly writing practices, specifically those that draw on scholarship across national and disciplinary borders to challenge parochial understandings of all of the above" ("International"). The teaching of writing in international institutions has become more "systematic" and "institutionalized," though often under the auspices of North American scholars. Relatedly, writing center studies, another North American enterprise with English language roots, has affected the development of writing centers beyond US borders. Writing centers are an appealing export for international universities seeking to prepare students for global interactions in English.

Indeed, many international universities have established English-centric writing centers because they equate global engagement with westernized education and the English language. Wildavsky finds that "universities in non-English speaking countries are offering degrees in English to cater to Anglophone and non-Anglophone students alike" (43). There are fifteen institutions in my sample that have "American" in their name (i.e., American University of Cairo) or are satellites of US universities (i.e., Temple University in Tokyo or Northwestern University in Qatar). In Qatar, there are at least four English-centric writing centers located in Education City, a place where the royal family invited several U.S and Canadian universities to establish an "academic outpost" for Qatari students who wished to pursue a North American education (Wildavsky 57).

Other writing centers in non-English-speaking, Western countries prepare students for study abroad in English. The Academic Writing

Center at Pontificia Universidad Catolica de Chile provides English writing tutoring for "people interested in applying for study abroad" ("Academic"). Although two-thirds of the German universities listed in the IWCA directory have German-only writing centers, Leuphana University houses an English-only writing center, which bills itself as "a key component of Leuphana's international strategy" ("Writing Center").[7] Similarly, the Universidad de Magallanes in Chile created its English Academic Writing Center "in an effort to participate more fully in the global academic environment" ("Academic"). Of course, participation in the "global academic environment" can take place at home or abroad.

Take, for example, South Korea. On the one hand, the government sought to import westernized higher education into the country because of concerns about the steady increase of students choosing international study, resulting in an almost four-billion-dollar annual economic loss (Wildavsky 80). As a result, much like Qatar, South Korea created the Inchcon Free Economic Zone, a "52,000-acre complex," to attract "several dozen high-level research institutes," including the State University of New York at Stony Brook and North Carolina State University. In so doing, South Korea aspired to become "an international hub of research excellence" and compete for students and renowned US researchers (Wildavsky 75). On the other hand, some South Korean universities continue to prepare students for study abroad in English. Kyungbook National University has an International Writing Center with the motto "preparing students for a global future." This English-centric center aims to "enhanc[e] students' international competitiveness as they apply for foreign study programs, internships, and professional positions overseas" ("International"). Both the Inchcon complex and Kyungbook exemplify Korea's efforts to provide a westernized education with a "hearty embrace of English" so as to "prepare students for a globalized society in which English has become the lingua franca of both the scholarly and business worlds" (Wildavsky 75).

These English-centric writing centers in countries in which English is not the official language often articulate their missions in terms of access and inclusion. In Korea, Hanyang University's Center for Teaching and Learning English Writing Lab assists students who seek to "publish in English international journals" ("Center for Teaching"). Similarly, the Center for Academic Writing at Central European University in Budapest, Hungary has as its mission "to ensure high standards of written academic English throughout the university, by providing students with support and guidance so as to ensure that their work meets *the expectations of the international discourse community*" (emphasis added). Ironically, in equating "written academic English" with the 'international discourse community," Central European University implicitly acknowledges the dismissal of non-English speaking scholars from the globalized mainstream scholarly community. Canagarajah critiques the westernization of academic writing and publishing and its dominance by one language. He observes that the academic publishing industry is English-centered, and the West produces the academic databases. The few non-West journals that publish the work of scholars outside of North America in languages other than English "may not be visible or accessible to nonmainstream disciplinary communities" (*Geopolitics* 34-35). Canagarajah concludes that the English-centric academic community often ignores the work of periphery scholars who write in languages other than English, in nonstandard dialects of English, and/or in discourse considered unconventional by the mainstream. The language politics of globalization should give writing center professionals pause, particularly in light of the IWCA's "Diversity Initiative," which aims to engage "excluded and marginalized peoples." To apply Naydan's point about writers to writing centers, the "monolingual hegemony that is inherently at play works to colonize everything."

THE BENEFITS OF MULTILINGUAL WRITING CENTERS

True, English-centric writing centers in international locations do the important work of preparing students to participate as scholars in a monolingual, globalized world. In the US, however, the teaching of FL writing "has become more urgent," as Jean Marie Schultz argues, "because of globalization" (72). The MWC responds to this urgent need, articulated not only by Schultz but also in a 2014 joint letter from the US House and Senate to the American Academy of Arts and Sciences (AAAS):

> English is no longer sufficient as a lingua franca—neither at home or abroad. The percentage of the world's population that speaks English as a first language is declining rapidly; if

current demographic trends continue, only 5 percent will be native English speakers by 2050. At the same time, the ability to communicate in languages other than English has never been more important ... ("Letter").

The US House and Senate wrote this letter to request that the AAAS form a Commission on Language Learning that would study the "current state of language education" ("Commission"). Pointing out the demise of native English speakers, the letter states that English is not "sufficient as a lingua franca," which is not the same as claiming that English is no longer a lingua franca. Rather than simply dethroning English, the writers question the sufficiency of any lingua franca and, in so doing, challenge monolingualism. They suggest that FL learning breeds "greater international understanding and cooperation," which is necessary for solving problems—economic, scientific, diplomatic, technological, among others—from a global perspective. A report from the Modern Language Association (MLA) on degree requirements makes a similar connection between FL learning and international understanding: "[l]anguage learning ... improves sensitivity to cultural differences and awareness of one's linguistic and cultural particularities. ... Reading, writing, speaking, and listening in English are part of many disciplines; expanding these abilities in another language throughout the educational system can only benefit students" (Lusin 3). Similarly, the European Union (EU) "has designated language learning as an important priority" and central to the "efforts to promote mobility and intercultural understanding." The EU's language policy identifies "[m]ultilingualism" as "an important element in Europe's competitiveness." To that end, the EU holds "that every European citizen should master two other languages in addition to their mother tongue" ("Fact"). Echoing this declaration, the University of Helsinki's language policy states, "Language skills are a means to understanding foreign cultures" as well as one's own culture. As articulated in the policy, "the University promotes the language proficiency of its students and staff as well as supports their knowledge of different cultures. Multilingual and multicultural communities promote creative thinking" ("University). Thus, the US government and the EU, as well as various academic institutions within their borders, have pointed out the limits of a common language and argued for internationalization over globalization, inclusion over marginalization, and multilingualism over monolingualism.

MWCs build bridges to a multicultural and multilingual world, which students may first encounter through study abroad and then through their chosen profession. In the US, many students seek to acquire foreign language literacy skills and experience cultural immersion, often in languages other than English. A report issued by the MLA based on 2013 data reveals that there were over 1.5 million postsecondary students enrolled in non-English, modern language courses (Goldberg et al. 2). Further, 16.7 percent of all undergraduate enrollments in the modern languages were in advanced (defined as third and fourth year) courses (Goldberg et al. 40). As many of these students look forward to careers in the global arena, their immediate goals often include study abroad. According to the Open Doors Report published by the Institute of International Education (IIE), a nonprofit founded in 1919 with the purpose of creating educational connections between the US and other nations, 10 percent of US students study abroad during their undergraduate years ("Number"). Among the top study abroad destinations were several in which English is not the official language: Italy (11 percent), Spain (9.4 percent), France (4.9 percent), Germany (3.8 percent), China (3.6 percent), Costa Rica (2.5 percent), and Japan (2 percent). The IIE proposed the Generation Study Abroad initiative, which aimed to provide resources for 600,000 US students to study abroad by 2019. If institutions of higher education become increasingly more internationalized, will writing centers respond in kind? MWCs are sites where students develop intercultural competence and linguistic awareness. MWCs help students hone their literacy skills so that they can confidently join the global conversation as scholars and professionals in another language.

MWCs provide much needed access to the target language outside the classroom. Though not the true linguistic immersion of study abroad, the MWC functions as a language community in which writers practice the target language with proficient, sometimes fluent tutors. For those writers who may be anxious about expressing themselves in the foreign language, MWC tutors create a positive learning environment in which FL writers hone their literacy skills. The needs of FL learners vary considerably, as Melinda Reichelt suggests, since some students may arrive in college with no experience while others may have up to ten years' experience with the foreign language. Although bilingual classmates can be resources for practicing the target language, they may not be comfortable fulfilling that role and may create "linguistic insecurity in students" ("Key," 25–27). MWC tutors, who are not in language classes with writers, attend to the anxieties of second language learners by creating a supportive learning environment for them to build linguistic confidence. Welcoming writers into another linguistic universe, the MWC buttresses the classroom experience and opens doors to international engagement.

MWCs challenges the global narrative of monolingual hegemony by fostering a diverse and inclusive writing culture that dismantles the native (L1)/nonnative (L2) binary. Shawna Shapiro, Michelle Cox, Gail Shuck, and Emily Simnitt pose an important question about multilingual writers: "How can we treat students as developing writers/language users without promoting a deficit view of second language (L2) writers and writing, and without reproducing stigmatizing pedagogies and policies?" (32). In MWCs within institutions that have a FL graduation requirement, all writers and tutors, both domestic and international, are first and second language learners. Because all tutors and writers are multilingual, international students for whom English is an additional language are no longer stigmatized for their supposed uniquely confounding and substandard literacy skills. Instead, the struggles and challenges of L2 learners of English are suspiciously similar to those of FL learners. The literacy skills of L2 learners of English are highlighted and revalued when those tutors serve as authorities on their native academic and writing cultures. The existence of writing tutors assisting in their L2 calls into question the "de facto authority and privilege" of native speakers (Kramsch 359). Native speaker privilege is disrupted when native speakers on campus become nonnative speakers in the MWC. The MWC, then, functions as an inclusive environment that supports "the multiple possibilities for self-expression in language" (Kramsch 368). In this space, multilingualism is the norm as writers work between and within languages toward their writing goals.

MWCs also decenter English as the dominant language. While English functions as a lingua franca—or the language all tutors and writers have in common—it is not *the* target language but one of several target languages. Given the complex variety of language learners and their diverse writing goals, multilingual writers and tutors move freely among whatever languages enable learning. Thus, the MWC does not elevate, restrict, or devalue English but, instead, recommends its strategic use. For example, a common question for tutors-in-training is what language they are supposed to use in their tutoring sessions. Experienced tutors tell them that it depends—on the level, confidence, and ability of the writer. Tutors working with heretofore English monolinguals who are beginning to write in a second language tend to communicate mainly in English while the reverse may be true for advanced writers. In fact, an exchange student from Argentina who used the MWC told of his experience taking a third language (Italian) in his second language (English). After struggling with a brief writing assignment, he made an appointment with an Italian writing tutor. When the writer expressed confusion about verb tense, the tutor started explaining Italian verb tense in English. The writer described how difficult it was for him to understand a fine point about Italian grammar when the tutor explained it in English, his second language. Fortunately, the tutor was able to explain it again—but in Spanish. Thus, while English remains a lingua franca, it is one of many languages in which conversations about writing can occur.

Pedagogically and practically, the MWC complements and extends the teaching of FL instructors. Seeking to study trends in college-level FL writing instruction, Mary E. O'Donnell surveyed the directors of sixty-six Spanish, French, and German programs across the United States. She found that 68 percent required four or more writing assignments in their courses (658). Yet, while revision is "perhaps the most important work that is required of students in a language classroom," one-third did not require revision and of the remaining two-thirds, half required only one revision and half required two. For several, workload was the issue as large-sized classes forced them to forego revision (664). Still, despite large classes, the majority managed to provide feedback in some form (666). O'Donnell's research illuminates the dilemma many college instructors face: that their wish to employ best practices often conflicts with workload pressures, most notably large classes that make it difficult to sustain a continuous cycle of drafting, feedback, and revision. An MWC provides trained writing tutors who can offer quality feedback and assist students with revision, thereby enabling instructors to teach the writing process while making the workload more manageable.

MWC tutors can also attend to the individualized needs of multilingual writers. Rosa Manchon, Lourdes Ortega, and Melinda Reichelt et al., distinguish between FL writing pedagogies, namely writing to learn the language (i.e., grammar, mechanics, vocabulary) and learning to write (Manchon; Reichelt et al.). They describe the needs of FL learners who "may be simultaneously (a) learning and creating content, (b) learning to write about it, and (c) learning to use a new language both to learn and create the content and write about it" (Ortega 245). In the classroom, instructors are challenged to address the overlapping needs of multiple and diverse individuals. Ortega finds that the "compartmentalization" of student and teacher learning goals can "lead to a misalignment between teacher and student." She cites a study of Spanish instructors who used writing to help students learn the language. The study revealed that the instructors failed to recognize the learning needs of heritage speakers who could speak fluently but wanted to learn to write (243). To address all kinds of learners in the classroom, Ortega urges instructors to merge learning-to-write and writing-to-learn approaches in "a productive, symbiotic relationship" (249). MWC tutors offer a solution to the problem of compartmentalized goals since they provide one-on-one assistance, meeting multilingual writers at their level and working with them on their individual goals.

Linguistic Diversity and Translingual Tutoring Practice

With the 2011 publication of "Language Difference in Writing: Toward a Translingual Approach," the translingual theorists offered an alternative to monolingualism—one that has implications for MWCs. Bruce Horner, Min-Zhan-Lu, Jacqueline Jones Royster, and John Trimbur define the "translingual approach" to working with multilingual writers as one that acknowledges students' right to their own languages; views language norms as "heterogeneous, fluid, and negotiable"; and maintains a "more tolerant and accommodating" view of error (303–06). In so doing, they embrace multilingualism over linguistic assimilation, allow for fluidity rather than conformity to convention, see the value of "experiment" or "error," and seek to preserve the original voices of students. It is worth considering how translingualism does and does not help theorize MWC practice, while acknowledging that "[t]ranslingual pedagogy isn't yet fully articulated" and specific classroom applications "have thus far remained limited" (Schrieber and Watson 96-97; Gevers 76).

Critics of translingualism have pointed out some problems that arise when practitioners convert translingual theory into a pedagogy and a genre—the code-meshed essay. Paul Kei Matsuda warns about the uncritical enthusiasm he has observed in "conference presentations and workshops" when teachers express a "strong interest in incorporating translingual writing . . . into their teaching." This "pedagogical imperative" has pushed against the primarily theoretical model ("Lure" 479), resulting in some practitioners assigning essays that require code-meshing. Jeroen Gevers questions the effectiveness of translingual code-meshing and "whether multilingual students experience the need or desire to code-mesh or to negotiate translingual identities as writers" (74). Carol Severino also points out how translingual practices "stres[s] readers' accommodations of multilingual writers" at the expense of "writers' second language writing development" ("Multilingualizing'" 13). In defense of translingual practice, Brooke Ricker Schreiber and Missy Watson argue that "flawed" teaching practices are "an inevitable part of the work of educators" who are grappling with new paradigms (97). Reasserting the core value of translingualism to "avoid the perpetuation of the monolingualist paradigm," they assert the need to think "beyond code-meshing" (97). These points of contention around issues of writer's purpose, imagined audience, and written product have implications for the MWC.

For example, in this chapter, I have discussed the problem of English-centric writing centers participating uncritically in the globalization of the English language. That critique resonates with translingualist concerns about enforcing standardized language usage. Dylan B. Dryer rejects the notion that standardized tests like TOEFL, IELTS, SAT, among others, are "politically neutral." Instead, they "shape the contexts of teaching and learning they measure" (277). The colonizing force of monolingualism calls attention to "recognizable differences in language" that then serve as "justification for prejudicial treatment" of groups of people (Lu and Horner 213). To counter the "unidirectionality of monolingualism" and all of its exclusionary politics, translingualists hold that all language users are "constantly negotiating multiple languages, conventions of writing, and linguistic loyalties" (Trimbur 226). Thus, translingualist theory posits a process and ethos for FL writing tutors—namely, to help writers produce meaning across language difference while remaining judgment-free.

Yet this privileging of language difference/variation over standardization is a potential problem if it is not rooted in students' learning goals, which are the foundation of writing center practice. Translingualism has emerged from among a group of North American scholars in English-dominant educational contexts (see Canagarajah, "Translingual"; Guerra; Dryer). Because English is an international lingua franca, the majority of people—"well over 80 percent"— who speak it are bilingual/multilingual, and monolingual English speakers are members of a "dwindling minority" (Kirkpatrick 355, 346). Given the existence of World Englishes produced by the large percentage of multilinguals, there may be an audience of students attracted to translingual approaches if their goal is to learn English to communicate with nonnative speakers of their own "native speaking culture" (Kirkpatrick 351). I found this is not always true of FL learners. Quoting Severino, I asked a group of MWC tutors who were all US domestic students—one year before Horner et al. published their seminal article on translingualism—whether they thought their role should be to assimilate writers to a standard, or to negotiate "hybridized 'culturally balanced' styles that will be acceptable" in both cultures ("'Doodles'" 56). One tutor quipped that the question was "very American." Several chimed in to explain that professors overseas do not care if a student comes from another country; they expect international students to assimilate to the new academic culture. In answer to my question, one tutor shared her strategy of temporary erasure when she offered the phrase "dual identity" in place of "hybridity." She explained, "When I am in France and I write, I try to be as French as I possibly can. When I am in America, I write as an American." Some students choose to "go native," immerse themselves in another culture, and assimilate for a time. While the tutor who strived to become "as French as she possibly can" betrayed in her very language the fact that she can never totally assimilate, she nevertheless revealed her language-learning goal—one that did not value "hybridity" or "linguistic heterogeneity." A critique made by L2 writing scholars about translingual writing in English applies to foreign languages as well: the translingual approach can "overlook . . . multilingual students' own goal to continue developing as . . . language users" and "obscure . . . situations where writers make the rhetorical choice not to deviate from the dominant practice" (Shapiro et al. 31-32; Matsuda, "Lure" 481; Severino, "'Multilingualizing'" 13–14). Thus, it is important for FL writing tutors to understand students' goals for learning the language so they can adjust their approach accordingly.

The "main proponents" of translingualism take issue with an over-emphasis on "instructed code-meshing," preferring to stress how the theory emphasizes "prioritized critical awareness" (Gevers 76). As Matsuda observes, "the process of negotiating assumptions about language is more important than the product" for translingualist theorists ("Lure" 481). In this sense, translingual writing process pedagogy carries rich possibilities for the MWC. The translingualist critique of monolingualism potentially supplants error correction with an awareness of language difference. Trimbur traces translingualist process theory to Mina Shaughnessey's and David Bartholomae's work on error, which is foundational not only to translingualism but also to writing center practice. Error analysis employs close reading to identify patterns of error and then "explicate the logic of error" (221). Viewing error as "evidence of intention" allows practitioners to reimagine students as orderly thinkers rather than illiterate scribblers of unconventional or idiosyncratic writing. Yet, as Trimbur explains, for Shaughnessey and Bartholomae the end game is the eradication of error and the reinforcement of standardized English. Conversely, for the translingualists, close reading and error analysis expose "not just the logic of error but also the logics of difference" without mandating that linguistic variation should be replaced with standard forms (225). In a similar way, Dryer imagines standardized tests that no longer measure students' abilities to master standard usage but to "work across language variation" (277). Similarly, Juan C. Guerra wants his students "to develop a rhetorical sensibility that reflects a critical awareness of language as contingent and emergent, rather than as standardized and static" (228)

The debates between translingualists and second language writing scholars reveal the principles that they hold in common: a shared notion of linguistic diversity as "promoting a positive, inclusive view of language" that regards multilingualism as an "asset or resource" and "valu[es] multiple linguistic codes" (Shapiro et al. 31). Ultimately, translingualism offers the MWC a means to interpreting the conversations between writers and tutors—ones in which the writer and tutor routinely move between languages to consider "what the writers are doing with language and why" (Horner et al. 305) Foreign language writing tutors do this when they embrace linguistic diversity, "linguistically inclusive practices," and "the concept of student agency" (Shapiro et al. 32). As one team of writing program administrators asserts of their strategic plan for training faculty, they have "purposefully avoided top-down, prescriptive approaches in favor of collaboration and dialogue," arguing that "increasing students' knowledge of language differences will produce more informed students and better writers as a result" (Lovejoy et al. 319).

According to these scholars, then, a pedagogy that respects language diversity is not "top-down," stresses "student agency," and favors conversation and collaboration—all values and practices of writing centers. To illustrate how tutors can mediate agency in translingual moments, here is a transcript of a session between a Spanish language learner and a writing tutor who is an exchange student from Argentina. The writer has brought in a blog reflection on "service experiences in the fields and in the clinics" and has asked the tutor to "go over the grammar." The following translingual exchange occurs in the middle of the conversation:

Writer: Pienso que nuestro rol como intérprete joven es beneficioso para todos los trabajadores porque nosotros representamos el futuro de nuestro país. [I think that our role as young interpreter is beneficial for all the workers because we represent the future of our country.]

Tutor: Perfect. So pienso que nuestro rol como so nuestro is plural so it's intérpretes. And here the same: jovenes [young]. And you know here you . . . like just want to explain to you that this is something cultural, you know, that good writing varies according to cultures and in the Spanish speaker's sphere in general, we prefer this kind of construction, talking about *us*. It's called—

Writer: The collective.

Tutor: Yes. Like humble.

Writer: Like it's not just—

Tutor: It has limits, humble condition. Okay like this is very like— bear that in mind because you have done good here. Like you could have said like in the United States style—

Writer: Like *my* role.

Tutor: Yes, *I* as a young interpreter.

Writer: Individual.

Tutor: Yes, but just want to say that this is very good.

Writer: I never thought about that. That's a good observation.

Tutor: Yes.

After pointing out to the writer an agreement error, the tutor identifies the cultural implications of a rhetorical move that the writer makes when they choose to use the first-person plural. Even though the writer admits, "I never thought about that," they catch on quickly and label the move "the collective" as soon as the tutor points out the use of "us." As Schrieber and Watson state, "pedagogy is translingual not merely by exposing students to language diversity . . . but by asking students to investigate/consider how language standards emerge, how and by whom they are enforced, and to whose benefit" (95). Though the tutor (in training at the time) moves too quickly to the next issue, he gives the writer agency to make an important rhetorical choice. With experience, tutors ideally will come to teach—and not just give—agency. In this case, he could have asked the writer if they knew why the culture values the collective voice and its connection to humility, who uses it, when, and why. This could have resulted in a conversation about language, power, and society as the writer determined why they would or would not want to use the collective/humble voice. In so doing, writer and tutor would actively negotiate language difference.

Language Diversity and the Multilingual Writing Center

In the previous section, I described a pedagogy of linguistic diversity that arises from linguistic and rhetorical awareness of difference, writer agency, and a translingual writing process. Such a pedagogy develops in students a habit of mind that views language and culture in descriptive rather than prescriptive terms; dismantles unhelpful binaries like standard/nonstandard, native/nonnative, correct/incorrect; and exposes the social politics embedded in language use. Yet linguistic diversity is not only important in the session but also in the center. The time is ripe for WCAs to consider the broader political implications of monolingualism. Schultz, for example, labels English the "Microsoft of languages" for its "dominant role in the marketplace" and voices the concerns of FL scholars who fear that "learning languages other than English will fall away and that the cultural differences that are so valued in the field will be reduced and over time irrevocably lost to the lure of American materialism and economic forces" (69). Reacting to a report from the Modern Language Association that 651 foreign language programs in US colleges and universities were cut between 2013 and 2016, Ruth Ben-Ghiat warns that "fewer Americans learning foreign languages means more Americans deprived of the openness of mind and understanding of other cultures." In an MWC, linguistic diversity is embodied not just in the translingual/multilingual interplay of writer and tutor; it also arises from the belief that knowledge of languages and literacy practices contributes to greater understanding of the people and cultures that routinely interrelate in a globalized world.

It would benefit WCAs in the US and worldwide, particularly in institutions with strong global education missions, to reflect on the implications of supporting English monolingualism at the expense of linguistic diversity. Consider, for example, the IWCA "Diversity Initiative":

1. The IWCA recognizes the necessity of cultivating and honoring the participation and leadership of historically excluded and marginalized people.
2. The IWCA recognizes that its outreach efforts to historically excluded or marginalized communities must be shaped by the express needs and interests of those communities.

The first statement seeks to include "marginalized people—defined in terms of race, sexualities, "abilities, economic needs, and linguistic expression." The phrase "linguistic expression" refers to multilingual writers who are marginalized because of their nonstandard dialects. The second statement qualifies the first by acknowledging that marginalized communities should set the terms of their inclusion. When read in light of Canagarajah's argument about the hegemony of English and the exclusion of periphery scholars, the two statements raise questions. Who is excluded or marginalized by writing centers that promote the English language and North American rhetorics, genres, and educational practices in international sites? To what extent do English-centric writing centers help the West dominate the intellectual community and at what cost? How can writing centers educate writers about and resist the linguicism that permeates contemporary life? While not directly addressing linguistic diversity, the "Diversity Initiative" carves a space for it. I would argue that the "Diversity Initiative," which clearly embraces multilingual writers, should also include—even issue a challenge for—linguistically diverse writing centers.

Given the growth of global education initiatives in higher education, the importance of FL study, and the international character of the writing center community, it is time for writing center scholars to tackle the language politics of English-centric writing centers. In his controversial critique of linguistic imperialism, Robert Phillipson asks, "What does the expansion of English signify for the future of other languages of scholarship? How should the education system create proficient users of English, and how can this goal be achieved in harmonious balance with proficiency in other languages?" (211). Echoing Phillipson's concerns about the global dominance of English, John Harbord, Director of the Center for Academic Writing at Central European University, asserts: "the great global power and reach of the English language should not repress the legitimacy of local languages or endanger *academic* literacy in other countries where English is *not* the national language" (1). While writing centers are implicated in this charge, they are also uniquely positioned to build on their already strong commitment to multilingual writers and support diverse languages, rhetorics, and discourses along with English in all its varieties. By opening their doors to the wide world, MWCs counter the master narrative of English monolingualism and foster cultural understanding through written language.

2 Holistic Tutoring Practices: Toggling Between the Parts and the Whole

Foreign language writers complicate and extend the best practices of English-centric writing centers, much in the same way that so-called English as a second language (L2) writers once did. Take, for example, the higher-order concern/lower-order concern (HOC/LOC) binary.[8] The earliest training advice to tutors of first language (L1) English writers was to treat HOCs before LOCs, essentially hierarchizing the binary. Soon tutor-training guides adapted the HOC/LOC hierarchy to L2 English writers (Caposella; Gillespie and Lerner; and Ryan and Zimmerelli). The HOC/LOC hierarchy was also embraced by second language acquisition researchers. In an oft-cited essay about L2 English writers, Vivian Zamel asserts, ". . . we need to refrain from reading texts the way most of us currently do. We should hold in abeyance our reflex-like reactions to surface-level concerns and give priority to meaning . . ." (96). Soon, however, scholars of L2 English writing came to view the HOC/LOC binary as more of a double bind, which they subsequently dismantled. Musing over the plight of tutors who are trained to start with HOCs and L2 English writers who want to start with LOCs, Susan Blau and John Hall conclude that "tutors can interweave global and local concerns rather than prioritizing them" (42). Pointing out "the unique issues second language writers bring to the writing centers," Matusda stresses the need to "reexamine some of the fundamental assumptions of the writing center," in particular "the common practice of focusing on global issues (e.g., content, organization, idea development) before local issues (e.g., grammar, style, and mechanics)" ("Teaching" 47). Most recently, Severino and Cogie have referred to the HOC/LOC binary as a "false dichotomy." Borrowing a phrase from Blau and Hall, they suggest that tutors practice an "informed flexibility" when working with L2 writers. In other words, some sessions may "focus only on LOCs; or on LOCs before or at the same time as HOCs; or on some LOCs that interfere with communication and are therefore HOCs" (465). For Severino and Cogie, context should be taken into account when prioritizing "higher" and "lower" order concerns.

While such theorizing implies a sound pedagogical framework, tutors still wonder where to start, especially when writers defer to tutors for agenda-setting. Tutors of L1 English writers, in many cases, can still use the HOC/LOC hierarchy as a starting point. Conversely, FL writing tutors, who often work with true beginners, face a unique set of challenges as they consider how to initiate conversation about a writer's draft. In a staff training exercise in which I ask tutors to write about their most difficult sessions, many describe complex scenarios that involve essays riddled with global and sentence-level concerns. For example, here is one tutor's response to a training exercise that asks for a description of a "most difficult session":

> The student came to the session with the idea of working on so many things at the same time. You can notice that beyond the foreign language errors, the student has a lot of problems with developing ideas and sense of structure, even in English. And also, he's not very creative and he just repeats/writes what the professor says or translates from English using bad online translators. The result? A paper without sense, with a lot of grammar mistakes, and without ideas.

This tutor articulates well the competing challenges of FL writing tutoring, exemplifying Rafoth's point that tutors do not always know how "to easily separate less from more important problems" (47). This tutor may find that the writer is not only struggling to articulate a new language but may also be transferring ineffective writing strategies from the L1. Or maybe the task of communicating in the foreign language, as in the case above, is causing the writer to rely too much on the professor or to use an online translator. The tutor, then, must figure out where to begin. Do they start with the language errors or with idea development? Do they help the student revise a derivative essay—a summary of the professor's points that the writer composed in English and then submitted to an online translator? Or do they teach the writer how to prewrite a new draft? If they help the writer prewrite, do they encourage the writer to do so in the first language or the target language?

All tutors—whether they are working with L1 writers, L2 writers in immersion contexts, or FL writers—must decide how to begin the tutoring conversation. As experienced tutors know, there are multiple paths into a conversation—some that lead to dead ends and others that open up possibilities and generate discoveries. That said, while L1 and L2 tutors of English benefit from decades of research on best practices, FL writing tutors must look to writing center and second language acquisition studies to build a pedagogy. For one, there is no published scholarship (in English) on FL writing tutoring. For another, FL writing research is a relatively new field, which "has been quite limited" up until the last twenty years, and the canon of scholarship is still "relatively small" (Reichelt et al., 181). As one group of FL writing scholars conclude, "there is no critical mass of findings that allows for strong claims about the nature of writing in non-English L2s" (Reichelt et al., 185). Consequently, this chapter adapts, synthesizes, and reimagines writing center and second language scholarship to propose an approach to FL writing tutoring.

This historical lack of research can be attributed, in part, to the fact that not all FL instructors agree that writing is a necessary skill to master. Among classroom teachers, there is "resistance to composition instruction" as well as "skepticism as to whether writing needs to be taught at all in the FL classroom" (Reichelt et al. 34). Some instructors assign "writing" so that students can practice grammar and employ new vocabulary. In addition, among those who do teach writing as part of the foreign language, there are those who "assume that L1 writing skills will automatically transfer over to the FL and that FL writing is essentially an act of translation" (Reichelt et al. 34). Some instructors, then, may assign but not teach writing, and/or they may use writing for limited purposes.

Yet even when the instructor values writing and teaches it well, the students may dismiss the importance of FL writing or view it reductively. Foreign language writers are missing the experience of linguistic immersion, which threatens to undermine their "motivation and general acquisition" (Reichelt et al. 26). In addition, "some research has indicated the EFL [English as a Foreign Language] writers may perceive L2 writing as more useful than L2 writers of other languages do, primarily because they believe they will use it in their future work lives" (Reichelt, "L2 Writing," 181). Students who do value writing and seek to become literate in a foreign language may understand writing mainly in terms of language acquisition. According to Virginia Mitchell Scott in *Rethinking Foreign Language Writing*, research indicates that L2 "writers are focused on linguistic accuracy, nearly to the point of obsession" (48). At Dickinson's MWC, as is true of all writing centers, many students prioritize grammatical correctness over critical writing skills like idea development and organization. When students make an online appointment, a question on the appointment form asks them to identify what they "would like to work on." They are given sixteen choices that run the gamut of writing concerns, and they can choose more than one.[9] In the 2018-2019 academic year, for example, "editing for grammar mistakes" was a concern for 50 percent of L1 English writers. That percentage jumped to 72.5 percent for L2 English writers and 68 percent for foreign language writers.[10] A major charge for writing tutors is to help these writers identify the best starting point for revision—which may or may not be editing for grammar mistakes. This difficulty is compounded by the writers' ever-present first (and other) language(s) as when FL writers "lear[n] the appropriate vocabulary and grammar and overla[y] it upon English composition formats" (Reichelt et al. 27). Holistic tutoring, a specific kind of "informed flexibility," can help writers negotiate the writing process, global writing concerns, and sentence level issues.

This chapter argues for an MWC grounded in the best practices of what I call holistic tutoring. Holistic tutors recognize that FL writers are developing a second language writing process, learning writing conventions, and acquiring the language—all at the same time. When it comes to FL writing, students and even some instructors do not always think of writing in holistic terms—that is, as a complete system as opposed to the component parts. In fact, FL writing scholars categorize FL writing pedagogies in the following way: "(a) learning and creating content, (b) learning to write about it, and (c) learning to use a new language both to learn and create the content and write about it" (Ortega 245; Manchon, *Learning*; Reichelt et al.). The first model captures the heuristic potential of writing to solidify knowledge and to formulate ideas. The second model refers to writing as a form of communication through genres and their associated conventions. The third model synthesizes the first two and adds a new function—writing as a means to language acquisition. Only the last is holistic, for, as Ilona Leki's observes, "learning-to-write and writing-to-learn [the language] feed each other in ever expanding cycles" ("Learning" 105). A practical reflection of this theorizing, holistic tutoring involves the interplay between form, meaning, and writing process. First, while some writers reduce the written product to an exercise in language acquisition, holistic writing tutors toggle between global and sentence-level concerns with an awareness of their interconnection. Among the techniques they use are noticing, hypothesis testing, metalinguistic reflection, and negotiated interaction. Second, while some FL writers truncate the writing process into two steps (composing and editing) or three (composing in the first language, translating into the second language, and then editing), holistic writing tutors enlarge writers' repertoires of process skills. Tutors can assist writers who draft in the first language and then translate into the target language by distinguishing between translating and composing (or thinking not in terms of literal words but in terms of meaning). Inevitably, conversations about meaning lead to questions about purpose and organization. By tracing problems with the written product back to the writer's process and exploring the interplay between language acquisition and writing, FL writing tutors, as I will show, can help writers make connections between the parts and the whole. Consequently, the starting point for the tutoring conversation becomes less important than the outcome.

HOLISTIC TUTORING: NOTICING, HYPOTHESIS TESTING, AND METALINGUISTIC AWARENESS

It is commonplace for the English-centric writing center to define itself as *not* a "grammar fix-it shop." With the inclusion of FL writing tutors, that customary dictum would need to be heavily qualified. After all, FL writers are also learning the language, which causes them and their instructors to emphasize grammar, usage, and word choice more than L1 instructors and writers—maybe even at times to the neglect of writing concerns. Holistic tutoring practices bridge the gap between writing and language acquisition by helping students acquire the language as they learn to write in it. To explain this aspect of holistic tutoring, I will take a cue from Rosa Manchon, who examines several theories central to second language acquisition and applies them to FL writing studies to argue that writing has the potential to reinforce language acquisition.

Before explaining how tutors can turn second language acquisition theory into practices that assist writers, a brief (though not exhaustive) overview of cognitive aspects of language acquisition will help provide context. Cognitive theories seek to describe the mental processes involved in acquiring a language. Relevant to this discussion are the Input Hypothesis, the Output Hypothesis, and the Noticing Hypothesis. Considering the act of comprehension, the Input Hypothesis states that learners acquire language when they "understand language that contains structure that is 'a little beyond'" their current level (Krashen 21). The Output Hypothesis suggests that learners produce language when they attempt to communicate, fail, and then try again (Swain and Lapkin). However, self-correction does not occur without self-awareness. Thus, the Noticing Hypothesis questions the notion that language learning is an unconscious process and, instead, recognizes the need for learners to "pa[y] attention to language form" (Schmidt 149). Drawing on the Output Hypothesis, Manchon views writing as a form of "pushed output," an occasion in which learners are forced to produce language. In writing, FL learners produce language that is unavoidably flawed so that they can receive feedback and then practice making that language "more precise, more coherent, and more appropriate" ("Language" 47). To that end, Manchon recommends "feedback for acquisition," which she distinguishes from "feedback for accuracy" ("Language" 57-58). Whereas feedback for accuracy aims to correct errors, feedback for acquisition engages students in the "deep problem-solving" that leads to language acquisition. According to Manchon, through pushed output in the form of writing, instructors can provide "feedback for acquisition" that prompts students consciously and intentionally to employ language acquisition processes. However, as cognitive linguists point out, "attention is effortful," and students can receive only so much feedback before they suffer from cognitive overload (Van Patten 16). Foreign language writing tutors can effectively intervene in the writing process by directing writers' attention and managing cognitive overload. To extend Manchon's argument, writing tutors trained in these second language acquisition concepts can holistically support both writing and language acquisition goals.

Although Manchon addresses FL instructors, the practices she identifies are transferable to FL writing tutors seeking to provide feedback for acquisition:

1. *Noticing*: To acquire language, learners must notice the gap between actual and intended meaning. When writers produce language, FL writing tutors can help them identify what they are unable to do, making the writers aware of their gaps in learning.
2. *Hypothesis Testing*: To acquire language, learners use trial and error to test how the language works. Their own "internal feedback" or "instructor feedback" triggers hypothesis testing. In addition, FL writing tutor feedback can initiate hypothesis testing as well as prompt writers to "compare [instructor] feedback to what they actually wrote."
3. *Metalinguistic Awareness*: To acquire language, learners must become aware of the forms of language. When writers seek to master a new skill, like verb tense or transitions, FL writing tutors can heighten their awareness of how they are shaping language by asking them to reflect on the "forms, rules, and form-function relationship" of language (48).

Through writing, a form of pushed output, FL writing tutors can instill habits of mind like noticing, hypothesis testing, and metalinguistic awareness. Even more, in approaching sessions holistically, they can employ these techniques to aid in both the development of writing skills and language acquisition.

The following examples from interviews with Dickinson FL writing tutors illustrate how one tutor strategically implemented these techniques and another adapted them to her holistic tutoring practice.[11] Marco, a Spanish writing tutor, described a session in which he employed noticing, hypothesis testing, and metalinguistic awareness. He explained that when a writer has questions about grammar and usage, he begins by reviewing the rule: "okay, so I just helped you understand—I don't know—the preterit form of the past tense." He then asks the writer to "notice": "When we are going through and reading through this, I want you to tell me which word to you is the preterit or where should you use the preterit." Asking writers to notice enables him to offer feedback for acquisition rather than accuracy: "They're not just waiting for me to tell them to do the correction." Marco very consciously avoids even pointing out the problem as he gets the writer to discover where they use the preterit and then think about whether they should be using the preterit in that context. Marco even uses the writer's L1 to magnify the noticing. as he illustrated: "This is like what you just told me in English. Let me tell you what you just told me. Is that what you are trying to say? No? What's wrong there? Is the context okay? Yeah? So what's wrong? And then they tell me, 'Oh, the tense is wrong.'" He translates the writer's Spanish output into English to make the disparity between expression and intention even more apparent to the writer.

Marco positions the writer to test a language hypothesis by first asking the writer to clarify the intended meaning: "So are you trying to say that this happened or that it is happening right now?" He then prods the writer to develop a hypothesis about the correct verb tense: "So what tense do you use?" Marco finishes with questions that make the writer reflect on the rules about verb tense: 'Did it happen continuously, or did it happen one time? Imperfect or preterit?" Reflecting on his own tutoring practice, he concludes: "So I . . . tell them what they're telling me in their native language, so they see [notice], and then I ask them what is wrong. But they are telling me . . . 'this is wrong' and 'this is wrong' and they fix it themselves." The writer benefits from the guidance of a fluent tutor who can stimulate noticing, hypothesis testing, and metalinguistic awareness through conversation.

In this next example, Veronica, a French writing tutor, described how she used these same techniques holistically to help a writer toggle between sentence-level and global writing concerns. The writer set an agenda for the session: to work on transitions. A less adept writing tutor may have given the writer a list of French transition words and phrases and perhaps talked about the differences between them. Veronica described how she used a series of questions to help the writer think holistically about the draft: "What does this paragraph say? . . . What is the message? How do we move to the next message? What is the transition? So moving from organization to content to lower-order concerns, if you will, on the word level and in transition sentences." As Veronica and the writer move sequentially through the draft, Veronica urges the writer to notice the messages in each paragraph and then think about how they are connected. She encourages the writer to hypothesize about the transitions that best help her move from one message/paragraph to the next. In the process of repeating this cycle of questioning throughout the entire draft, Veronica instills in the writer the kinds of questions that stimulate metacognitive reflection. Whereas Marco sticks to the metalinguistic level in coaxing the writer to recall the rules for past tense in Spanish, Veronica's questions urge the writer to think about their thinking. In responding to Veronica, the writer must move from the global to the sentence level, metacognitively exploring how paragraphs logically connect to each other and then metalinguistically constructing the most appropriate transition.

As Manchon argues, writing fosters the "deep-problem solving" that results in "comprehensible output" but only under certain conditions. Writers need adequate time to write; they need to be prompted to notice, test hypotheses, and reflect on the metalinguistic level; and they need to work through the "iterative process of output + input + noticing/reflection + output" ("Language," 51-52, 57-58). While instructors can design classroom pedagogies and assignments to meet these conditions, FL writing tutors, as Veronica and Marco exemplify, can reinforce these problem-solving practices. Writers who make appointments in an MWC set aside time to work on a draft with FL writing tutors who guide them through the output-feedback-output cycle. Tutors trained in holistic tutoring practices can redirect writers' attention from "editing for grammar mistakes" and refocus it on "us[ing] grammar as a tool during the writing process" (Scott 48). Finally, holistic tutors can engage writers in the necessary metalinguistic and metacognitive reflection that will enable them to bridge the gap, in Veronica's case, between writing to learn the language of transitions and learning to write a logically connected argument.

HOLISTIC TUTORING: NEGOTIATED INTERACTION

Another best practice for FL writing tutors that draws on cognitive theories of language acquisition is "negotiated interaction." Renewed focus on the Interaction Hypothesis has informed recent L2 writing center pedagogies (Long). In the words of Jessica Williams, "the Interaction Hypothesis explores how *negotiation* of meaning among learners and their interlocutors aids in the acquisition of language" (81). Negotiated interaction is the alternative to "editing or appropriating" a writer's work; it is the "key" to balancing mutual engagement and helpful guidance. Negotiated interaction begins with noticing when the writer and tutor realize that they have "different understandings and, through negotiation, arrive at a mutual one" (Williams, "Undergraduate" 83). Or, as Jennifer Ritter puts it, "We can negotiate the meaning and form of a text when we want to confirm our understanding or when we do not know what the writer meant" (106). Thus, negotiated interaction rests on the understanding that "miscommunication promotes language learning" (Rafoth 59). A form of "deep problem-solving," in a negotiated interaction the "speakers have first to see that there is a problem, then agree to work on it, and then figure out what to do about it" (Rafoth 63). As writer and tutor "figure out" the miscommunication, "interpretation occurs constantly" (62).

Rafoth illustrates a negotiated interaction from a transcribed session in which the constant interpretation occurs as the tutor and L2 English writer negotiate the correct translation of an idiomatic phrase. The writer has used the phrase "country fashion" to describe a former classmate's appearance. Confused about the meaning, the tutor asks if the writer means "contemporary," rather than "country," and asks the writer if she would describe her own style as "country fashion." The writer rejects that interpretation and replies that her own "fashion is ordinary." The tutor then offers the phrase "plain clothes," but the writer remembers a word she heard in some US movies: "geeky." The tutor mentions some synonyms like "nerdy," "weird," and "strange." After a discussion about the various connotations of these words, the writer chooses "strange fashion" (a choice that seems to highlight difference without the stigma of nerdy or geeky). The tutor offers feedback for acquisition since she gets the writer to notice the gap between expression and intention, test several options, and develop an awareness of synonyms and their connotations.

Negotiated interactions can also be holistic, toggling between word choice and idea development. Veronica, the French writing tutor, shared a story of how one critical word shifted a writer's entire interpretation of a film character. Though French is her L2, Veronica helped the writer clarify meaning by finding the best English word and then using a dictionary to discover the proper French equivalent. A writer brought to the MWC a learning-to-write assignment: an analysis of the French film *La Reine Margot*. They were engaging in line-by-line editing when Veronica noticed that the writer had written: "*Margot à créer une révolution*—like she created a revolution." With this sentence, the session turned holistic. She asked the student why she used that word: "Do you really want to use the word *creer*, to create? Do you think that's the best word to use? And she's like, 'Well, that's just the word I know.'" In introductory-level courses in which writing assignments tend to be narrative or descriptive and emphasize language acquisition, tutors encourage writers to express themselves with the vocabulary they have learned. In more advanced courses in which writers are challenged to convey ideas and analyze with linguistic accuracy and precision, tutors assist writers with connecting word choice to overall meaning. Veronica tells the writer, "Give me English words that you think you want to use, and let's try to find the best translation." On the word level, she asks the writer to choose the best word in English and then translate it into French using a dictionary. As Veronica explained, "we ended up using *participer* which means to participate in. Because she [Queen Margot] didn't necessarily make it [the revolution]; she was a part of" the revolution. In this case, the writer's word choice, which affects the analysis of Queen Margot's character, resonates on the global and sentence levels.

In a session similar to Veronica's, Marco's native knowledge of Latinx culture proves crucial as he negotiates meaning with a writer of a literary analysis. Marco and the writer were discussing her interpretation when he became aware of a "contextual/cultural problem." She used the word "negro" to describe a dark-skinned, Latin American immigrant boy who grew up in an African-American neighborhood. Marco explained, ". . . in Spanish to call someone or to describe someone that has a darker skin usually—the word she used was the word negro . . . which, it has a very derogatory sense to it in Spanish because it's . . . the direct translation is black, sort of like the color black." He explains that negro would never be used "in academic writing" or in "speaking about a child." According to Marco, the writer was arguing that as a Latin American boy living in an African-American neighborhood, the child "was sort of like almost black," particularly to the neighborhood women who behaved as "mothers who are like family." He explained that the writer's use of the word negro completely undermined her argument that the neighborhood accepted the boy. Marco continued, "But when she used that word, it was derogatory—sort of like the entire neighborhood was like—oh, that dark skinned boy, like oooh no, wouldn't wanna have anything to do with that. Instead, what she was trying to convey was—Oh, he's dark-skinned like us. Not *dark-skinned*, but dark-skinned like us." Marco helped the writer negotiate her meaning by bringing his knowledge of culture and idiom to the session. He stated, "I tried to help her to change to *moreno* . . . which is dark skinned. And then it was about a child so we make it— it's called a diminutive—so *morenito*. So it was interesting to see how that single word changed how the neighborhood would see the person, and the reader completely was thrown off by the one change." This tutor fulfills an important rhetorical function when he helps the writer imagine an authentic cultural audience, which she does not have access to as an FL writer. The proficient writer with whom he worked "benefit[s] from a native speaker's intuitions and corrections because" she is "ready to take on the finer points of style and usage learned mainly from experience and feedback" (Rafoth 46).

Both Veronica and Marco describe negotiated interaction in a way that goes beyond negotiating idiomatic expressions. Their concern with the writer's word choice had less to do with the meaning of a discrete word and more to do with their writers' overall analyses. Veronica's and Marco's training in holistic tutoring enabled them to think more broadly and connect global and sentence-level concerns. In addition, because holistic tutoring demands flexibility and the toggling between concerns, the starting point of their sessions mattered less than the outcome of the sessions. By linking writing and second language acquisition, they were able to keep several goals simultaneously in play. Told together, their narratives reveal the benefits of L1 and L2 speakers/writers of the target language in the MWC, as Veronica (L2) was able to model how to use the dictionary and Marco (L1) was able to conjure an authentic audience for their writers.

HOLISTIC TUTORING: THE ROLE OF TRANSLATION IN THE WRITING PROCESS

Thus far, I have defined holistic writing tutoring as the iterative movement between the global and sentence levels as the FL writer and tutor construct meaning. However, holistic writing tutors must focus not just on pushed output but also on the writing process. For example, FL writing tutor Mindy described in her session log her efforts to develop a writer's process:

> Laura brought in a draft for an essay that was due in two days. When I asked Laura what she wanted to work on, she said she wanted help making sure her sentences were free of anglicisms. During the session, we talked about how to make sure that she focused on conveying her thoughts through her sentences, as opposed to translating word-for-word. We also discussed how to order her sentences in a way that contributes

to the overall purpose and organization of an essay. By the end of the session, Laura better understood how to practice focusing on conveying the meaning—as opposed to the literal words—of her points, as well as strategies for effectively organizing the components of her essay and said she planned to incorporate these suggestions in her final draft.

There are several ways, some more effective than others, to approach sessions in which writers seek to eliminate anglicisms from their writing. Anglicisms occur when writers take an English word and make it sound like a word in a foreign language. For example, the writer who invents the word *librario* rather than *biblioteca* for the noun "library" has created a Spanish anglicism. Some anglicisms are word-for-word translations of English idioms such as the German word *gesichtspalmieren* for the English expression "face palm." After "noticing" the anglicisms, tutors could engage in negotiated interaction, show writers how to use the dictionary or simply tell them how to express the word or phrase in the target language. In this session, Mindy considered the writing process as she tackled the underlying cause of anglicisms: translating from the first language. Distinguishing between composing and translating, Mindy helped the writer think not in terms of "literal words" but in terms of "meaning." Their discussion about meaning then led to questions about purpose and organization. By tracing problems with the written product back to the writer's process, Mindy helped the writer see yet another interconnection between the parts and the whole.

Foreign language writers, like all writers, need to develop functional writing processes. Foreign language writing tutors, like all writing tutors, should be trained to assist them with prewriting by demonstrating heuristics; revising by tracing lines of argument, developing ideas, and organizing points; and by modelling the "slowed down form of reading" that will allow them to notice how words fit together to make meaning (Bartholomae 264). However, unlike their L1 writing tutor counterparts, FL writing tutors must deal with their writers' first (and other) language(s). It is inevitable that FL writers will compose translingually. Beginners may compose a draft in the first language and then translate it into the foreign language, and non-beginners may think in the first language as they formulate ideas (Cohen and Brooks-Carson 183). However, I refrain from using the phrase "L1 interference" with its negative connotation because the first language can help writers effectively produce the target language. Foreign language writing tutors need to learn different strategies for working with writers who use the first language to make meaning in the target language versus writers who make meaning in the first language and then use an online translator. This section will begin by considering a bona fide hindrance to the writing process, online translators, before examining how holistic writing tutors can work with writer-generated translations as they help writers establish functional writing processes.

THE TROUBLE WITH GOOGLE TRANSLATE

Foreign language writing tutors will frequently encounter writers who circumvent the writing process and use online translators, most notably Google Translate. A study of German language students' use of online translators revealed that despite being expressly prohibited from using technology in the writing process, students reported using it for 27.7 percent of their assignments (White and Heidrich 242). Google Translate, which was first launched in 2006, enables students to receive at the click of a mouse a translation of a word, phrase, or even entire document in any of 106 languages. Some FL departments view the misuse of Google Translate to translate whole sentences, paragraphs, or essays as cheating. Learning to write in the target language is a student learning outcome, and students who use Google Translate flout that learning goal. Back in 2006, FL instructors could rest assured that students who resorted to Google Translate did not get away with much because the translations were often incomprehensible. But Google Translate continues to improve the quality of its translations—a fact that excites computer programmers much more than FL writing instructors.

While the intricacies of Google Translate are best left to computer scientists, FL writing tutors and instructors would benefit from understanding how machines learn and why the translations produced by Google Translate continue to improve. Jeremy Howard, an expert in machine learning, explains that before machine learning, computers performed tasks only when they were given complex and detailed step-by-step instructions. Then computer scientists became interested in programming computers to do things that the programmers could not do themselves—like beat world champions at *Jeopardy* or predict the movies that millions of Netflix viewers would want to watch. According to Howard, computer scientists developed algorithms that enabled computers to learn by processing large batches of data, thereby making step-by-step programming unnecessary. Geoffrey Hinton developed a groundbreaking algorithm called "deep learning," which was "inspired by how the human brain works" (Howard). There were no "theoretical limitations" on the algorithm; instead, the more data and time that the algorithm was given to compute, the better it worked. The deep learning algorithm enabled Richard Rashid to take "a large amount of information from many Chinese speakers and produce a text-to-speech system" (Howard). Rashid's algorithm could convert spoken English into comprehensible, if not perfect, written and spoken Chinese. A group of researchers from Switzerland, none of whom spoke Chinese, created an algorithm that understood Chinese "at about native Chinese speaker level" (Howard). As Howard contends, "Deep learning now in fact is near human performance at understanding what sentences are about. . . ."

An example of deep learning, Google Translate is an evolving force of which FL writing tutors must take heed. In its first incarnation, Google Translate was more like a digitized phrasebook, operating vis a vis a phrase-based machine translation algorithm that "breaks an input sentence into words and phrases to be translated largely independently" (Le and Schuster). In other words, the phrase-based algorithm worked like a digital dictionary, translating word-by-word or chunk-by-chunk. In September 2016, Google introduced its multilingual neural machine translation (MNMT) algorithm "that is entirely based on deep learning" (Castelvecchi). In the human brain, neurons communicate information in the form of electrical and chemical impulses to other neurons through synapses. Similarly, computer scientists create abstractions of neurons and connect thousands of these neurons together in a multilayered network. Google's MNMT algorithm "combine[s] artificial neural networks—layers of computational units that mimic the way neurons connect in the brain—with enormous data sets" (Castelvecchi).

While the phrase-based algorithm "simply memoriz[ed] phrase-to-phrase translations," the MNMT algorithm searches for patterns in linguistic data and "encod[es] something about the semantics of a sentence," in effect, creating its own "interlingua" or artificial language (Schuster, Johnson, and Thorat). The formation of an interlingua enabled Google Translate to produce "zero-shot translations." For example, the MNMT was provided Korean to English, and English to Japanese translations. It was then able to formulate Korean to Japanese translations even though the system was not directly fed such translations (Castelvecchi; Schuster et al.). The Google team concluded that the MNMT "surpasses all currently published results" and "deliver[s] high quality translations"— in some cases, with "the accuracy achieved by average bilingual human translators." Compared to the phrase-based algorithm, MNMT "delivers roughly a 60 percent reduction in translation errors on several popular language pairs" (Wu et al. 20). If Google's claims are true, Google Translate should be able to translate, for example, an English sentence into Spanish and then back into English, and the input and output English versions would be very similar, if not the same.

> *English original*: Assimilation is the process through which a person takes on the language, religion, values, and customs of another culture.

> *Google Translate Spanish Translation*: La asimilación es el proceso mediante el cual una persona asume el lenguaje, la religión, los valores y las costumbres de otra cultura.

> *Google Translate English Re-Translation*: Assimilation is the process by which a person assumes the language, religion, values and customs of another culture.

In this example, Google Translate produces an accurate translation. There are two differences in the input and output English sentences—"through which" is replaced with "by which" and "takes on" is replaced with "assumes"—and these differences are standard English alternatives that do not alter the meaning of the original. The improved Google Translate is a nuisance to FL writing teachers and tutors when writers question the value of "learning a foreign language if [they] are able to produce an acceptable L2 text from [their] own L1 writing, instantly and with no financial cost" (Groves and Mundt 113).

However, whether Google Translate is able "to produce an acceptable L2 text" in every case is questionable. In practice, there are limitations to Google Translate as a tool for FL communication and, in particular, academic writing. Since Google's MNMT launched in September 2016, the research community has not had adequate time to examine the accuracy of its translations, although there is a body of research on Google's phrase-based algorithm, and some of the implications of that research apply to MNMT. Research on the phrase-based algorithm has pointed out that the accuracy of translations between different languages varies depending on the language; namely, the translations among European languages are better than those among Asian languages (Aiken and Balan). Further, a study of Google Translate that sought to determine the accuracy of translations from Chinese and Malay into English concluded that the they were "riddled with errors" and fell short of a "polished or professional standard of language." As such, writing produced by Google Translate for an academic audience would "necessitat[e] post-editing to achieve truly high-quality outcomes" (Groves and Mundt 118). For example, below is the same English sentence that Google Translate successfully rendered into Spanish above, only this time translated into Chinese and then back into English.

> *English original*: Assimilation is the process through which a person takes on the language, religion, values, and customs of another culture.
>
> *Google Translate Chinese Translation*: 同化是一個人接受另一種文化的語言，宗教，價值觀和習俗的過程。
>
> *Google Translate English Re-Translation*: Assimilation is the process of a person accepting another culture of language, religion, values and customs.

Compared to the input English sentence, the output English sentence contains grammatical errors that obscure the meaning of the original. A collocation problem, the phrase "process of" is generally followed by an -ing verb, not a noun ("a person"). "Culture of" does not equate with the possessive "culture's." Thus, there is some evidence to suggest that like the phrase-based algorithm, the MNMT produces English-Chinese translations that fall short of a "polished or professional standard of language," and students who use Google Translate would need to thoroughly edit their work to make it comprehensible.

An analysis of a longer passage of academic writing translated by Google Translate into French and Korean reveals that Google Translate's inability to understand rhetorical context compromises the comprehensibility of its translations. Here is the original passage in English, taken from an article I published in *Writing Lab Newsletter*:

> In the Multilingual Writing Center, we grapple with determining the appropriate balance between global revision and sentence-level editing. Depending on the writer's level, the hierarchical categorizing of global revision issues above sentence-level concerns may not be useful. Instead, we train tutors in "holistic tutoring"—a challenging practice that involves toggling between local and global issues while being keenly aware of their interconnection. Ultimately, the Multilingual Writing Center model raises a whole new set of questions about the teaching and learning of writing in international contexts for writing centers and, by extension, foreign language instructors. (Lape)

This passage was uploaded to Google Translate, which then generated a French and a Korean version. To understand how writing tutors read Google Translate documents, I asked two tutors on my staff—a French heritage speaker and a Korean native speaker—to create literal English translations of the Google Translate versions.

Not surprisingly, the French is more comprehensible than the Korean version. Although usage errors are at a minimum, the translated text is plagued by word choice problems. The issues with word choice arise from the fact that the specialized vocabulary of writing studies (which, as mentioned in chapter one, is a North American construct) did not translate culturally.

> In the Multilingual Writing Center (MWC), we try very hard to determine the appropriate balance between global revision and the editing of sentences. Based on the author's level, the hierarchization of global editing questions above preoccupations at the level of sentences may not be useful. Instead of this, we form tutors in "holistic tutoring"—a difficult practice which implies going back and forth between local and global questions all the while being deeply conscious/aware of their interconnection. In the end/ultimately, the model of the

> MWC raises an entire set of questions on the teaching and learning of writing in international contexts for writing centers and, by extension, the monitors of foreign languages.[12]

The translation starts off well with a clear articulation of the "global revision"/"editing of sentences" binary. However, Google Translate fails to grasp foundational concepts of the writing center community that frame conversations and theorize practices. For example, the next sentence conflates those terms in the phrase "global editing" and replaces the word "concerns," which has a specific connotation as the root of HOC and LOC, with the much less precise "preoccupations." Then Google Translate substitutes the phrase "train tutors" with "form tutors," a dissonant phrase that denotes the directive molding of identity and runs counter to the writing center community's shared goal of developing tutor autonomy. "Instructors of foreign languages" become "monitors" or persons who simply observe the progress of their students. As the authors of a study on German language students' use of online translators conclude, the students reported that online translators do "not necessarily [produce] writing that they would call their own" (White and Heidrich 242). Similarly, Google Translate makes the author of the passage appear to be an outsider to the writing center discourse community precisely because Google Translate is unable to take into account the rhetorical situation. To properly present the above passage to a French audience, the writer would need to unpack the implicit assumptions—about revision versus editing, the training of tutors and their agency as practitioners, and the role of FL writing instructors—for a French readership who does not have the same understanding of "tutor" as the US author of the passage. As FL writing tutors can make clear to Google Translate users, Google Translate may be able to produce some fairly comprehensible language, but it cannot approach a text rhetorically—it cannot write.

Apparently, sometimes Google Translate constructs its own rhetorical context as in the case of the Korean translation of the passage. In the Korean version, not only does the specialized language of writing centers not translate, but as the translator Diane Lee notes, some aspects of the Google translation are in the language of geology.

> In the multilingual writing center devotes on deciding the appropriate balance between global reform and sentence level editing. Depending on the writer's standard, it may not be

useful to stratum-ically categorize entire-area changing problems that are higher than sentence-level concerns. Instead, we teach instructors at "(untranslatable) personal instructions." This is a defiant practice that toggles regional and global problems while being familiar with the interconnection at the same time. Ultimately, the multilingual writing center model raises an entirely new question about teaching and learning writing in an international environment for the writing center as well as for foreign language instructors.[13]

Compared to the French version, this translation is riddled with usage errors that are arguably less pressing than the word choice errors. The central concept of the passage, "holistic tutoring," translates to "(untranslatable) personal instructions." According to Lee, the untranslatable phrase refers to "a theory that looks at the entire thing" but the language is "very broken." Another key concept, "global revision," becomes "global reform," which suggests the act of changing the world. The seemingly accurate translation "sentence level editing," Lee notes, could be interpreted as "editing on a sentence-level basis" or as "changing the level of the sentence." As in the French example, Google Translate has difficulty translating concepts written for a US writing center audience into the Korean language.

However, in this case, Google Translate stumbles onto the language of earth science. Its translation of "hierarchically" is "stratum-ically," which, as Lee notes, is not an English word but in Korean "connotes sedimentary rock or earth layers." Lee also observes that "regional and global" in the final sentence is "strictly geological language." Google Translate's use of geological language may also account for why the phrase "global revision" in the original English becomes "entire-area changing problems" in Korean. The French and Korean Google translations show that rather than making FL writing easier, Google Translate creates writing problems because it cannot translate accurately across disparate rhetorical and cultural contexts. Foreign language writing tutors confronted with Google Translate drafts are put in the position of working through complex rhetorical problems and negotiating idiosyncratic meanings created not by a writer but by a machine.

That said, Google's pronouncements about the "high quality translations" of the MNMT should not be dismissed since Google uses crowdsourcing to make the MNMT evolve. The Google Translate landing page invites users to "Join the Translate Community" by identifying the languages they know from a drop-down menu and then opting to "Translate" or "Validate." The "Translate" link prompts users to translate a phrase into another language. The "Validate" link offers a phrase and several possible translations. Users are asked to choose the translation that is "error-free," "natural-sounding," and precise in "meaning." The website looks like a game with badges and statistics to encourage participation. Assuming that good faith "players" outnumber the trolls, the Google Translate community will change the neural network of the algorithm, resulting in more accurate translations over time.

As for now, students who use Google Translate to tackle reading and writing assignments run the risk of creating problems for themselves. There are several reasons why some FL writing students use Google Translate and chance committing an academic integrity violation. First, some suffer from FL anxiety (the topic of the next chapter) that makes them worry about their ability to create correct prose. Others, particularly adult learners in introductory courses, feel frustrated and impatient because they cannot express themselves in the L2 as well as they can in the L1. They use Google Translate because they cannot reproduce the mature and sophisticated sentences of their L1 in the target language. Still others use Google Translate knowingly and intentionally to cheat. None of these students fully comprehend the limits of the tool. Foreign language writing tutors need to understand how Google Translate works and acquire strategies for helping writers compose on their own.

FL writing tutors can learn to spot Google-translated drafts so that they and their writers do not waste time working on language generated by a machine. The following tips (along with the words of Dickinson FL writing tutors gleaned from session logs) coupled with the kind of close reading modelled earlier in this chapter can help FL writing tutors detect the signs that a writer has used Google Translate.

1. *Sentences literally translate but lack meaning because they retain the grammar and syntax of the first language instead of producing the grammar and syntax of the target language.*

    - "Many of his sentences make very little sense even though they might directly translate. I am not sure if this is from Google Translate or another form, but many of the sentences do not come across as I believe he wishes them to."

2. *The text contains multiple grammar errors because the translator incorrectly transferred English grammar rules to the target language.*

    - "It was the first composition she had written in Spanish and she had used a translator to work through her paper. It resulted in a lot of grammatical mistakes and Spanglish."

3. *Key words are archaic, stilted, or direct translations of idioms, indicating a lack of understanding about word connotations and culturally-specific idiomatic expressions.*

    - "There were issues of word choice that came from his use of Google Translate as a dictionary, which I explained was not sufficient because you need to know how and why you use different words in specific contexts."

4. *The parts of speech are confused.*

    - "I noticed a number of times that she used nouns in place of adjectives or adverbs and also had a huge amount of trouble with gender/number agreement. She also rather indiscriminately used the subjunctive and mixed up personal pronouns with possessive pronouns. I wondered if perhaps Google Translate had been used too liberally. . . .

5. *The writer cannot explain the reasoning behind awkward phrasing.*

    - "Most of her errors sounded like they were made by translating text online because she could not explain the awkward phrasing to me."

This last point, in particular, illustrates how tutors can waste time working with writers who have used Google Translate. To fix awkward phrasing the tutor would need to interact with the language producer. David Bartholomae, in his explanation of error analysis, explains why.

> An error (and I would include errors beyond those in the decoding or encoding of sentences) can only be understood as evidence of intention. They are the only evidence we have of an individual's idiosyncratic way of using the language and articulating meaning, of imposing a style on common mate-

rial. A writer's activity is linguistic and rhetorical activity; it can be different but never random. The task for both teacher and researcher, then, is to discover the grammar of that coherence, of the "idiosyncratic dialect" that belongs to a particular writer at a particular moment in the history of his attempts to imagine and reproduce the standard idiom of academic discourse. (255)

When a tutor asks a writer to explain an incorrect grammatical structure, poor word choice, or awkward phrasing, the tutor is searching for "the grammar of that coherence," a revelation of the writer's "intention." If an algorithm has created the language in question, the tutor ends up helping the writer understand and edit an error made by a third party, thereby compromising the writer's language learning and the purpose of the tutoring session.

There are several interventions tutors can make when they suspect that a writer has used Google Translate. Most simply, they can ask the writer if they have used Google Translate. In fact, FL writing tutors report that many writers do not realize that there is anything wrong with using Google Translate, and so they do not hide the fact that they used it. Once a tutor ascertains that the writer has used it, the tutor can explain the limitations (as discussed earlier in the chapter). To demonstrate those limitations, tutors have asked writers to craft a few sentences in the L2 and submit those to Google Translate for translation into the L1, and then analyzed the output sentences with the writers.

Google Translate and other online translators thwart FL students' acquisition of writing skills and undermine FL writing tutoring sessions. Foreign language writing tutors trained to understand how Google Translate works are able to converse with writers about how online translators will not only sabotage their language learning but also produce incomprehensible prose. However, even before the advent of online translators, second language writers incorporated translation into the writing process—they just did the translations themselves. Some less proficient writers compose in the first language before they translate into the target language; other more proficient writers think in the first language as they write in the target language. In fact, the role of translation in the writing process of L2 writers has been studied since the 1980s when L2 research began to evolve. At first, scholars held that any writing in the first language would inhibit the acquisition of the second language "due to transfer of structures and vocabulary from the first language in an incorrect way" (Friedlander 109). This led practitioners to urge students to think and to write only in the target language. However, in her recent review of FL writing research, Reichelt sums up the current research when she states "that it is not uncommon for writers to employ their L1 while composing in the L2, and that doing so is not necessarily detrimental to writing quality" ("L2 Writing" 190). Early studies of translation in the writing process found that L2 writers tend to switch languages and translate, subprocesses that prove to be beneficial for some writers (Krepels; Woodall). By generating content in the first language, writers reduce cognitive overload, thereby freeing up their working memory so that they can produce the target language (Cohen and Brooks-Carson 181; Van Weijen et al.). In one study of college-level L1 English speakers who were learning to write French, the best writer hardly ever incorporated English into the writing process while the second strongest writer frequently thought in English. The researcher concluded that the use of the L1 does "not necessarily result in a problematic performance" because the L1 is often "the carrier of meaning, the vehicle for formulating or reviewing content, throughout the thinking process" (Knutson 103). These studies suggest that, at least beyond the beginner level, writers who incorporate translation into the writing process would be more apt to think holistically—toggling between meaning, form, and language—than would writers whose meaning-making occurs in a language in which they are limited.

These studies of translation in the writing process have pedagogical implications for FL writing tutors. First, FL writing tutors should consider language level when determining whether to challenge a writer to think in the target language. When low proficiency writers compose in the L1, translation helps them overcome their limited vocabulary and range of syntactical forms. Yet the writing of advanced students may not always benefit from their translating the native language into the target language (Kobayashi and Rinnert). Second, FL writing tutors should ask about the instructor's writing goals or learning outcomes. If the instructor aims to develop fluency in writers, then writers may benefit from prewriting and composing in the target language. However, if the instructor wants writers to think deeply, then writers might benefit from composing in the L1 (Bean et al. 232). Finally, FL writing tutors should consider the assignment in relation to the writer. One study showed that students wrote better essays when they composed in the language in which they learned the subject matter. Chinese international students in a college-level English composition course were given two different letters. One letter came from the Director of International Students who asked them to explain the Chinese Qingming festival to US students; the other letter was from the Director of International Student Orientation who asked them for advice on issues related to college life for a revised orientation program. Some writers planned their essays in the language in which they acquired the knowledge and others did not. The researchers discovered that students who drafted in Chinese on the Chinese subject and English on the US subject scored significantly higher on the essays, wrote longer plans, and composed longer essays in English than did the mismatch group (Friedlander). Thus, FL writing tutors might choose to work with a writer in the first or target language based on the language in which the writer has attained knowledge of the subject.

Rather than developing a hard and fast rule about the use of writer-generated translations in a session, FL writing tutors should make that decision based on contextual factors (like those mentioned above). Ultimately, a pedagogy of "informed flexibility" would dictate "strategic use" of language switching during the writing process (Woodall 23). One such strategic approach would be for FL writing tutors to show writers the "double benefit" of "composing or inventing in their home language" and then "composing again" in the target language (Bean et al. 235). Foreign language writing tutors may also need to warn students about becoming too dependent on translating, particularly since such overdependence hampers fluency and prevents writers from imagining an audience comprised of target language users—the exact problem with the Google translations (Kobayashi and Rinnert). Students preparing to enter a second-language immersion context would especially benefit from composing in the target language while imagining an authentic target-language audience when they write.

Although translation is not always and immediately to be discouraged, writer-generated translations can also be marred by a myriad of problems, especially if the L2 writer is not a strong writer in the L1. The following list of tips on tutoring students who bring their own translations to a session are derived from the session logs of Dickinson FL writing tutors.

1. When writers translate words using only a thesaurus, show them how to use dictionaries to understand connotations.

- "We talked about how to choose words in Spanish based on the connotation as opposed to the exact English translation."

2. When writers' translations of phrases and sentences lack clarity, use the negotiated interaction technique.

    - "I asked L. how she could say it differently, and she was able to come up with new, more understandable constructions."
    - "She admitted starting from English and trying to translate into Italian some concepts/ideas. We read together each paragraph and worked on them individually. I suggested to re-formulate in English AND in Italian what she meant to say in order to find synonyms and easier ways to express herself. She would soon recognize the English-looking-like-sentences and would try to fix them."

3. When writers non-strategically compose entire essays by translating a draft composed in the first language, help them practice thinking in the target language.

    - We "talked a bit about how to start writing by thinking about words that she knew in Spanish instead of thinking in English first and then trying to translate it as she wrote."
    - "At first glance, on the sheet of paper that he brought in, he had an entire paragraph written on the subject in English. Then beneath that, he had short sentences in English with the Italian translation below them. Upon reading the short sentences, it became clear that a lot of work needed to be done. So much so that I simply had him turn over the piece of paper and start from scratch."

As FL writing tutors practice holistic tutoring, good pedagogy starts with calling attention to how language choices affect meaning and how writing process behaviors influence the written product. MWC directors can train FL writing tutors to instill the habits of mind and writing behaviors that help students acquire language: noticing, hypothesis testing, metalinguistic reflection, negotiated interaction, the avoidance of online translators, and the strategic use of translation in the writing process. Even more, they can use these tools holistically to toggle between the global and sentence levels, the written product and the writer's process. The next chapter continues the exploration of holistic writing tutoring by taking into account the FL writer as a whole person, considering the difficulties posed by FL writing anxiety, offering suggestions for developing a positive learning environment in the MWC.

3 Holistic Tutoring Practices: Creating a Supportive Learning Environment

Writing in a foreign language can be both mentally and emotionally stressful. Many L2 writers struggle to make meaning from a limited vocabulary and abstruse grammatical rules while, at the same time, doubting the clarity and maturity of the language they produce. Some writers bring their stress and discomfort into their sessions with FL writing tutors. Take the example of a German writing tutor who reported in a session log that after she helped a writer "rewor[d] some of her sentences so that they best reflected what she was trying to say," the writer "voiced her frustration about when her thoughts are more complex than she can put into words in German." The tutor, for whom German is a second language, revealed that she "sympathized immensely," commiserating with the writer: "it is a challenge to simplify sentences without simplifying meaning, but learning that balance is all part of the process!" Having experienced the language learning process, the tutor could empathize with the writer's struggle to negotiate her complex thoughts and limited language ability. An effective holistic tutor understands the process, including the frustrations of writing and language learning, and tends to the writer's whole person by cultivating a supportive learning environment. Such tutors make their sessions holistic by not only engaging with the piece of writing on the table but also supporting the person who wrote it.

This chapter argues that FL writing tutors should be trained to create a learning environment that sustains language learning—one in which writers feel safe to take risks and make mistakes. A supportive environment can increase motivation while the opposite can undermine students' confidence and decrease motivation (Ambrose et al,

79; Barr 5). In his Affective Filter Hypothesis, Stephen Krashen considers how anxiety, self-confidence, and motivation are interconnected when it comes to language acquisition: namely, anxious students have less self-confidence and motivation. This is problematic because learners who experience low-anxiety, high motivation, and high self-confidence are more successful in acquiring a language. Under these ideal emotional conditions, the affective filter is low, and language learners are more likely to absorb new linguistic input (30-32). Conversely, when the affective filter is high, students have more difficulty learning since the cortisol that the body produces under stress causes "short-term memory loss and impedes long-term memory retrieval" (Rubio-Alcala 198). In some ways, FL learning is particularly fraught as "few Americans who claim to speak a non-English language say that they acquired those skills in school." According to the Pew Research Center analysis of the 2006 General Social Survey, among US adults, a mere 25 percent reported that they speak a foreign language, and only 43 percent of those say that they do so "very well." Of this proficient subset, 7 percent indicated that they learned the language primarily in school (as opposed to home) (Devlin). While outdated pedagogies and the lack of an immersion experience account, in part, for the fact that a small percentage of students said they learned a language in school, learning environment is likely another important factor, particularly when that environment is unsupportive or students perceive it to be so because they suffer from FL anxiety.

Because learning environment can either exacerbate or soothe anxiety, FL writing tutors should intentionally build a foundation upon which language learning flourishes. Foreign language writing tutors can learn proactively to create a supportive relationship with all writers, especially given the fact that anxious writers are not always easy to spot from mere observation. As I have argued elsewhere, many tutor-training guides prepare tutors for encounters with distressed writers by defining or categorizing the problem types and suggesting how to approach them. The guides contain sections like "The Writer Who Comes at the Last Minute," "The Unresponsive Writer," "The Antagonistic Writer," "The Writer Who Selects an Inappropriate Topic or Uses Offensive Language," "Tutoring in Emotionally Charged Sessions" and ". . . Engaging Reluctant Writers." Emphasizing affective issues that are externalized and observable, these tutor-training manuals employ a rhetoric that may place new tutors in a defensive position—

on alert, waiting for the inevitable problem person to arrive (Lape, "Training" 2). Rather than posing a reactive approach to potential problem situations, I will examine how to create a supportive learning environment that directly addresses those with FL anxiety but, ultimately, benefits all writers. Such an approach focuses tutors on what they can control (learning environment) rather than on what they cannot control (emotional writers). This chapter will explain the obstacles FL anxiety creates for language learners and then offer tips for creating a learning environment that attenuates anxiety. The chapter ends with four case studies from FL writing tutors who intentionally created supportive learning environments in their sessions.

FOREIGN LANGUAGE WRITING ANXIETY

The phrase "foreign language writing anxiety" conjures dramatic images of writers who panic when it comes to tackling an assignment. In such scenarios, tutors easily recognize anxious writers who "fidget," "stutter and stammer," act "jittery and nervous," tense their jaws, appear wide-eyed, and avoid eye contact (Young 429; Rubio-Alcala 207). Once the session begins, these anxious writers are overly sensitive to feedback, defensive, and doubtful about their ability to succeed in learning the language (Rubio-Alcala 206). Far outside their comfort zones, they become easily frustrated and resort to procrastination. Professors and tutors may judge them to be lazy or unengaged (Horwitz et al. 127). True, some writers will manifest these physical and behavioral cues, but not all writers telegraph their FL anxiety. Some anxious writers may just seem shy when, in fact, they are passive and disengaged, reticent about participating in conversation or error correction (Young 429; Rubio-Alcala 207). Other writers who want to protect their self-image may appear to be quite cooperative, "smiling and nodding frequently . . . seldom interrupting . . . giving frequent communicative feedback such as 'uh-huh'" (Young 429). The students who are struggling the most may not even look as if they are terribly anxious or frustrated.

In understanding these writers, it helps to go beyond the overt signs and understand the "distinct complex of self-perceptions" that characterize FL anxiety (Horwitz et al. 128). Countering assumptions that FL anxiety is generalized anxiety transferred to the FL situation, Elaine Horwitz, Michael B. Horwitz, and Joann Cope posit that FL anxiety is actually a constellation of "performance anxieties" rooted in dysfunctional self-perceptions, specifically about foreign language learning (127). By understanding the research on self-perceptions and their connection to writing, FL writing tutors can construct a learning environment that offsets anxious and dysfunctional thinking, regardless of whether the student is overtly panicked or not.

While much of the research on FL anxiety does not specifically focus on writing, the conclusions regarding dysfunctional self-perceptions apply to the act of producing a FL, whether it be oral or written. Dysfunctional self-perceptions are fears and/or erroneous beliefs that can stall or sabotage learning. For example, some students are overcome by the enormity of the L2 learning task. They may be astounded by having to learn so much vocabulary and so many language rules that the idea of acquiring the target language seems impossible (Horwitz et al. 128; Van Patten and Glass 96). Other students are stymied by the "self-exposure" involved in learning another language (Gkonou 270). For adult beginners, the issue may be "sounding like a child who makes simple utterances with simple ideas" in the target language (Van Patten and Glass 92). The learners may feel profound embarrassment at their perceived "infantilization" (Rubio-Alcala 207). Alternatively, the risk of exposure can come from expressing oneself in a language without being fully aware of "linguistic or socio-cultural standards" (Gkonou 270). In these cases, anxiety arises from the perceived "disparity between the 'true' self" of the L1 and the "more limited self" of the L2 (Horwitz et al. 128). Still other perfectionist students have unrealistic expectations about their progress in acquiring the L2. They believe they cannot communicate effectively unless they understand every word of an utterance (Horwitz et al. 130). They impossibly strive to "sound like a native speaker" and believe they "should be fluent in two years" (Young 428). All of these self-perceptions can lead to a reluctance to take risks for fear—"real or imagined"—of being judged negatively by instructors and peers (Horwitz et al. 128). If students fear being judged harshly for trying and failing, they will avoid orally or in writing "uncertain or novel linguistic forms" that would expand their linguistic repertoires (MacIntyre and Gardner 112).

CREATING A POSITIVE LEARNING ENVIRONMENT

By creating a supportive learning environment, FL writing tutors preclusively address both explicit and implicit FL anxiety. Researchers have found that "a positive classroom experience is associated with positive academic outcomes at the college level including adjustment, learning outcomes, and retention" (Frisby and Martin 147). Thus, a positive learning environment in the MWC could help writers adjust to the discomforts of learning/writing a foreign language, understand and achieve the instructor's learning goals, and perhaps even persist in their language studies. A positive environment is also a "safe space," to use the contemporary parlance, "that allows students to feel secure enough to take risks, honestly express their views, and share and explore their knowledge, attitudes, and behaviors" (Holley and Steiner 50).

Conversely, a negative or unsafe learning environment can cause students to develop FL anxiety. Several scholars of FL anxiety have pointed to the "language learning experience" and teaching methods as a cause of FL anxiety (Young 429; Horwitz et al. 175). Addressing the specific problem of L2 writing anxiety, Ilona Leki argues: "Dislike of writing stems from a variety of sources, most of which, are, sadly, the probable results of education experiences" ("Techniques" 65). One such notable education experience is error correction. While receiving feedback on errors and making corrections is central to the learning process, Young cautions instructors (and, by extension, tutors) to consider "the *manner* of error correction—when, how often, and most importantly, how errors are corrected" (429). Writers can internalize feedback in a way that strengthens or diminishes them. Many writers have had the experience of internalizing an encouraging instructor's voice as they write; unfortunately, others hear only the carping criticism of an overly critical instructor. The learning environment as constructed in and through the feedback voice exceeds time and space; students can carry learning environment—for better or for worse—inside them.

Foreign language writing tutors have no control over writers' past or present classroom struggles, but they can and do play a role in counterbalancing dysfunctional learning environments. Peer tutors are key to language learning because a "comfortable peer climate enhances positive student outcomes" (Frisby and Martin 148). For students who fear being judged negatively when they express themselves in a foreign language, tutoring can serve as a type of "exposure therapy" in which writers practice the language in a social setting, ideally in front of a nonjudgmental, "more fluent" peer who is also a "sympathetic reader" (Oxford 184; Leki 77–78). In fact, both FL and L2 writing scholars have argued that "supplemental instruction," peer tutoring, "small group and pair work," and "personalize[d] language instruction" can reduce foreign language anxiety (Young 431; Van Patten and Glass). A study of Turkish EFL students with writing anxiety concluded that peer review decreased writers' anxieties and increased their confidence. Their collaboration "enabled them to learn from each other and made the learning environment less anxious and stressful" (Yastibas and Yastibas 537) Hence, FL writing tutors are ideally positioned to create an optimal environment that sustains learning.

In a supportive learning environment, FL writing tutors employ "motivational scaffolding" and "politeness." Analyzing transcripts of writing tutor-student conversations, Jo Mackiewicz and Isabelle Thompson show the importance of "building rapport and solidarity with students and attending to their motivation during writing center conferences" (66). To flesh out their important points in a FL writing context, I have synthesized research on classroom climate/learning environment from the scholarship of teaching and learning, second language acquisition, and FL writing studies. However, research in those fields focus solely on instructors, and so I have reframed the advice for FL writing tutors who, as I argue above, are often overlooked as potential contributors to a positive learning environment for FL writers.

Build rapport. Most writing tutor-training manuals stress the importance of establishing rapport—"an interpersonal relationship based on harmony, connection, and mutual trust" (Barr 2). Tutors must not only build rapport but also nurture and sustain it throughout a session and across subsequent sessions when writers return to work with the same tutor. Researchers of classroom rapport, Brandi N. Frisby and Matthew M. Martin, have speculated: "It is possible that rapport is built through several interactions and channels both within and outside of the classroom" (160). While Frisby and Martin define outside interactions as emailing the professor and attending office hours, FL writing tutors can supplement (or even undermine) classroom rapport. A study to define the instructor behaviors that students perceive as rapport-building identifies five that tutors can enact in sessions.

1. "Uncommonly attentive behaviors"—The tutor remembers the student and their individual needs while "displaying a positive, enthusiastic attitude."
2. "Connecting behaviors"—The tutor connects with the student by being "funny, easy going, approachable, informal, calm, and collected."
3. "Information sharing"—The tutor offers clear advice and feedback while "smiling, nodding, and making eye contact."
4. "Courteous behaviors"—The tutor is "flexible, supportive, inclusive . . . and willing to listen" so that the writer feels welcome to speak and to ask questions.
5. "Common grounding"—The tutor "speak[s] on the student's level and find[s] similarities with students." This rapport-building behavior is even better suited to peer tutors than to instructors. (Webb and Barrett 19-21).

These behaviors coincide with the "politeness behaviors" that operationalize "motivational scaffolding," which Mackiewicz and Thompson analyze in tutor conversations: "praise," "encouragement/optimism," "demonstration of concern for students," "statements of sympathy or empathy," "reinforcement of student ownership" (50-51). By consciously enacting these behaviors, tutors infuse the learning environment with positivity, which has the potential to become a state of mind that writes carry with them.

Manage Error Correction. Because L2 writers are acquiring the language as they are learning to write, proofreading for grammatical errors subsumes all or part of most tutoring sessions. Conscientious FL writing tutors often have the impulse to help writers eradicate all of their errors, including the ones instructors may have chosen not to mark. For some writers, though, the sheer amount of errors that need correction can cause great anxiety. Maybe the writer is a perfectionist who will not risk communication that is bound to contain errors, or maybe the writer is overwhelmed by the prospect of mastering so many grammar rules. Tutors can help such writers by showing them that their errors do not necessarily impede communication. They can show that "there is more to language learning than just grammar rules and forms" (Young 432). For those who think errors are a sign of failure, tutors can create a supportive learning environment through "selective error correction" (Gkonou 277). In so doing, writers can experience success in communicating meaning and even mastering some new grammatical forms instead of feeling inarticulate and overwhelmed by the enormity of creating standard expressions.

Understand the Language-Learning Process. Some FL writers may give up on learning a target language because they have incorrect assumptions regarding how long it should take to become fluent and how easy that process should be. They may believe that FL writing tutors have a knack for languages that makes language learning especially easy for them. Severino argues for L2 writing instructors of English to undertake "second language learning experiences" so as to develop "the humility and empathy necessary . . . to 'multilingualize'" their teaching practices ("'Multlingualizing'" 17). Similarly, FL writing tutors need to tap into their own L2 writing experiences when they work with writers. Supportive tutors can disabuse students of their erroneous ideas by disclosing their personal challenges and the obstacles they surmounted as they learned a foreign language. Specifically, FL writers need assurance that learning grammar is a slow process, and all who study a foreign language make errors. Adult learners with a limited FL ability will struggle to express themselves, but language learning is developmental and requires patience and persistence to reach higher stages. Further, receiving feedback on the meaning-making process is necessary, even though the learner can feel vulnerable and exposed (Van Patten and Glass). By sharing their own language journeys, FL writing tutors provide the positive reinforcement students need to discover their motivation and to speak confidently about their language learning (Oxford 184). (See Appendix E for a tutor training exercise designed to address this issue.) Ideally, writers who internalize tutor encouragement and engage in positive self-talk develop a mindset that informs other FL learning environments.

Tutors Building Positive Learning Environments

In the remainder of this chapter, I will bring in the voices of FL writing tutors—one from a session log and three others from interviews—who consider the affective needs of individual learners. Since I conceive of this next section as a tool for tutor training, I will provide the entire scenario, as told by a FL writing tutor, followed by an analysis of the techniques the tutor employed to create a supportive learning environment. Among other things, tutors may consider:

- What techniques does the tutor employ to build rapport, manage error correction, and/or construct a positive learning environment for the writer?
- What are/might be the effect of those techniques?
- What other techniques might the tutor have used?

In tutor training, tutors should read and discuss the scenario before proceeding to the analysis.

> *Sharing Information.* "I worked with a 100-level Spanish student. She was a first year, and she was asking me amazing questions. She brought in a very simple descriptive paragraph about her family, but it was very good. We finished going through it in fifteen minutes, and then she started asking me questions about when to use *esta, este,* or *esto,* which depends on the sex and on if the noun is tangible or intangible. Usually, people don't ask me that question until they are in 200-level Spanish. But she was asking those questions now, so I asked her: 'Do you want to pursue Spanish? What are you trying to do?' For the rest of the session, we talked about her plan to go abroad to a Spanish-speaking country."

This brief scenario highlights the point that creating a positive learning environment need not be a response to a writer's feelings of frustration or strife. The Spanish writing tutor, a heritage speaker who immigrated to the US as a child, and the writer, an introductory Spanish student, both exhibited "uncommonly attentive behaviors" during this session. The writer asked the tutor to explain an advanced grammar rule, and, rather than dismissing her question as premature, the curious tutor asked why she wanted to know and learned about her goal to "go abroad to a Spanish-speaking country." The writer made a self-disclosure that students are not always invited or willing to make in a public and formal classroom. By sharing information with her about the fine points of Spanish grammar and about life abroad, the tutor created a learning environment in which the writer felt free to express her personal motivation, engagement, and goals for future study.

> *Nurturing Motivation.* "As a writing tutor, I consider myself a representative of the Middle East Studies Program, as someone who just loves Arabic. I want to get writers on a path where they can love learning Arabic and where it's not a pain

so that it makes the learning process easier. Arabic is so difficult. I think it's one of the five most difficult languages for an English speaker. It requires a lot of focus on your part, and the easiest and most pleasant way to get in that kind of zone is when someone is trying to take care of you as a learner rather than just making sure that the language is . . . getting up to the level that it needs to be. So when I approach things holistically, I'm thinking about the student and what they're trying to learn. It creates a safer space for them to make mistakes and for them to learn from what is happening, but it's also easier for them to understand the concepts when they are being surrounded by it. You know what I mean? When you're not just saying that this is a grammatical concept because of the way it is, but when you're trying to relate it to something else that they know, bringing in other aspects of them as a student. This makes a lot of sense in how they feel about Arabic, and then how they study it.

It's kind of a "you can lead a horse to water" situation. Sometimes students are really just not into it. They are not having whatever you are trying to give them. I am a thoroughly energetic tutor. Not all of them want that, especially at 10:00 p.m. I would say most of my students really appreciate that I want them to succeed, and I ask them how class was, and they tell me their stories. But some of them just want me to sign off on their paper so that the professor knows that they came. And . . . if I want to take the time to go over how to use a dictionary rather than just being a dictionary for them, they get frustrated, and they never want to come in again.

But there's a point where you can convince them to be receptive to Arabic. I had a student who came but for a while was not enthusiastic about it. He didn't really understand the commitment that it would take, and, over time, I sort of pushed him towards it. I knew he was on a sports team, so I said: "You know, that's okay if you want to make the very last appointment for every time we're in here. That's okay. I can block that for you, and it will be after practice. You'll have time to do your homework, and you can come in." Now he's willing to come in and sit down and talk about his work.

> He came in the other day and rather than using me as a dictionary, he had the entire thing written and we could go through it. He still had a lot of errors because we were talking through it as he went. But he came in, and it was done, and it was really quite good, and I was so proud of him. I really just tried to get him to the point where he felt comfortable coming in when he wanted help with Arabic, writing and speaking, and it has made it better for him. He's enjoying it more than he was at the beginning.

This writing tutor, for whom Arabic is a second language, has an ulterior motive that influences her approach to establishing a supportive learning environment: she views herself as a "representative of the Middle East Studies Program, as someone who just loves Arabic," and she wants "to get [writers] on a path where they can love learning Arabic." She wants to "mak[e] the learning process easier" and "convince [writers] to be receptive to Arabic." This tutor describes two ways of helping students enjoy learning Arabic and persist in their language learning. First, she creates a "safe space" in which writers can "make mistakes" through careful rapport-building in which she "tak[es] care" of writers as "learner[s]" as opposed to attending solely to linguistic output. Second, she reinforces this strategy when she admits to going beyond explaining the "grammatical concept" in order to "relate [their writing] to something else that they know, bringing in other aspects of them as a student." In other words, she hopes her "connecting behaviors" will affect "how they feel about Arabic, and then how they study it."

Cognizant of writers who lack motivation and view her as "a dictionary" or an extension of the professor, she keeps the learner's needs in the forefront. She realizes this writer does not grasp the language-learning process—namely, "the commitment that it would take." Displaying "uncommonly attentive" and courteous rapport-building behaviors, the tutor convinces the writer to schedule evening appointments after his athletic practice, giving him time to prepare for the session. As a result, he came to his session with a complete rough draft that was "really quite good." The tutor's attitude of positive regard for and connection with writers, even those who are initially reluctant and disengaged, fuels her desire to make this writer feel "comfortable" as well as her pride when she realizes he is "enjoying" Arabic. Her efforts to nurture his motivation lead to his growing engagement with learning Arabic.

> *Building Confidence.* Recently a student came in—she's a senior I believe. She had this Hebrew paper, and she didn't trust herself as much as she should. She filled in a lot of words in English. But as we were working through it, I said: "You know the sentences you have in Hebrew are really good and you just have these random spots. Let's think about really easy Hebrew words you know and try to say what you're trying to say in English in the words that you do know." So working together she was able to translate all her English words she had written down.
>
> She had just gotten defeated—like, "I don't want to think of this. I'm terrible with words and my tutor can translate it for me." That was the specific issue: she didn't know certain words. I think looking at the bigger issue or the bigger picture, we realized together that she didn't know how to say what she wanted to, so I told her in the future if you're ever writing, think about how much you do know how to say because you know how to say a lot. Recognizing her skills was the bigger picture and then translating the small words was the smaller picture.
>
> I tried to give her the confidence of letting her know—and I see this with a lot of students, not just this one—they know more than they think they know. A lot of times when you come in to get tutored, you sort of rely on the tutor and bank on the tutor telling you what you know. So it is important for the tutor to help them realize they know a lot more than they think. The role of the tutor is to say, "I might know more than you because I've taken Hebrew for longer, but that doesn't mean you're not good at what you're doing." I am almost like their friend who is helping them with their homework. If they wanted to talk to their professor about this, they would go to office hours, but they specifically come to me for a reason. I'm not grading them—that brings down another wall. I'm not judging them.

Like the Arabic writing tutor, the Hebrew writing tutor sees beyond the paper on the table to the person who wrote it. In this case, the writer presented a draft that was composed in Hebrew with English words inserted when the writer's limited vocabulary failed her. As discussed in the previous chapter, this kind of translingual drafting can be a functional aspect of an L2 writer's learning process. A tutor focused only on process and product might proceed, as did the Hebrew writing tutor, by helping the writer access her new vocabulary: "Let's think about really easy words you know and try to say what you're trying to say in English in the words that you do know." However, as the tutor points out, this was the "specific issue," but there was a "bigger picture."

The bigger picture was that the writer wanted "to use bigger words" and had "just gotten defeated." According to the tutor, the writer "doesn't trust herself as much as she should," a dynamic the tutor has observed "with a lot of [Hebrew] students, not just this one." In response, the tutor uses several techniques to build a supportive learning environment. She reassures the writer and helps her understand the developmental nature of the language learning process by reinforcing the importance of employing the vocabulary that is readily available to her. She re-focuses the writer on "really easy words" because adult FL learners often avoid the vocabulary they have been taught when it does not fit the mature and complex ideas they wish to express. Consequently, the writer's anxiety about linguistic infantilization may be lurking beneath the surface of this session.

In addition, the tutor draws on "courteous behaviors" when she praises the writer and quells her anxieties: "I said, you know the sentences you have in Hebrew are really good and you just have these random spots." The tutor even theorizes her approach, positing the importance of "recognizing [the writer's] skills" and "just giving her the confidence of letting her know—and I see this with a lot of students, not just this one—they know more than they think they know." Finally, the tutor articulates her desire to connect with the student on "common ground"—a powerful position unique to writing tutors and a "wall" that instructors cannot scale. She describes being "almost like their friend that's helping them with their homework"—that is, someone who is "not grading them—that brings down another wall, like I'm not judging them." For FL writers who are anxious about being judged, the Hebrew writing tutor consciously inhabits an ethos of "friend" rather than "expert" to build confidence and motivation while lessening the writer's anxiety.

Disarming Stress. A student came to the MWC with her Portuguese essay, which had feedback from the professor, but she hadn't made the changes by herself first. I told her the Writing Center policy states that the student makes the alterations by herself first before the tutor helps. I told her I would give her a few minutes to work on it before we started the session.

She got angry and was a little rude. I remained calm and explained to her that this policy exists so she can learn from her mistakes and the professor's feedback instead of just coming here and expecting the tutor to give the answers. She started doing some of the changes and then apologized for her behavior. I told her I know she didn't mean it and that I could see she was stressed out, and I didn't take it personally. She thanked me and started crying nervously. She told me she feels frustrated for having so much work and not having enough time, and I tried to calm her down. I told her that I would help her make the alterations because I saw she was in no condition to do it by herself.

I helped her throughout the whole process, but she was proactive, trying to get the answers right. In the end of the session, when she was calmer, I told her that it is okay this time, but next time she needs to try to make the first changes by herself because this is important for her development as an autonomous learner. She thanked me and hugged me in the end. I am very worried about the level of stress she is experiencing though.

This scenario speaks to the importance of establishing rapport and sustaining it throughout a session—and even beyond. For the FL writing tutor, this session starts poorly when the writer flouts MWC policy by coming to her session without having attempted her own corrections, and then responds with anger and rudeness after the tutor explains MWC policy. Rather than react to the writer's tension and anger, the tutor remains calm and collected, important connecting behaviors. She then expertly finesses the situation and creates a positive learning environment. She gives the writer emotional and physical space to work on proofreading. The writer self-corrects, apologizes for her behavior, and makes herself vulnerable to the stranger she just treated rudely. In other words, the writer assumes "common grounding" with the peer tutor and is rewarded for taking a risk. The tutor responds with "courteous behaviors," keeping the goal of re-establishing a positive learning environment in view. She accepts the writer's apology as is evidenced by her willingness first to listen to the writer disclose her frustration and stress, and then to try to "calm her down." The tutor succeeds because she is able to separate herself from the overwrought writer. As she admits, she "didn't take it personally."

The tutor also makes the controversial decision to break with (but not abandon) MWC policy and help the writer correct her errors "because she was in no condition to do it by herself." The tutor's breaking with policy is a "demonstration of concern for the writer," a key aspect of motivational scaffolding. Rather than being rigid and inflexible about the rules, she finds a middle ground on which she balances best practices and concern for the writer. It is unclear whether the writer was mainly overwhelmed by the errors in her draft or by the demands of her studies in general. Nevertheless, the tutor imparts a functional practice of error correction. Although she helps the writer "throughout the whole process," the writer is "proactive," making her own corrections under the supportive gaze of the tutor. Sensing the writer has regained her emotional calm, the tutor reminds her that she needs to "make the changes first" because it is "important for her development as an autonomous learner." By the end of the session, the tutor has "reinforce[d] . . . student ownership" and conveyed an important aspect of the language learning process—autonomy (Mackiewicz and Thompson). The session that began with the writer's rude outburst ends with the writer hugging the tutor, and the tutor empathetically expressing her continued concern for the writer's well-being to the instructor via the session log.

If, as Krashen and others hypothesize, FL anxiety threatens to undermine the success and persistence of language learners, an MWC staffed by trained peer writing tutors can prove to be a powerful intervention. Rather than succumb to the stress and anxiety of FL learning, writers can work with FL writing tutors who are trained not necessarily to diagnose problem situations but to understand the mentality of struggling language learners, build a supportive learning environment, and sustain it through as many sessions as the writer attends. That said, those who train FL writing tutors must do more than recruit empathetic students and expect that empathy to emerge and transfer to their FL writing tutoring; instead, WCAs must facilitate explicit conversations about the importance and characteristics of supportive learning environments. Positioned to affect significantly the mindsets of FL learners, FL writing tutors create a kind of transportable learning environment that can sustain (or undermine, in the worst case) the acquisition of FL literacy and fluency. By building rapport, placing errors in perspective, and demystifying the language learning process, FL writing tutors mold the transportable learning environment by becoming a positive voice that echoes in the minds of writers.

4 Helping Writers Understand Writing Culture Shock and Develop Intercultural Competence

As FL writers focus on how to make meaning in the target language, they must write about something—and that something often involves culture. Based on courses recently taught by my colleagues, FL writers may encounter topics like Russian popular culture and news media, soccer in Latin America, rituals and celebrations in Hispanic culture, minority cultures in Germany, food and French cultural identity, Japanese film and literature, among many others. Considered a "World Readiness Standard for Learning Languages" by the American Council for Teachers of Foreign Languages, cultural understanding is thoroughly interwoven into FL curricula. To fully support learning-to-write assignments, then, FL writing tutors need to be trained to address culture in all its manifestations. An MWC that does not tangle with culture ends up supporting language instruction within a vacuum.

By "culture in all of its manifestations," I do not mean just cultural knowledge—though, of course, FL writing tutors can and should help demystify aspects of culture of which they have knowledge. While FL writing tutors are not content-area tutors nor can they all be expected to have equal knowledge, for example, of soccer or news media or food culture, etc., there are aspects of culture, namely intercultural rhetoric, that all FL writing tutors can learn to address. Foreign language writers do not always consider how culture inflects writing—both process and product. An instructor of Russian whom I interviewed for the final chapter stated of her students, "knowing writing genres and knowing about writing differences culturally is an important part of building cultural knowledge and cultural appreciation." This chapter discusses how to internationalize the writing center by training tutors to engage with the cultural aspects of writing.

When FL writers transfer their knowledge and expectations about academic writing from their home to their study abroad culture, they may experience writing culture shock. Culture shock occurs when a sojourner encounters unwelcome or unexpected differences between the home and abroad culture, which lead to "increased ambiguity and uncertainty" (Hess 140). Foreign language writers face writing culture shock when they realize that their assumptions about the development of writers and the criteria for "good writing" differ across cultures. Even the most smart and savvy students can be taken unawares, as is true of Catrina, a French writing tutor, who described in an interview her "ambiguity and uncertainty" as she sought to tackle academic writing assignments at a French university:

> It just was so counter-intuitive to the way I was used to writing that I just felt like I was lost for a long time. I'd be writing in my room, and my host mom would say, "Oh, how's it going?" And I was like, "I don't know! I don't know what's going on!" It was this awful experience. "I don't know how to write. What am I doing? I'm just like a poor excuse for an English major. Why am I here?" You know, those moments of self-doubt. That was really surprising. I know how to write, I think. So taking that experience and trying to move forward with it and not be totally crippled by this weird form that I was forced to use.

Catrina's writing culture shock surprised her and left her in a paradoxical position. On the one hand, she wanted to assimilate, to perform correctly the writing task that her teacher had assigned. On the other hand, she admitted to feeling "forced" into using culturally-specific academic writing conventions. Her shock is evident in the language she used to describe these conventions: "counter-intuitive" and even "weird." Discursively adrift, she lamented her "awful experience" and devolved into crushing "self-doubt"—not surprisingly, since culture shock often leads to "questions about . . . personal competence" (Hess 140). Ultimately, Catrina made "the rhetorical choice not to deviate from the dominant practice" but to master the culturally-specific, French writing skills that had eluded her at first (Matsuda, "Lure"

481). In an MWC that seeks to be truly internationalized, FL writing tutors can demystify intercultural encounters, whether at home or abroad, by talking to writers about language, writing, and culture. Such conversations train FL writing tutors to embrace a mindset of cultural relativism in which writing reflects culture as opposed to an ethnocentric mindset in which US writing conventions and practices are deemed universal while all others are "weird." Drawing on interviews with students, this chapter lays a framework for intercultural conversations by examining some conditions that create writing culture shock— namely, culture-specific academic genres and conventions, absence of support for the writing process, and conflicting definitions of "good writing." The chapter ends with techniques tutors can use to help writers develop the intercultural competence that will enable them to reframe their shock and navigate new writing cultures.

CULTURE-SPECIFIC ACADEMIC WRITING

FL writing tutors need to examine the ways in which writing is a cultural construct. The connection between writing and culture was first made by Robert Kaplan whose famous "squiggles" of Oriental, Semitic, English, Russian, and Romance writing illustrate his premise that "thought patterns" arise from "cultural patterns" ("Cultural" 12). Assuming a stance of cultural relativism, he argues that international students are not necessarily poor but "different" writers who "employ a rhetoric and a sequence of thought which violate the expectations of the native [English] reader" ("Cultural" 13). As is true of Catrina's experience writing abroad, international students, according to Kaplan, have "a rich inventory of various genres; the problem is that those genres may be utterly inappropriate in an English-speaking [i.e., foreign] academic context" ("What" xi). Based on an analysis of six hundred student essays, he concludes that the English thought pattern is "dominantly linear," and then contrasts it to the other four cultures ("Cultural" 13). The "Semitic" pattern "is based on a complex series of parallel constructions" (15); "Oriental" "turn[s] around the subject and show[s] it from a variety of tangential views" (17); and "Romance" and "Russian" take different kinds of "digressions" (18-19). While scholars today credit Kaplan with starting an important conversation, they also critique many of his essentialist assumptions. Kaplan suggests that when given an assignment, students will revert to prior knowledge of culturally-determined thought patterns. He assumes that international students have read and written texts frequently enough in their native languages to develop "a rich inventory of various genres"—an assumption that may not be universally true since at the time of this writing many international academic cultures would have assigned writing scarcely and infrequently. Further, rooted in a concept of culture that derives from a "colonialist, racist past" in which some groups were subordinate and "other," Kaplan's squiggles place writers of languages other than English in binary opposition to "linear" writers of English. The squiggles imply that culture is "deterministic" and writers are "cultural robots" when, in fact, "cultural mixing and meshing" occurs as writers construct a "variety of positions and identities" (Atkinson 560). Thus, scholars now dismiss Kaplan's theory of contrastive rhetoric and, in recent years, "cultural influence on L2 writing often seems to have become a topic either to critique or avoid" (Atkinson 546).

Seeking to recuperate the scholarly conversation, Ulla Connor reconsiders contrastive rhetoric, pointing out the essentialist and binary logic that it replicates and the "need to move far beyond such binary distinctions as linear vs. nonlinear discourse, Japanese prose versus Finnish prose, inductive versus deductive logic, and collectivist versus individualist norms" (304). Instead, she imagines a multidimensional theory of "intercultural rhetoric" that moves beyond textual features and examines writerly behaviors: "[I]t needs to describe the vast complexities of cultural, social, and education factors affecting a writing situation. It must attempt to understand why and how individuals behave rather than simply study cultural artifacts and products. We need to understand the speakers, writers, and readers. We need to know what went into the processes of writing as well as the historical background" (304). Alternatively, some scholars, like Matsuda and Dwight Atkinson, observe the broader social contexts that shape texts: "many people in CR [contrastive rhetoric] agree that language/culture/educational contexts and individual differences, the socio-historic moment, economic conditions, and many other things—such as conventions of the publishers and the scholarly societies—play roles in shaping any given written text" (284). Still others focus on educational contexts, attributing difference to "course assignments, curricular writing instruction, institutional specifics, disciplinary writing cultures, as well as national or language-related aspects" (Chitez and Krause 156).

Because the differences among international writing cultures are multiply determined, and there is not a universal academic discourse, FL writers will encounter new genres and surprising prompts that can cause writing culture shock. The film *Writing Across Borders*, shown in many tutor training courses, begins with a poignant example of how an international student's socio-historic context resulted in her [mis]interpretation of an assignment. An African graduate student in public health describes an assignment that required her to evaluate the lunch program of a US middle school. To do so, she had to assess whether or not the meals were nutritionally balanced, and the school followed federal regulations. Her failure to produce the appropriate genre had less to do with her replicating essentialist African thought patterns and more to do with her conditioning as an African citizen. She explains, "if I go back to my country where I come from, Malawi, before 1994 it was so hard for us to criticize anything related to the government . . . it was so hard because if we do that, most of the times people were arrested or something done to them by the government." In the case of this student, the main rhetorical move required to craft a successful evaluation was literally shocking to her since she perceived that move—finding fault with a government agency—as potentially life-threatening. While this example is extreme, it raises the issue of how the rhetorical awareness writers need to tackle assignments may run counter to the rhetorical awareness they develop as students in a particular educational system or as citizens in a particular country.

Similarly, US students who write in a foreign language must also deal with writing culture shock. As Christiane Donahue remarks, "a broadly ignored area of composition work is that of US monolingual students' experiences when they go overseas to study or work and find themselves in universities or workplaces with different rhetorical, discursive, and sociolinguistic expectations, whether that work is being done in English or another language" ("Internationalization" 218). Eileen, a French and English writing tutor who studied abroad in France for her junior year, recounted how unstated genre expectations caused writing culture shock for her when she was assigned a *con détaillé* for her very first assignment. She explained, "I asked a person that I knew and she said, 'Oh, it's just an outline, don't worry about it.' I asked my host parents, 'Oh, it's just an outline, don't worry about it.' So I didn't worry about it, and then it was something to be worried about when I got to class." Assuming that genres are universal, Eileen resorted to her prior knowledge of outlines that she learned in the US: "So I thought it was like an American style outline and it's just a couple bullet points. On this part, you'll say this, this part you're going to say that, this part you're going to say that. Fine, over with, done. One page tops. So that's what I did." The shock occurred when she realized she had profoundly misinterpreted the French meaning of "outline": "But I get to class the week after when it was due and the person [sitting next to me] pulled out this giant packet of every single spaced, every single, tiny detail of this topic. So it's basically writing a paper but just in outline form with endnotes and stuff." To her credit, Eileen turned her shock into writing culture knowledge and awareness: "So that was a bit of shock in that the *détaillé* really meant details. That was kind of typical, you had to be very organized, very detailed, very conscious of these things when writing things." Like the student from Malawi, Eileen learned how culture shapes genre, turning her (mis)interpretation into a newfound awareness of the detailed outline in French academic writing culture.

Support for Writers

Foreign language writing tutors need to be aware that in other countries educators have different assumptions about how writing is taught and learned (and, consequently, supported). While many international writing cultures expect students to demonstrate writing proficiency—often in the form of a thesis—to earn a degree, many assume that "writing development and pedagogy" are "transparent or even inevitable" (Russell and Foster 7). Conversely, in the US where writing studies developed as a discipline, cognitive researchers determined in the late twentieth-century that writing could and should be taught. According to David R. Russell and David Foster, the "prevalence in US universities of general writing courses," however, "strikes teachers in many other nations as strange" (7). When academic writers come from the US where writing is taught as well as assigned to countries in which writing is either rarely assigned or assigned but not taught, the conditions are right for writing culture shock.

Several writing studies scholars have commented on international academic cultures in which educators presume that writing development is "inevitable" and writing skills are "transparent." Lisa Ganobcsik-Williams describes her realization, as a US exchange student in

England, that she would receive no "guidance on expectations for writing in a higher education culture" because faculty believed that "students learned to write (or didn't) through acculturation" (500). Similarly, Paula Carlino finds that in Spanish and Latin American universities, faculty presume that students learn to write during their "compulsory education" years and that reading and writing are "general abilities that can be transferred to any context" (489). Thus, in Spanish and Latin American universities, instructors do not offer "guidelines" for writing or feedback on writing, and they have no need for writing-in-the-disciplines pedagogy (489-91).

In 1999, the Bologna Declaration brought about changes in writing culture across several European institutions of higher education. Some institutions began to assign more writing, albeit outside the context of a structured writing program in which students were taught to write. The twenty-nine European countries that signed the Declaration agreed to 1.) make all European diplomas comparable, 2.) align their degree programs by instituting a three-year bachelor's, two-year master's; three-year doctorate; 3.) create college credits that were transferable across European universities; 4.) establish "quality assurance"; and 5.) simplify student and instructor movement among European universities (Dysthe 239). The statement on "quality assurance" had the greatest impact on writing culture. For example, in Norway before the Bologna Declaration, universities tended to assign undergraduates "little or no compulsory writing" and "training in sustained writing was lacking" even though graduate degrees were contingent upon writing ability (Dysthe 238). At the same time, "critics of the Norwegian university system for decades ha[d] deplored the lack of undergraduate writing" (Dysthe 246). When the Bologna Declaration's "quality assurance" standard called for active learning and the assessment of student learning, Norwegian professors started to assign more writing and to provide more feedback, thereby engaging students in active learning while providing formative assessment (Dysthe 239, 246). Still, the reforms occurred outside of structured writing programs that would "ensure a sensible progression throughout a student's educational trajectory" (Dysthe 251).

Similarly, in Italy and France, more writing was assigned, though not taught, after the Bologna Declaration. Historically, in Italian higher education, the *corso universitario* (lecture) was followed by an oral exam. After four years of oral assessment, students were required to produce a *tesi di laurea*—a final thesis—for which they had no preparation. The Bologna Declaration inspired Italy's institutions of higher education to increase the amount of writing. Candidates for a bachelor's degree now write a *prova finale* (final thesis), and candidates for a master's degree write a *tesi di laurea magistrale*. In addition, some professors began to assign more writing in courses, like the *tesina* (researched argument) and the *saggio* (essay) (Chitez and Kruse 170-71). The increase in assigned writing without formal writing instruction was also the case in France. However, in France, there are multiple academic genres like the *commentaire* and *dissertation*, that have strict rules and unique formats. (Chitez and Kruse 164). Some institutions offer "*methodologie universitaire*" courses, but these focus on "acculturation to university work in general" rather than writing instruction (166). While there has been scholarly work published on French academic genres, little is known about whether students are taught writing process skills (Chitez and Kruse 166).

Among European countries, Germany is the exception in that many German institutions of higher education privilege writing as a form of learning and also provide support for writers vis a vis German-language writing centers. Gerd Brauer cites the "pressing needs stemming from the Bologna Reform" as causing "students and teaching faculty alike" to "act in a way that finally supports process writing and the long-term development of academic writers" (481). Unlike Italian universities, for example, which have relied on the oral exam to assess student learning, German universities have historically employed writing as a form of learning. In the nineteenth century, Wilhelm von Humboldt restructured German education and created the "research seminar," and "for the first time in university education," writing "became the main teaching and learning agent" (Chitez and Kruse 168). Student writing was the means to provoke discussion among seminar participants. Students were also asked to choose a subtopic in a "research field," "define" and "narrow" the subtopic, and then conduct their own research. While formative feedback from the professor was not part of the process (Chitez and Kruse 169), German-language writing centers have proliferated across Germany to fulfill that need. These writing centers offer writers "one-on-one interaction" with tutors, train faculty in writing process pedagogy with emphasis on "regular feedback of different kinds," conduct extracurricular writing workshops for students, offer writing instruction through "lectures and workshops" and beginning writing courses, and facilitate writing groups and/or collaborative writing projects (Brauer 474-75). In short, writing centers address the need for writing instruction and faculty development in German institutions.

When FL writers travel abroad to writing cultures in which writing is assigned but not taught, they may find themselves struggling to write without guidance or feedback on the process. An anthropology major and an MWC tutor in Spanish and English, Zoey traveled to Cuzco, Peru to study indigenous people and globalization. She described writing assignments in disciplinary as opposed to cultural terms. As an anthropology student, Zoey was told to keep a field journal in Spanish in order to write a long, researched essay about an aspect of her field experience. While she understood the assignments and felt comfortable with the expectations, she found herself experiencing a writing culture that was, as she described it, "different than the writing process and evaluation and professor feedback" culture of her home institution.

Zoey's writing culture shock arose from the feedback experience. In the US, she had come to expect that her classroom instructor would provide feedback so that she could assess and then improve her writing performance. Yet this was not the rhetorical situation that informed the giving and receiving of feedback in Cuzco. Whereas in the US Zoey "would usually use the first assignment to gauge . . . performance" and "better craft [her] second paper," in her Cuzco course, "we didn't receive our papers back before we turned in the second one." She also learned to her surprise that the feedback she received was abridged. At the end of the course, she requested a transcript for her home institution, only to discover that "they had written a short paragraph about the paper itself, strengths, weaknesses, overall successes that they hadn't included on the papers that they'd given back to us. *So it was kind of weird* that there was this whole section that they weren't really giving to us; you had to ask for it [emphasis added]." She described the feedback she received: "they would circle things or underline things and make general comments" like "elaborate more here or incorporate sources better here" while "the more extended version was more specific." Zoey concluded that in the US, feedback was part of the student's learning process while in the Cuzco program, feedback was more important for administrators. Finally, because the course was team-taught, she did not know who assessed her writing. Zoey reflected, "*It was weird*, I guess I never really thought about it [emphasis added]. I just assumed that the professor who was reading it was correcting. But in December when I asked for the summary of the evaluation of my paper, it was the other person [another instructor] who sent it to me." Like Catrina, Zoey used the adjective "weird" to denote practices that differ from those of US academic culture—ones that create uncertainty and ambiguity. "Weird" is an adjective that signals writing culture shock or the cognizance that US writing conventions and processes are not universal.

Zoey described the even more dramatic writing culture shock of other students in the program who tried to navigate a low-guidance, low-feedback writing culture. In one instance, a professor issued an oral prompt for an assignment: "She said make a compare and contrast, design a compare and contrast essay based on several of the readings that we've read up to this point." According to Zoey, the prompt "sent them [her fellow students] into a tailspin and they were just panicking" as they tried to guess what "several" and even "compare and contrast" meant. Zoey attributed the shock, on the one hand, to a lack of guidance and feedback: "I guess for other students, they were more accustomed to a stronger rubric and a stricter list of expectations that . . . spelled out explicitly exactly what they were to do." Zoey further surmised that the instructor "probably didn't understand how much the students were used to having things enunciated step-by-step-by-step." On the other hand, she ascribed the writing culture shock to lack of preparation on the part of her peers who had not mastered compare and contrast, "a basic writing skill." Quite insightfully, Zoey concluded, "it was a giant mix of expectations, languages, backgrounds, which really complicated the professor getting clear and soothing the students' worries for the first assignment. . . ." While Zoey conceded that the students had "practice in the first assignment" to prepare them for the second one, she admitted "but then again, they didn't have feedback on the first assignment" and she did not know if her panicky classmates "went to the professor afterwards to say, 'Hey, did I do this right?'" As US students write in FL classrooms and study abroad, they may find themselves immersed in academic cultures in which writing process pedagogy, which had been institutionalized in US K-16 settings for several decades, does not exist, resulting in writing culture shock. Writing tutors who have had experiences like Zooey can share with writers bound for study abroad the cultural differences that frame writing in and for international institutions.

UNCLEAR RULES AND EXPECTATIONS

Besides unfamiliar genres and lack of writing support, FL writing tutors need to learn to talk to writers about how study abroad often requires writers to decipher the criteria for "good writing," which may not only be unstated but also different across cultures. For example, in a cross-cultural study of "good writing," Melinda Reichelt asked English teachers in the US and Germany to assess three different literary analysis essays written by US secondary school students. She found some key cultural differences regarding what each group valued in the writing. German teachers favored content and organization, specifically essays that answered the assignment prompt, exhibited a "logical" and "understandable" organization, and contained "ideas and analysis." US teachers praised a predictable structure—that is, a clear thesis statement, congruence between the points stated in the thesis and the body, and a five-paragraph essay organization ("Defining" 110-11).

Like Reichelt, Xiao Ming Li studied the concept of "good writing" among US versus Chinese educators. Starting with the belief that Chinese and US teachers have different "educational philosoph[ies]," Li describes the "arbitrariness and cultural situatedness of the criteria for good writing" (2). According to Li, the Imperial Exam, which was administered to Chinese students from 587 CE to 1905, continues to influence Chinese educators, resulting in "well-developed theories and praxes of composition, as well as widely accepted criteria for 'good writing'" (4). To explore cultural differences in writing assessment criteria, Li conducted an ethnography in which two teachers from the US and two from China were invited to contribute five or six of their students' "best personal narratives" and to explain why the essays were the best. Next, all four teachers commented on a subset of six essays from both countries and discussed their comments with each other. Four of those six essays were distributed to a larger group of about thirty teachers from both countries who were then asked to rank the papers and explain the reasons for their rankings (5).

While there was not unanimity among all teachers of the same country, Li identified several distinct cross-cultural differences between the Chinese and US teachers. "Obliged by the Chinese tradition and the current political system to be the gatekeepers of social morality and ethics," Chinese teachers favored tradition, "social impact," and "honest, strong, sincere emotions" (115, 126). US teachers valued self-expression, realistic detail, and lack of emotions (126). In terms of narrative style, Chinese teachers rewarded a "selective and suggestive narrative style" and "poetic images" (121). In Li's words, they liked "the mingling of the qing (human emotions) with jing (natural scenes) and their preference for a 'dragon's eye' at the end to bring the piece to a definitive closure" (126). The US teachers preferred narratives with "flawless logic," an "opening that leads the reader immediately to the action," and an "ambivalent and provocative ending." A major difference of opinion centered on the role of emotion in writing, for the US teachers found the Chinese essays to be "uncontrollable, almost peevish," and "over dramatic and overly sentimental" (122-26). An implication of Reichelt's and Li's studies is that students need tools to uncover the often-unarticulated expectations of "good writing" when they find themselves in a different writing culture—whether it be during study abroad or simply in a FL classroom.

In the case of Morgan, who studied in Italy, undefined expectations coupled with second language challenges caused her to resort to writing behaviors she had outgrown in order to tackle "foreign" assignments. She chose not to approach her instructors for clarification because she perceived them to be "aloof": "the professor will lay out the lesson and just lecture and then kind of walk away, end of class." In addition, she understood writing to be not an important measure of learning but practice for oral examinations. She mentioned one class in which writing assignments "weren't really graded as essays but they were more given to sort of help us prepare for our oral exam at the end of the lesson." When asked directly if she had understood the criteria of good writing, Morgan said Italian papers needed "to have a main point" and that examples as evidence were "really essential," but, as opposed to English, a "very clear-cut thesis that is very argumentative" was not important. She inferred that her professors expected her to write "coherently in another language," and so their main concern was whether or not the paper "made sense."

Confronted with an unfamiliar use of and criteria for "good writing" coupled with the challenge of composing in a second language, Morgan adapted by developing a reductive version of her English writing process. She eliminated the formal planning stage because it was "hard for me to completely plan out everything . . . I kind of had main headings of main ideas that I wanted to focus on and then just kind of wrote from there and revised as I went along." She described her Italian writing process as "less structured, less organized, more kind of write as you go and then revise afterwards." To bring structure back into her process, she resorted to the five-paragraph essay, which, as she said, she had "definitely got away from once I started college, but in [Italy] since my papers were a little bit shorter and it took longer for me to write them because they were in another language, I felt like if I had introduction and conclusion and three really, really good points then my paper was okay. So my writing was a little bit more structured in that way. I'd look at the length of my paragraphs and judge by that, if I had examples." Although she was an advanced writer and an experienced writing center tutor, Morgan, like many struggling writers, gained control of the messy writing process by making three points and estimating the quality of her writing by the length of her paragraphs. As a result, meaning-making and argument took a backseat to organization and correctness (i.e., understandability). Morgan was hampered because she did not know, nor could she infer, what her Italian professors considered to be good writing. As a result, she shifted into survival mode, abandoned the planning stage, and resorted to the five-paragraph essay. To prevent FL writing tutors from universalizing US writing practices, WCAs can help them investigate the varieties of international writing cultures and identify culture-specific notions of "good writing."

Writing Culture Shock and the Politics of Acculturation

Catrina's, Eileen's, and Morgan's frustrations arose in large part from a desire to understand and, ultimately, succeed in an international writing culture. Their experiences underscore a central conundrum for FL writing tutors: how should tutors help writers position themselves in FL writing? As Li concludes in her study of Chinese versus US definitions of good writing, "To write to different standards . . . is to do more than switch linguistic codes: it is a process of acculturation" (127). In other words, when FL writing is done for purposes other than reinforcing language acquisition, FL writers must take on the writing practices, rhetorical situations, and conventions of another culture. Rather than FL writing tutors assuming their preferred stance toward acculturation, they should converse with writers about the writers' goals, particularly in relation to acculturation. Severino, for example, identifies three potential pedagogical stances in second language writing classrooms. Assimilationist instructors, often concerned with the demands of the job market, expect linear and thesis-driven arguments written in idiomatic standard English that "eradicate linguistic and cultural differences" ("Sociopolitical" 187). Oppositely, separatists "celebrate linguistic diversity" in order to build a society that accepts multiple cultures and their differences. However, students of separatists, the most vulnerable to future writing culture shock, may find themselves in uncertainty and ambiguity "when the next teacher, tutor, or employer they encounter tends toward an assimilationist stance" ("Sociopolitical" 188). Synthesizing these opposing approaches, accommodationists (acculturationists) help students "acquir[e] new discourse patterns" by balancing "both linguistic differences and societal conventions" ("Sociopolitical" 188-89). Accommodationists, then, respect students' own language while helping them function linguistically in the English-speaking world.

When FL writing tutors (or teachers) assume a particular stance, they take the choice of language-learning goals away from students. Ruth Spack's longitudinal study of Yuko, a Japanese international student in the US, reveals a researcher whose accommodationist philosophy seems, at times, to conflict with the student's stated assimilationist goals. Throughout the study, Yuko is a conscious assimilationist, uncomfortably so, even placing US above Japanese educational approaches. In fact, Yuko's choice to attend a US college "was tied to her resistance to the education she was receiving in Japan" (34). She chooses to learn in the "American style" because she thinks "independent and creative learning" is lacking in Japan (21). Yuko paints a stark contrast between Japanese and US writing: "the former being a repetition of the ideas contained in a reading and the latter being an original opinion provided by the (student) writer" (28). (As Spack comments, Yuko's "Japanese" writing, namely summary, is quite common in the US.) Further, Yuko frames her "failures" as a developing writer in nationalistic terms. She is displeased with a B+ on a political science essay because she wrote the paper "'the way I always did it in Japan'" rather than "'like an American'" (25).

Yuko's desire to assimilate—learn "the American way"—at first confuses Spack who is "puzzled by Yuko's apparent acceptance of the system." Spack then claims to have misread Yuko's assimilationist stance for while Yuko rebelled against Japanese education, she also "was skeptical about American discourse practices," which, to her, "lacked subtlety and implication" (35). Spack resolves the assimilationist conundrum by dubbing Yuko an "emancipated learner" (35) and concluding that it is important "to accept wider varieties of expression and be careful not to insist on students' conforming to one way of communicating" (38). But does Spack place her pedagogical stance above Yuko's learning goals? Perhaps like Catrina and Eileen who desired to master French writing conventions, Yuko wanted to learn "the American way." It would make sense that writers who seek a linguistic immersion experience but plan to return to their native country would be more favorably inclined toward an assimilationist approach than writers who have immigrated or plan to immigrate. Temporary sojourners might choose to immerse themselves in another culture and assimilate. Spack's study of Yuko leaves the reader wondering if Yuko's choice to assimilate is pragmatic, experimental, misguided, or ethnocentric. Ultimately, Yuko's story highlights the importance of instructors and tutors talking to FL writers about their language-learning goals.

In fact, as FL writers consider (and reconsider) whether they want to assimilate, acculturate, or separate, FL writing tutors trained in intercultural competence can support them and help them strategize their goals. Intercultural competence involves the ability to think critically about an intercultural situation, "asses[s] global perspectives," and "understand other worldviews" so as to exhibit "*effective* and *appropriate* behavior and communication in intercultural situations" (Deardorff 66, 68). Thus, intercultural competence shifts the focus from the politics of acculturation to the ethics of intercultural understanding. When writers experience writing culture shock, or even before they do, an interculturally competent writing tutor can help them strategize how they position themselves culturally as writers.

TRAINING FL WRITING TUTORS IN INTERCULTURAL COMPETENCE

In the field of intercultural competence, there are several versions of a heuristic that helps students confront (conscious and unconscious) ethnocentrism, mediate culture shock and the disorientation that accompanies it, and think critically about their intercultural positioning.[14] This heuristic prompts students to describe and then interpret an intercultural event. First, the student/writer recognizes a "critical event" or an occurrence that breaks with "routine" (for a writing culture example, an assignment prompt that does not require an argumentative thesis). Next, the writer asks someone from the culture for information that will help them understand the critical event. Finally, the writer formulates a new interpretation and adopts a new behavior. This heuristic rests on the assumption that the "ability to perceive reality, especially in cross-cultural situations, is limited" (Hess 25).

As a first step to building intercultural competence in writers, FL writing tutors need to develop a nuanced understanding of international writing cultures so that they can offer writers tools for positioning themselves interculturally. Training exercises can prepare FL writing tutors to recognize "critical events" that break with routine—to identify those seemingly unconventional conventions. Drawing on the work of JoAnne Liebman, Severino turns her writing tutors into amateur ethnographers to better assist international students with their English writing. Severino's tutors prompt L2 writers of English to "describe their native writing instruction and experiences" as well as how writing for US teachers differs from writing for teachers in their native countries. The tutors, then, ask students to consider how "cultural values differ" and how "these differences influence writing and writing pedagogy" ("'Doodles'" 49; "Writing" 56). Adapting this as an exercise for FL writing tutors, I facilitate discussion around four questions that focus on writing in different cultural contexts:

1. How would you describe your native writing instruction and experiences?
2. What surprised you most about your study abroad writing instruction and experiences?
3. What was most familiar to you about your study abroad writing instruction and experiences?
4. How would you describe native and study abroad writing experiences when you tutor?

FL writing tutors work in language teams to generate answers to these questions.

When discussing the lists across language groups, the tutors begin to see areas of commonality but also evidence of culturally-specific writing conventions. For example, the Chinese writing tutors pointed out that Chinese writers use symbolism and complex sentences that are difficult to understand, making the reader tease out the "mystery," to quote one tutor. Chinese writers also use historical stories as examples, but they are not expected to document them. At one meeting, when the discussion turned to how cultural conventions influence tutoring, the tutors shared that they had, at times, experienced difficulty convincing writers of the accuracy and authenticity of conventions, mainly because the conventions ran counter to the writers' US-based prior knowledge (i.e., always document sources; spell things out for the reader in an authoritative voice; eliminate redundancies, etc.). Through this discussion, the FL writing tutors begin to see how writing culture shock inflects their sessions.

After prompting FL writing tutors to reflect on their own critical events regarding writing culture shock, the following case studies based on surveys with FL writing tutors can be used in tutor training. The exercise is followed by a close reading that unpacks the case scenario. In tutor training, tutors should read and discuss the scenario before proceeding to the analysis.

> *Understanding the Critical Event and Gathering Information about the Culture:* Grace, Lila, and Amelia are senior French writing tutors who just returned from their junior year abroad in France. They each took courses at the French university where they were required to read and write in French. They are talking about their experiences in the MWC when Jake, a sophomore, walks in and overhears their conversation. He joins the conversation, sharing that he is in the process of applying to the same program, but he is nervous about studying and writing in French, his second language.
>   Lila remarks that French writing assignments are "far more structured and less open to the creativity/originality of students." Grace agrees with her, noting that "formatting is important." Amelia echoes their observations, stating that "following the recipe" helped her complete the assignments. Jake is not sure what to make of this information as he notes that format is also important in his current courses. Lila attempts to explain, "Disputing the professor's ideas or those of

a critic is not encouraged and perhaps discouraged." Grace jumps in to add: "Personal voice is not very important. If I want a good grade, I need to write like a professor." She continues, "The professor is God. Do not contradict unless you're feeling *reeeal* [sic] confident." And Amelia concurs, "Do exactly what the professor says. . . . You have to spit out what you've learned for a good grade."

1. In what ways might Lila, Grace, and Amelia be expressing writing culture shock?
2. How did the shock denote a break with routine for them?
3. What caused the writing culture shock?
4. What information about the writing culture might Lila, Grace, and Amelia be missing?
5. Where might they go to find that information?

Formulating a New Interpretation: In the middle of the conversation, Melissa, another French writing tutor, arrives for her shift, and Lila draws her into the conversation. Lila explains that they had been telling Jake about what French professors expect of writers. Melissa quips, "The French adore structure, to the point that it's almost rigid." She elaborates, "In literature, French professors often ask for a *commentaire composé*; a very intense, detailed close reading on one particular section of a work, rather than an essay that treats an entire piece. Even larger essays, called *dissertations*, are different and then incorporate multiple works to show one's knowledge of a subject as a whole." Also, essays begin with the *problématique*, which is "different from a thesis statement. Essentially, the *problématique* asks the question that a thesis statement would answer."

1. Has Melissa also experienced writing culture shock?
2. How does her explanation of French writing culture differ from Lila's, Grace's and Amelia's?
3. What might their differing perspectives suggest about how they approach tutoring?

Grace, Lila, and Amelia were seniors who had spent their junior year abroad at a French university. On the one hand, they had taken a course that introduced them to the basic French genres—*commentaire de texte, dissertation,* and *exposé oral*—that form the basis of French university writing (Donahue, "Lycee" 136). On the other hand, the bulk of their previous academic writing in the US mainly involved literary and cultural analysis in which they were taught to argue a controvertible thesis, develop an original analysis, and craft an organic line of argument. Their US professors encouraged them to offer counterarguments and to debate their sources, including the professor. The critical event that resulted in writing culture shock occurred when they experienced a classroom environment that they perceived to be rigid, impersonal, and authoritarian. Lila described the academic writing assignments at the university as "far more structured and less open to the creativity/originality of students." Grace remarked that "formatting is important." Just as Morgan reverted to the five-paragraph essay when writing in Italian, Grace admitted: "I tend to cling to form a bit more in French, where I am less masterful.' Amelia echoed the observations of both Grace and Lila when she noted the importance of "following the recipe."

All three connected the strict adherence to formula to what they perceived as an authoritarian rhetorical situation. Lila stated, "Disputing the professor's ideas or those of a critic is not encouraged (perhaps discouraged?)." Grace more emphatically described how professorial authority silenced authorial agency: "Personal *voice* is not very important. If I want a good grade, I need to write like a professor." She continued, "The professor is God. Do not contradict unless you're feeling *reeeal* confident." And Amelia concurred, "Do exactly what the professor says . . . You have to spit out what you've learned for a good grade." For these three writers, the US focus on argument competed with the less palatable (perceived) emphasis on form. Amelia's metaphors—"formula" and "recipe"—connote lockstep rigidity; Lila contrasts the professor's demand for "structured" writing with her desire for "creativity/originality"; Grace "clings" to form—for survival, it seems, within a rhetoric that forces her to erase her "personal voice" and form an obedient and submissive relationship to the professor-reader. Her uncomfortable ethos of submission resonates when she refers to her professor as "God"—and a "critical" one at that. She imagines the possibility of developing an argument, but only in the case of extreme confidence. Lila has learned not to talk back or "dispute" the professor or even a critic that she cites, although she questions how egregious an act of defiance would be. (Would it be not encouraged or outwardly discouraged?) Like her peers, Amelia explains the importance of sublimating self to "do exactly what the professor says"; once again waxing metaphorical, she demotes her writing to saliva, something she has to "spit out" in order to earn a "good grade." An effective FL writing tutor would help these writers develop intercultural competence by understanding other worldviews.

To do so, the FL writing tutor would guide them as they gather information about the culture, preferably from a native informant (possibly even the tutors themselves) and use that information to revise the original assumptions and reframe the writing culture shock. As is evidenced by Lila, Grace, and Amelia, US students who study in French universities often find themselves in a writing culture that is only vaguely familiar. Traditionally in France, four basic genres comprise the foundation of university writing: the *commentaire composé*, the *etude d'un text argumentatif*, the *dissertation*, and the *discussion* (Donahue, "Lycee" 136). While these four genres are distinct in terms of conventions and purposes, Donahue identifies some generalizable characteristics of French academic writing:

- an easily recognizable and repeatable external structure
- the absence of first person even as students express opinions
- a strong reliance on paraphrase without citing
- frequent explicit transitions
- a statement of "the problem" and "the plan" at the beginning
- a thesis statement at the end
- support for claims and assertions through short examples from literature, sociohistoric events, or current events. ("Lycee" 136)

Several of these characteristics would stymie a US international student who had not been taught French writing: the formulaic structure that differs according to genre, the lack of citations, and the concluding thesis statement. However, in many ways the rhetorical context is just as confusing, particularly the subject position of the writer (hinted to in the above list as the "absence of first person") and the writer's proper relationship to the audience. Donahue describes French academic writing as the "systematic study of established knowledge about a topic, and the incorporation and synthesis of diverse sources of this knowledge into an authoritative viewpoint" ("Lycee" 156). She likens it to the German *wissenschaftliches Schreiben* in which writers forego "personal views" to establish an authoritative voice that synthesizes sources into an academic conversation (Foster 219). In an article on German academic discourse, David Foster tells of one German student, albeit an exception to the rule, who admitted that she "felt silenced" by the demands of "incorporative rhetoric" (220).[15]

With an understanding of the writing culture, writers can be brought to recognize that genre conventions and the criteria of "good writing" in the US are not shared by all cultures. Then FL writing tutors can assist them in formulating a new interpretation of the critical experience. A fourth student who studied in France, Melissa, provides a counterpoint. While Lila, Grace, and Amelia experience a loss of personal voice at the hands of "god-like" professors, Melissa does not express a loss or even much of a conflict as she focuses more on genre expectations than the perceived power dynamics of the rhetorical situation. Unlike Grace who finds French form confining, Melissa quips, "The French adore structure, to the point that it's almost rigid." In addition, she has developed an understanding of French academic genres: "In literature, French professors often ask for a *commentaire composé*; a very intense, detailed close reading on one particular section of a work, rather than an essay that treats an entire piece. Even larger essays, called *dissertations*, are different and then incorporate multiple works to show one's knowledge of a subject as a whole." Her cross-cultural knowledge extends to conventions, like the *problématique*, which, she explains, is "different from a thesis statement. Essentially, the *problématique* asks the question that a thesis statement would answer." In contrast to her peers, Melissa has a framework that enables her to make sense of the differences. She depersonalizes the rhetorical relationships and refers to "the French" and "French professors." At worst, her criticism is faint: the French are "almost rigid" and "intense." She can clearly explain French genres and criteria of good writing (i.e., they "adore structure."). Rather than writing culture shock, she displays her intercultural competence and participates in writing culture immersion.

These varying conceptions of French academic writing have implications for the mission of an MWC, the role of FL writing tutors, and the unique interventions those tutors can offer FL writers. Tutors with intercultural competence, like Melissa, can help writers adapt—that is, cross confidently into the new academic culture. She represents the potential of FL writing tutors to demystify the language-specific writing culture by explaining rhetorical relationships, genre, and discourse conventions. Foreign language writers with writing culture shock, however, can be taught intercultural competence as they are prompted to identify critical events, uncover the necessary information from native informants, and then reinterpret the critical events from the culture's point-of-view. Once writing culture shock is resolved and FL writers are no longer reacting to their perceived discomfort, they are in a better position to choose whether they want to assimilate, separate, or acculturate.

While the critical event in the above example arises from a lack of awareness of culturally-specific writing conventions, this is just one way that culture can inform an FL writing tutoring session. A critical event can happen when FL writers analyze historical and cultural events or works of art through an ethnocentric lens. The lens could be ethnocentric because, on the one hand, it reproduces stereotypes, or, on the other hand, it results in a reductive interpretation that overlooks cultural nuances. In these cases, FL writing tutors can move beyond the language on the page and use their cultural knowledge to help writers broaden their perspective and view the target culture with more complexity. Relatedly, a critical event can occur when an FL writer misconstrues a cultural audience. For example, Spanish, Argentinian, and Russian international students have told me that emails from US students and instructors come across as rude, direct, and abrupt. Based on their cultural expectations about appropriate formality, the writers do not exhibit politeness and deferential indirectness or, what one called, the "humble perspective."[16] In other words, FL writers may produce drafts in which they simply and unreflectively translate their US voice into the target language without awareness of the cultural audience. These writers would benefit from working with FL writing tutors who have "been there" and who can serve as "cultural informants" of German or Spanish or Chinese culture—academic or otherwise (Powers 41). What Judith Powers states of writing tutors working with English L2 writers applies also to writing tutors working with L2 writers of other languages: "Part of what [writers] need from us is knowledge of what that unknown audience will expect, need, and find convincing" (41) Foreign language writing tutors can intervene by becoming what Miyuki Sasaki terms an authentic "imagined community" that helps writers to imagine their cultural audience, craft a personal voice, and create an intercultural writerly identity. In a study of

EFL students in Japan, Sasaki measured the writing skills of students who studied English only in the FL context versus those who studied abroad and learned English in an immersion context. Sasaki concluded that the students who studied abroad showed greater improvement in their writing skills because their motivation grew as they formed "L2-related imagined communities," which enabled them to "imagine themselves writing in the L2 for communicative purposes" (170). As interculturally competent informants, FL writing tutors can demystify audience and make it an "imagined community." The imagined community helps writers to learn the target language and to construct an identity as a member of that community (Huhtala and Lehti-Eklund 277-78). The imagined community also optimizes the learning environment for writers who cannot always be in an authentic immersion context.

Whether the critical event involves misunderstanding culturally-specific writing conventions, interpreting a culture through an ethnocentric lens, and/or misconstruing a cultural audience, FL writing tutors can prompt writers not only to seek knowledge that sheds light on the critical event but also revise their rhetorical strategy and reformulate their interpretation. Thus, training in intercultural competence prepares FL writing tutors to tackle their multiple and shifting roles: to help students understand culturally specific genres and rhetorics, to serve as useful guides as students transition to another writing culture, and to impart the tools that would enable them to resolve writing culture shock. As I have shown in these last three chapters, a solid tutor training pedagogy that takes into account the unique context and challenges of FL learners is essential to developing an MWC. Yet it is equally important to build a solid administrative infrastructure in collaboration with FL colleagues—the subject of the last two chapters.

5 Working with Stakeholders to Develop and Administer a Multilingual Writing Center

When I have presented on Dickinson's MWC at professional conferences, my WCA colleagues have expressed curiosity about similar things. How did I secure funding for the MWC? And how did I get the FL faculty to participate? For some, no doubt, these two questions arise from experiences with fraught institutional dynamics. Writing centers have had a history of marginalization, some might even say second-class citizenship, and many WCAs have struggled (and still struggle) to obtain appropriate resources. As Linda Poziwilko observes, "We complain and fret to each other about being given quarters in the darkest corner of the basement of the humanities building" (4). Indeed, such complaints abound throughout writing center scholarship. One writing lab is housed in a "dimly lighted, ill-equipped broom closet that masqueraded as an office" (Davis 16); a second "is, of course, in the basement, two or three floors away from the Arts and Sciences offices . . ." (Farkas 3) and a third exists in "one small room, too large to be a closet, too small to be anything else" (Kossman 1).[17] Poziwilko contends that WCAs "are not always eager to explore the avenues that will help us secure a more prominent place in our institutions" (4). She warns WCAs about focusing on writing at the expense of engaging in the kind of "institutional politics" that will enable them to secure better spaces and adequate funding (4). Yet many WCAs have not received professional training as administrators; instead, they are left to their own devices when it comes to engaging in institutional politics, arguing the merits of their projects, and winning resources.

Further, some WCAs work in a campus culture with a strong silo mentality—in other words, like-minded individuals in different departments may be seeking solutions to similar problems, but they choose not to share information or collaborate; instead, they guard their territory and resources for fear of losing them. I would go so far as to argue that, historically, writing centers have constructed their own silos. In "The Idea of a Writing Center," an early and oft-anthologized essay that defines the mission and purpose of writing centers, Stephen North declares independence from classroom teachers: "we are not here to serve, supplement, back up, complement, reinforce, or otherwise be defined by any external curriculum. We are here to talk to writers" (440). Yet, a few paragraphs later, he reconsiders this claim: "I suppose this declaration of independence sounds more like a declaration of war, and that is obviously not what I intend, especially since the primary casualties would be the students and writers we all aim to serve. And I see no reason that writing centers and classroom teachers cannot cooperate as well as coexist" (441). North's argument came at a time when writing centers were proliferating in colleges and universities across the country. His essay, in part, seeks to defend writing centers from the criticisms of skeptical faculty who did not understand the idea of a writing center and viewed tutors with suspicion—at best, as incompetent helpers and, at worst, as violators of academic integrity. In the essay "Revisiting 'The Idea of a Writing Center,'" North reflects that his words "gave lots of ignorant but essentially well-meaning people pause" (9). Today, North's declaration still resonates in writing center practices like prohibiting instructors from viewing writing center session logs. While "The Idea of a Writing Center" aims to disabuse faculty and administrators of their "ignorance," it does so by putting the writing center and faculty in separate silos.[18]

More recently, administrators throughout higher education have considered the disadvantages of the silo mentality. In an article in *The Chronicle of Higher Education,* Holden Thorp and Buck Goldstein explain "How to Create a Problem-Solving Institution." They argue that the "silo mentality" often undermines an institution's "discussions of innovation and how to attack big problems." On a campus with a silo mentality, there may be faculty across FL departments who are concerned about helping students develop the full range of literacy skills, but these faculty never converse. While a WCA may see the value, for example, of expanding an English-centric writing center into an MWC, and FL faculty may desire writing support for their language learners, they may not know how to "build a collaborative mind-set based on mutual self-interest" (Thorp and Goldstein). And, in some cases, WCAs may be loath to engage faculty in such discussions, especially if they feel marginalized and/or unauthorized to quit their silos.

In this chapter, I will address the problems of securing funding and collaborating with FL faculty while outlining a strategic approach for directors who are considering expanding their English writing centers into MWCs. This chapter shows how WCAs proposing new initiatives like an MWC can engage effectively in institutional politics by taking into account mission and goals, creating buy-in, and then choosing the appropriate data-driven appeals for a proposal. By approaching the task rhetorically, WCAs can craft proposals and enter budget talks strategically and persuasively. Having put forth a path to funding, the chapter will then discuss building and maintaining relationships with FL faculty that are focused on student learning needs. In fact, without the support of faculty from the foreign languages, an MWC is not sustainable. Ideally, by shaping a committee that functions in multiple ways—planning, advising, and acting as a community of practice, a WCA can create an MWC that persists.

Taking into Account Institutional Culture

Many WCAs, myself included, look forward to attending professional conferences and learning about exciting new innovations. We imagine adopting them in our own writing centers, and we envision how these innovations would enhance the writing cultures on our campuses. Such a potentially top-down approach, though, has a great risk of backfiring and reinforcing existing silos. While the well-intentioned WCA with a strategic vision may be able to see the benefits of an initiative, their colleagues may not—or, at least, not at first. For that reason, WCAs should take the time to explore with potential stakeholders if and how an innovation meets student learning needs and fits the campus culture. In the words of Marcia Dickson, "the only way to direct a program is to let the individual program shape itself according to the beliefs of the people who make it up and existing power structures of the institution in which it is located" (147). In *The Impact of Culture on Organizational Decision Making,* William G. Tierney suggests a method for shaping a program to an institution when he outlines an ethnographic approach to administrative work. Rather than rushing to make changes, implement imported models, and/or solve problems,

Tierney advises administrators of all kinds to gain "an understanding of [the] organization's culture" in order to approach "the organization as an . . . interpretive undertaking." Such "cultural understanding" is "essential" for those who want to "foment change in the organization" (3). Tierney cautions administrators not to presume "that all organizations should function similarly" and, instead, to develop "a schema to diagnose their own organizations" (39). To do so, he suggests that administrators act as "researchers" who, like participant-observers, "do not enter the field with preconceived notions about the problem to be studied but, instead, attempt to understand the problem 'from the native's point of view'" (14). The researcher-administrator explores a "variety of settings" to "uncover informational data such as language habits, forms and patterns of written communication, and the agendas and interactions at various kinds of meetings" (15). In diagnosing and interpreting an organization, the researcher-administrator uses the qualitative tools of an ethnographer, like observations and interviews, that are structured and open-ended (Tierney 15). Implicit in the ethnographic approach is a collaborative ethos that runs counter to the silo mentality and "places the power in the hands of *all* faculty, giving them the means to influence the direction of the program they form . . . " (Gunner 14). As Jeanne Gunner states of WCAs "We cannot in good faith endorse collaboration as a pedagogy and turn away from it as an administrative model" (14).

I realize the ethnographic approach may be controversial to some WCAs. Echoing North, William J. Macauley, Jr. raises an important question: "How far should the writing center go in acculturating to an institution and its administration?" (57). In *The Everyday Writing Center,* Anne Ellen Geller, Michele Eodice, Frankie Condon, Meg Carroll, and Elizabeth H. Boquet critique the belief that WCAs are "more effective if we can 'translate' our work to our institutions." On the one hand, they see the value in learning the "language of the administration" but warn that there is "baggage" that accompanies that strategy. They hold that "our role is or should be so much more than receiving, accepting, and manifesting the values, traditions, and habits of mind and knowledge production that are identified and defined by others— the institution, the administrations, the faculty" (117). Conversely, Macauley contends that "writing centers don't work in a vacuum." He challenges WCAs to "engag[e] those around us in order to accomplish more for our centers" (58). He warns that WCAs disregard "institutional priorities" at the risk of "resource reductions" (59). Instead, "the more we reach out, the more options we have—and the more ways we have to access, see, and understand our work and the work that is possible for us" (78). For Macauley, breaching the silos is heuristic: connecting to the larger institution helps WCAs see the possible directions for writing center work.

Drawing on the heuristic potential of Tierney's ethnographic approach, I embarked on an "ethnographic tour" of my institution.[19] The purpose of the ethnographic tour was to explore the writing culture, pinpoint silos, and/or identify opportunities for collaboration. At the time, I was a new hire and uniquely situated for the role of participant-observer. WCAs who have worked at their institutions for many years, though, still can survey and interview faculty to gauge their needs and interest. When I interviewed my colleagues, I posed the same five questions:

1. How do you implement the college's "three-tiered" writing program in your department—that is, first-year seminar, writing intensive, and senior capstone writing courses?
2. Where is writing taught in your curriculum?
3. How do you teach majors the writing specific to your discipline?
4. How do you teach the writing process?
5. What kind of support can the writing program provide for you?

For FL faculty, I added one additional question: Do you teach your students to write US academic discourse in the target language, or do you teach them the rhetoric of the target culture? In addition, I kept field notes and collected writing artifacts (e.g., syllabi, writing guides, email follow-ups).

The ethnographic tour revealed that FL faculty, as a cohort, had much in common. As a group, they assigned multiple essays in a variety of genres that grew in length and complexity as the students progressed through the curriculum. Most of them had experimented with different writing pedagogies—particularly peer review. Some faculty were wary of the limits of peer review after observing non-fluent L2 learners lead one another astray, but they were reluctant to abandon it all together since they valued revision. They saw a possible solution in the writing center. Because all full-time faculty must teach a writing-intensive First-Year Seminar once per sabbatical cycle, FL faculty understood first-hand how the writing center supported students writing in English, and they could imagine the benefits of employing trained undergraduate writing tutors to work with their second language writers. In addition, prior to my arrival at the college, many had recommended talented bilingual students for the tutor training course. When those students became tutors, they would work with writers not only in English but also in foreign languages as needed. Thus, the writing center had provided FL tutoring informally and irregularly; further, some departments, like French and Spanish, had tried to develop their own tutoring support. In both cases, the tutors were not given any special training. Finding these limited interventions helpful, faculty across the languages supported the idea of a centralized writing center staffed by trained and fluent undergraduate peer writing tutors, some of whom were foreign exchange students. The ethnographic tour enabled me to breach the silos, engage with the FL departments, and learn about how they valued peer review and revision. This led to my working with a group of FL faculty to propose an MWC in which US students, international students, and foreign exchange students would work with writers in Arabic, Chinese, French, German, Hebrew, Italian, Japanese, Portuguese, Russian, and Spanish.

SECURING RESOURCES THROUGH CULTURAL APPEALS

The first step to proposing an MWC is to convene a planning committee comprised of stakeholders: WCAs, FL faculty, multilingual writing specialists, and global education staff, to name the obvious. A successful proposal will justify the worth of an MWC to the institution. With that purpose in mind, I will discuss three types of data-driven rhetorical appeals that WCAs will find helpful as they navigate institutional politics. The value-added *cultural appeal* uses qualitative evidence grounded in an understanding of the writing culture and the mission of the institution to (re)imagine the worth of the writing center. The *quantitative appeal* uses statistics—usage numbers, for example—to support requests for a larger personnel budget, a better space, or new computers, to name a few. The *value-added quantitative appeal* measures ways in which the writing center adds value to students' learning experiences. In the case of Dickinson's MWC, I will explain how the three types of appeals were used to acquire resources, sustain operations, and establish the value-added of the MWC.

Value-added cultural appeals to upper administration can bring innovations, like an MWC, to fruition. As Macauley suggests, it is important for WCAs to "engage institutional statements, objectives, and goals" by mining them for "language" and "priorities" (59). Tierney explains the importance of a clear mission when he asserts that an institution "is in charge of its destiny if it understands itself" (18). The data from the ethnographic tour enabled the committee to connect value-added cultural appeals to the college's mission and values in the MWC proposal. Those appeals fell into several categories:

1. *The appeal to the institution's mission.*

    An MWC would reinforce Dickinson's mission to prepare students "to become engaged citizens by incorporating a global vision that permeates the entire student experience" ("About").

    - The MWC would bring a global vision to the writing program.
    - The MWC would underscore the importance of foreign languages in the lives of engaged global citizens. Foreign language are distinctive programs in which "students have countless opportunities to practice speaking and translating."[20] With the development of an MWC, we would add writing to this list as well.
    - The MWC would help students deepen their literacy skills for study abroad in a second language.
    - The MWC would serve as a positive post-study abroad experience by providing an opportunity for returning students to apply their newly acquired global knowledge and linguistic skills as peer writing tutors.

2. *The appeal to the institution's strategic plan.*

    An MWC would address an important strategic goal: "We need to take full advantage of our students' abilities to contribute to their peers' learning process."[21]

    - An MWC would provide a consistent slate of undergraduate peer writing tutors who could assist their peers in developing FL literacy.

3. *The appeal to implicit core values (in this case, distinctiveness and cross-disciplinary collaboration).*

   - An MWC is distinctive since there is no established model for an MWC—one that builds bridges between the writing center and language departments.

4. *The appeal to organizational values like sustainability and efficiency through centralized resources.*

   - An MWC would provide an institutional structure for the tutoring of FL writers. Language learners would be able to seek support in one location rather than track down tutors in individual departments. Foreign language faculty would benefit from collaborating with the writing center and its solid infrastructure, including a multilingual specialist, to train tutors and evaluate their success.

While not an exhaustive list of appeals, these are examples of mining the institution for values and goals in order to imagine a program that fits the campus culture. Ultimately, the proposal succeeded because it was able to dismantle silos and bring together the writing center, foreign language, and global education stakeholders. The proposal also complemented the mission(s) of the institution and supported our most valuable asset—the students. Thus, value-added cultural appeals, gleaned from the ethnographic tour and reinforced by the planning committee, justified the worth of the MWC initiative. As a result, the Provost funded the pilot and, a year later, the MWC received a permanent budget line.

Sustaining the MWC through Quantitative Appeals

While value-added cultural appeals provided a rationale for an MWC, quantitative appeals helped develop and sustain the MWC over time. In "Counting Beans and Making Beans Count," Neil Lerner describes an all too familiar scenario: a "late-night phone call from [his] department chair, telling [him] of impending budget cuts." His response is to produce quantitative data since "college administrators often want numbers, digits, results" (2). Pointing out the writing center community's proclivity for qualitative methods, scholars like Lerner, and

Peter Carino and Doug Enders have led the charge to "use quantitative research to gain some answers to a question [that] could not have [been] addressed as efficiently using only qualitative methods" (Carino and Enders 83). Quantitative appeals indicating, for example, growing usage numbers and/or the writing center's contribution to retention support bids for better space and more resources. Quantitative data in the form of usage numbers have proven valuable to developing Dickinson's MWC.

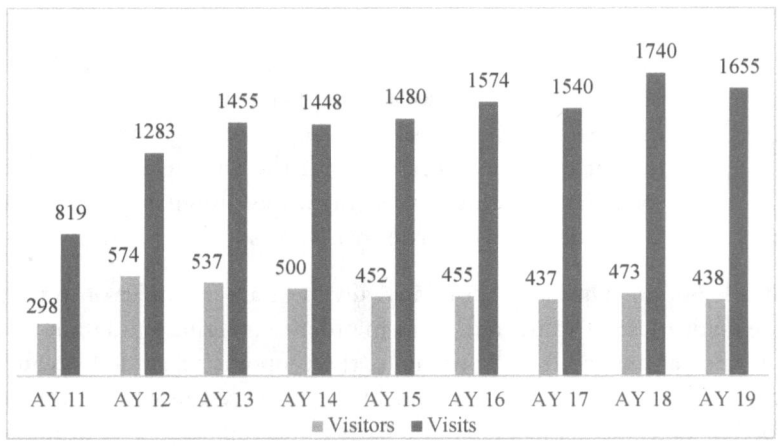

Figure 2. Foreign language writing visitors and visits by academic year

Usage numbers are the most familiar and basic type of descriptive statistics that scheduling software, like WCONLINE, makes incredibly easy to collect. At Dickinson, the number of FL writing visits increased by 112 percent between 2011 and 2018. The 438 students who used the MWC in 2019 represent 19 percent of the student body. Quantitative data, as Lerner suggests, can be used for multiple purposes: evidence of assessment for external accreditors, potentially replicable findings for the scholarly community, and proof of the writing center's value. In each case, the WCA would need to interpret the data and answer "So What?" since assessment data and research results do not automatically translate into project funding (Lerner 3). For external accreditors, usage data could be used to indicate, for example, that an institution is meeting a strategic goal related to learning support. For the scholarly community, a synthesis of usage data by institution size and type, like that collected by the National Census of Writing, could be used to establish national usage averages. For campus administrators, usage data could be used to argue for space and resources, as in my case. Dickinson's MWC, like the writing centers mentioned earlier, originally occupied a "dark corner": a storage room in Media Services, which was located in the basement of the foreign language building. Because usage data showed a dramatic and then steady increase in demand, the MWC was moved to a larger space in a choice location: the college library.

A more complex type of quantitative appeal is the value-added quantitative appeal, which employs statistics to make inferences about a population by assessing the strength of the relationship between dependent and independent variables. Carino and Enders, for example, created a statistical correlation study that measured student satisfaction with the writing center. When they found a correlation between "number of visits and student satisfaction," they considered it "ammunition in arguing that the writing center has a positive effect on student writers' perception of improvement" (99). Value-added quantitative appeals draw on such data to make effective rhetorical arguments for "when the Dean comes knocking" (Carino and Enders 102). With data showing a correlation between visits to the writing center and improved writing of first-year students, Lerner crafted a successful value-added appeal in which he argued that the writing center aids the retention effort since it contributes to first-year students' academic success.[22] In addition, such data are beneficial not just to individual institutions but to all writing centers by providing "large-scale evidence that writing centers can and do make a difference" (Lerner, "Counting" 1, 3). Value-added quantitative appeals can help WCAs establish the credibility of their centers and win the (continued) support of campus stakeholders.

Wanting to assess how the MWC contributes to students' academic success, I conducted an "effectiveness study" that addressed the following question: "Do students who use the [MWC] get better grades . . . than students who do not use the [MWC]?" (Lerner, "Choosing" 2). To answer this, I obtained the final course grades of all students who had taken a FL course in one year, identified the students who had and had not visited the MWC, and compared the grades of both groups. I chose to analyze the data by course level since the purpose of writing shifts from writing to acquire the language in 100-level courses to writing for academic purposes in 200-level and above courses. (This is not a strict binary—rather, a shift in emphasis.) In 100-level courses, there was a higher percentage of "A" grades among students who visited the MWC versus those who did not visit the MWC, and this difference is statistically significant (p <.01).

Table 1. Comparison of final course grades of all 100-level foreign language students (N=1067) who did and did not work with a writing tutor.

	MWC Visits		No MWC Visits		TOTAL	P-Value
A	11	47%	310	7%	421	0.005
B	8	38%	354	2%	442	0.18
C	3	10%	107	3%	130	0.21
D	5	2%	23	2%	28	0.59
F/W	7	3%	39	5%	46	0.27
TOTAL	34		833		1067	

In courses above the 100-level, there was a higher percentage of "A" grades among students who visited the MWC versus those who did not visit the MWC (p <.05). There was also a lower percentage of unproductive enrollments (F and W) among students who visited the MWC versus those who did not visit the MWC. Both of these differences are statistically significant (p =.05).

Table 2. Comparison of final course grades of 200-level foreign language students (N=1037) who did and did not work with a writing tutor.

	MWC Visits		No MWC Visits		TOTAL	P-Value
A	97	56%	26	48%	523	0.02
B	17	33%	66	39%	383	0.56
C	2	9%	1	9%	93	0.97
D	5	1%	8	1%	13	0.75
F/W	4	1%	21	3%	25	0.05
TOTAL	55		682		1037	

Value-added assessment is a complex process that takes time because each assessment can (and often does) raise questions that warrant further assessment. For example, when the data in both tables are aggregated, there is a higher percentage of "B" grades among students who made no visits to the MWC versus those who visited the MWC. Because this difference is statistically significant (p =.01), it raises questions for further study. Did students who would have received "B" grades earn "A" grades with help from the MWC? Did a shift occur across all grade categories? Is there a significant difference in "A" grades because the already motivated students chose to make appointments in the MWC? One potential follow-up assessment study could focus on the correlation between course grade and MWC visits of motivated versus less motivated students, thereby qualifying and deepening the current analysis. This initial study, though, offered promising evidence to an in-house audience of a correlation between visits to the MWC and academic success in FL classes.

Before making a project proposal, WCAs should fully analyze the rhetorical situation. As Lerner states, "What is most important is that you recognize the audience, purpose, and context for your assessment efforts and that you know how best to appeal to a dean or administrator who favors quantitative or qualitative evidence" ("Of Numbers," 113). For a developing center, qualitative arguments may be less compelling than quantitative evidence of growth. A marginalized or fossilized center could revive itself via an ethnographic tour that results in a revised strategic plan and value-added cultural appeals for fiscal support. Conversely, a well-established center would not need to argue about quantities in the way that a new center would. In the case of English-centric writing centers seeking to become MWCs, value-added cultural arguments place proposed changes in the broader contexts of the writing culture and the institution. By closely analyzing the rhetorical situation, strategic WCAs can engage institutional politics and develop their MWCs.

PLANNING AN MWC WITH FOREIGN LANGUAGE FACULTY

To sustain an MWC, WCAs need to forego their silos and continue the conversation with FL faculty, utilizing their sophisticated collaboration skills honed in the writing center. In her seminal essay, "Collaboration, Control, and the Idea of a Writing Center," Andrea Lunsford points out that collaboration "aids in problem finding as well as problem solving," results in "sharper, more critical thinking," and "promotes excellence," among others (5-6). Her points about the powerful interactions between tutors and writers hold true for WCAs and faculty: collaboration breeds innovation. WCAs will successfully navigate institutional politics when they take their well-honed collaborative skills across institutional boundary lines and build committees where ideas can incubate.

In building an MWC, the most effective committee is fluid, adapting its purposes strategically to meet evolving goals. The committee with whom I collaborate originally convened to plan the MWC, and then shifted into an advisory body that often functions as a community of practice. As I explained earlier, the committee's initial task was to plan and propose the MWC. To that end, we identified a mission, values, and learning outcomes that fit the college culture.

> The FL writing tutors support the mission of the FL departments to develop students' critical thinking skills and fluency in writing. The tutors assist writers of all levels and abilities who are working on essays written in Arabic, Chinese, French, German, Hebrew, Italian, Japanese, Portuguese, Russian, or Spanish. Trained tutors and Overseas Assistants will work one-on-one with writers on a variety of concerns.
>
> You should visit a writing tutor in your target language if you want assistance with the following:
>
> - developing ideas;
> - understanding genres;
> - organizing material;
> - crafting sentences;
> - analyzing and correcting patterns of error;
> - discovering a writing process that works in a foreign language;
> - realizing the difference between composing and translating;
> - understanding how cultural differences manifest in writing. ("Foreign")

This statement not only takes into account the mission of the foreign languages but also synthesizes writing center and FL-learning best practices. After articulating a mission and vision, we crafted a proposal and budget for the MWC. I have discussed proposal appeals earlier in this chapter, and so I will focus here on the budget. The challenge with the budget was anticipating the staffing for the MWC. Because some languages (like Spanish and French) had many more enrollments than others (like Hebrew and Portuguese), we knew the need for tutoring would vary across languages. I prompted the committee members to consider their enrollments and propose a number of tutoring hours per week for their languages. Wanting both geographical natives and nonnatives as tutors, most agreed to assign their Overseas Assistants (exchange students employed part-time to teach students language and culture) weekly shifts in the MWC. As a result, we negotiated a plan that took into account differing enrollments.

Table 3. Budget overview of the MWC

Item	Amount	Funding Source
Personnel		
Student Assistant/Receptionist		
OSAs		
Undergraduate Peer Tutors		
Additional Training Meetings		
Total		
Nonpersonnel		
Computers		
Furniture		
Supplies and Photocopying		
Software		
Dictionaries and Books		
Total		
GRAND TOTAL		

Table 4. Breakdown of budget for writing tutors by language

Language	OSA Hours	Peer Tutor Hours per Week
Italian	1 OSA for 2 hrs.	8
Spanish	3 OSAs for 4 hrs. each	16
German	2 OSAs for 2 hrs. each	6
Chinese	0	6
Japanese	0	6
Russian	1 OSA for 2 hrs.	8
French	1 OSA for 2 hrs.	10
Arabic	0	8
Hebrew	0	4
Portuguese	1 OSA for 8 hrs.	0

A committee that collaborates equates with faculty buy-in, which in itself was quite persuasive when it came to securing funding. Ultimately, the MWC planning committee conferred the leadership role on the writing center with the understanding that there would be continued collaboration with the language departments regarding staffing, training, pedagogy, and policy. In its current configuration, the MWC reinforces the global education goals of the college and FL departments even as it maintains its integrity as a writing center.

Developing an MWC with Foreign Language Faculty

Having completed the planning phase, the MWC planning committee became the MWC advisory committee. While the latter retained the representative membership of the planning committee, the committee took on new functions like recommending potential tutors, training them, and establishing policies. The single most important goal for any WCA is to recruit and develop the best possible staff. Unless a WCA is a genuine polyglot, it would be impossible for one person to vet the writing abilities of tutor recruits in multiple languages. Instead, WCAs must rely on FL experts on the MWC advisory committee. Those invested stakeholders discuss potential tutors with their departments and then compile a list of recruits as determined by departmental consensus. Not only does this process identify excellent tutors, but it also strengthens buy-in as FL faculty feel comfortable promoting an MWC staffed by tutors whom they have determined to be the most competent and capable.

As evidence of true collaboration, the MWC helped some FL faculty reflect on how they chose their OSAs. Anecdotes and informal observations led me to wonder if there was a fundamental problem with tutor training because it seemed like the OSAs did not retain as much of their training as did the domestic students. Whereas the domestic students who became FL writing tutors focused on writing as well as sentence-level concerns in their sessions, the OSAs seemed to focus mainly on sentence-level issues. Wanting to further investigate this suspicion, I analyzed the session log narratives written by tutors. After finishing a tutoring session, tutors write a session log or brief descriptive narrative of the interaction, using the following template:

> (Writer's name) brought in a _____ (draft, outline, notes, copy of the assignment, etc.) for a paper that was due in _____ (two hours, a week, two weeks, etc.). When I asked (writer's name) what they wanted to work on, they said _____(developing ideas, organization, grammar, etc). During the session we talked about/worked on _____. By the end of the session, (name of writer) understood _____ and said they planned to _____.

I chose to analyze session logs for several reasons. First, the structured template allows for coding and comparative analysis. Second, as opposed to session transcript analysis which is usually done with a small sample for the purpose of examining the micro-details of tutor-writer interactions (see studies by Mackiewicz and Thompson; Thompson and Mackiewicz), session log analysis enables a researcher to examine broader trends in a large sample—in this case, across ten languages. Some might argue that session logs reflect the values of tutor training more than the actual content of sessions. Given the large number of session logs (1000+) composed by sixty-two tutors, it is unlikely that all would be performing for the WCA all the time. Further, session logs are written not only for the WCA but also for the instructors whose values are multiple and do not consistently overlap with each other and/or tutor training. The logs were coded using the concepts of lower-order concerns (LOCs) and higher-order concerns (HOCs) from the scholarly literature.[23] The following is the rubric used to code session logs:

Table 5. Rubric used to code session logs

Type	Characteristics	Example
HOCs	Focus on the writing process (e.g., outlining, brainstorming, composing vs. translating), the assignment, genre, idea development, evidence, logic/coherence, organization, rhetorical situation.	A French tutor writes, "We spent most of the session working on understanding the assignment, on the organization of her future paper, and on understanding the text itself . . . I adviced [sic] her to read the text several times, looking up words that she did not understand. I explained the assignment to her, and made sure she understood the way her paper should be organized."
LOCs	Focus on grammar, spelling, punctuation, syntax, idioms, word choice.	A German tutor states, "We talked about prepositions and the difference between 'auf,' 'in' and 'bei,' as well as the usage of 'nach.' We also worked on word order and word choice, as well as grammatical accuracy."
HOCs/ LOCs	Focus on both higher and lower order concerns.	An Italian tutor writes: " . . . we focused on the structure of the paper. We talked about expanding the introduction and the conclusion. The professor also suggested to add details (characters and places' descriptions throughout the paper) so we explored some possibilities, i.e.: remove some less important details and expand others, summarize a few paragraphs that looked too long and repetitive, and finally, the usage of adjectives to talk about people and places."
Other	Focus on something other than a writing assignment.	A Russian tutor writes, "B has come today to the Multilingual Writing Center and asked to help him prepare for the quiz . . . During the session we translated the words and paid attention to their declination and conjugation."

Despite a tutor-training program that stresses writing and not just language acquisition skills, an analysis of session logs written by OSAs revealed that they spent more time on LOCs than on HOCs.

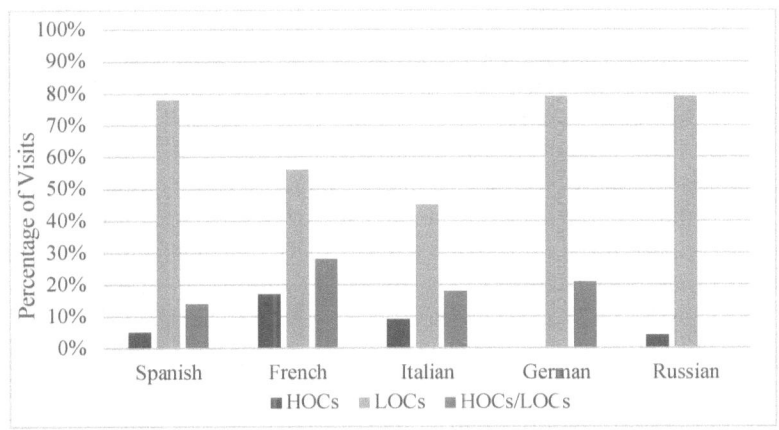

Figure 3. Comparison by language of the content of foreign language writing tutoring sessions, 2010-2011.

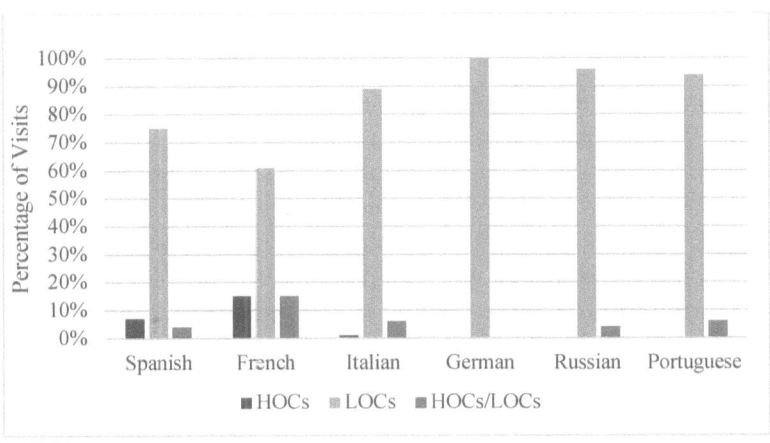

Figure 4. Comparison by language of the content of foreign language writing tutoring sessions, 2011-2012.

When I assumed that there was a problem with the training program, the MWC advisory committee identified several other factors that could also account for the OSAs' focus on sentence-level issues. First, several OSAs were majoring in translation studies at their home institutions, thus their proclivity for linguistic accuracy and correctness. Second, several committee members revealed that the writing skills of prospective OSAs were not always evaluated. To further investigate, the committee reviewed the results of that year's diagnostic writing test (at the time, the prerequisite for self-directed placement into a writing courses for international students). The diagnostic essay results revealed that three OSAs who were MWC tutors scored in the highest range, three scored in the middle range, and two scored in the lowest range. Hence, some OSAs may not have been equipped to engage students on the level of content, organization, genre, or rhetorical awareness, given their academic writing skills. This led the MWC advisory committee to discuss whether OSAs should be vetted for their writing skills, limited to sentence-level work, and/or allowed to assist with writing. Knowing that OSAs would be working with writers, FL faculty chose to more closely vet the writing abilities of future OSAs, and they re-emphasized the importance of writing skills as well as linguistic correctness during training.

The MWC advisory committee also helps to shape and deliver training. While all English tutors in the MWC take a full-credit tutor training course, the same is not possible for all FL writing tutors, mainly because English tutors-in-training are first-years and sophomores, and FL writing tutors (who are not OSAs) are most often seniors who studied abroad in their junior year. The latter two groups do not have as much leeway with their electives as do underclassmen. Mandating that seniors take a required tutor training course would cause scheduling problems that would deter qualified students from becoming tutors.[24] Instead, at the start of the academic year, FL writing tutors attend a mandatory, full-day training followed by monthly staff meetings throughout the year. (For a sample training schedule, see Appendix I). The first half of the training focuses on best practices for tutoring writers, stressing foundational concepts like agency and ownership, the arc of a tutoring session, directive and nondirective questioning, tutoring for language acquisition, tutoring to develop and organize ideas, and writers who translate. The second half of the training includes a panel discussion with experienced FL writing tutors as well as breakout sessions with FL faculty who discuss issues specific to the language with their tutor cohorts. Throughout the year, the topics of monthly staff meetings range from explaining cultural differences in writing, cross-training with English writing tutors, creating a supportive learning environment, and tutoring holistically. For the final meeting of the semester, FL faculty, MWC advisory committee members, and tutors attend a luncheon during which the tutors share their insights on L2 writing with classroom instructors. Though not the ideal full-credit course, MWC training benefits from a team-teaching approach in which WCAs, FL faculty, and experienced tutors combine their expertise to train writing tutors.

In addition, the MWC advisory committee often acts as a deliberative body that establishes policies. These deliberations occur between WCAs and classroom faculty and sometimes between classroom faculty and writing tutors. A case-in-point occurred when an instructor cried foul after finding a tutor's handwriting on a student's draft. A common practice in FL classrooms, particularly in introductory courses in which students write to learn the language, is for the instructor to mark errors on essays and then require the students to make corrections. The instructor was concerned that the tutor had corrected the errors that the student was supposed to correct and, in so doing, had violated the academic integrity code. Anonymizing the participants, I discussed the issue with the tutors. As it turned out, the tutors had broader frustrations related to sentence-level tutoring. Namely, some students did not know how to use the MWC correctly. They made appointments at the last minute and cajoled tutors into helping them correct errors that they had not tried to correct themselves. By the end of that meeting, the tutors had proposed a policy statement, "Working with Sentence-Level Errors," to the MWC advisory committee.

> At the November 10 staff meeting for the MWC, the tutors drafted a proposed policy for working with writers seeking feedback on sentence-level concerns.
>
> - Writers who have received feedback from professors and are seeking help with sentence-level errors should attempt to correct their own errors before their tutoring session. If they do not do so, tutors will instruct them to make such corrections on their own as part of the session.
> - There is some disagreement as to whether or not tutors should write on students' essays. Some faculty instruct tutors to record the writers' corrections on the essay. Others

tell tutors not to write directly on essays and to record any notes or reminders on a separate sheet.
- Each department should determine whether or not tutors should write on drafts and what they are allowed to write.
- Faculty should state the policy on course syllabi.
- Faculty should explain to their students how to use the MWC, stressing the dangers of procrastination and the importance of working through the corrections in advance. Alternatively, faculty can ask for a tutor to visit the class at the beginning of the semester and explain how to use the MWC.
- Faculty should provide students with a written copy of their editing symbols. They may also send those copies to the MWC to make available to tutors.

The MWC Advisory Committee discussed the tutors' policy statement and agreed on the need to be more transparent about their expectations for writers and tutors when it came to working on sentence-level issues. The MWC collected keys to editing symbols; the tutors refrained from writing on drafts; and the tutors required students to try to fix their own errors first. The committee members shared the policy with colleagues and explained how the tutors were trained to handle sentence-level errors so as to alleviate any concerns about academic integrity violations. Hence, in just this one instance, the committee's charge to establish policy yielded several important benefits: increased transparency and improved pedagogy in the MWC and FL classroom as well as an open line of communication and renewed trust between FL faculty and writing tutors.

Becoming a Community of Practice

I have attempted to illustrate the creative benefits of dismantling silos and crossing institutional boundaries in writing center work. Besides reimagining the writing center, rethinking the silo mentality also transformed the MWC advisory committee. Because the committee was open to collaboration, they were able to become a "community of practice," interrogating the interplay between writing center pedagogy, classroom practice, and the development of writing ability. As Etienne

Wenger, Richard McDermott, and William M. Snyder explain, "communities of practice" are "groups of people who share a concern, a set of problems, or a passion about a topic, and who deepen their knowledge and expertise in this area by interacting on an ongoing basis" (4). Unlike coworkers in silos, colleagues in a community of practice "share information, insight, and advice" and "help each other solve problems" despite the fact that they may not interact every day. They connect with each other through "the value that they find in learning together." Co-learning breeds a "unique perspective" on their topic and "common knowledge, practices, and approaches" (5). The true alternative to silos, communities of practice articulate common concerns and problems, share information, and explore solutions together.

The MWC originated with a call to form a community of practice. During the ethnographic tour, a FL faculty member asserted her wish for a writing center, which, she explained, would build bridges between language departments and bring together all FL faculty to discuss language instruction. That faculty member's wish was integrated into the vision of the MWC. For just one example, as a community of practice, the MWC advisory committee identified a common problem: students studying abroad often struggle with coursework in the target language and discourse. Conferring on this issue, the committee began to explore the possibility of establishing satellite writing centers in study abroad locations, and the French department was the first to act. In developing a satellite center, they anticipated issues that could arise when adapting the writing center, a US concept, to French academic culture. They also determined that the best way to create a staff would be to train exchange students from France to become tutors when they returned to the university.[25] As the progress of the Toulouse satellite writing center was reported to the committee, German, Italian, and Spanish faculty were increasingly inspired to pursue plans for their own satellite writing centers. The committee requested that the executive director of the center for global study and engagement attend a meeting, and she informed the group that most study abroad programs already had learning support funds built into their budgets. With funding no longer an obstacle, she invited the MWC Advisory Committee to consider the following questions:

1. What are your tutoring needs at your study abroad location? How many tutors/hours of coverage do you anticipate needing per week? For what courses?

2. Who will provide support? OSAs? Foreign exchange students? Dickinson students? What will you do if the OSAs/exchange students who were at Dickinson are not available to tutor in the following year?
3. How will you train the tutors? Is it feasible for you to train them here before they head overseas?
4. How will you sustain the satellite writing centers? How will you get our study abroad students to use the writing center?

Soon after the discussion, the Italian department used learning support funds to employ an OSA, who had tutored in the MWC, to work with students in Bologna. Alternatively, the Spanish department piloted online tutoring via Skype in which students studying in Malaga could make appointments with the Spanish writing tutors in Dickinson's MWC. While plans for satellite writing centers are still in the nascent stage, the committee, acting as a community of practice, shared insights about study abroad and helped each other come up with innovative solutions to the problem of language support for Dickinson students in immersion contexts.

Ensuring the Future of Writing Centers

An MWC may seem to be an overly-ambitious undertaking for writing centers that find themselves on precarious ground, struggling with budget cuts, absorption into learning resource centers, and, in the worst case scenarios, even termination. In "Some Millennial Thoughts about the Future of Writing Centers," Lisa Ede and Andrea Lunsford consider how writing centers "could strengthen their own institutional positions" (36). These matriarchs of model writing centers advise WCAs to "take advantage" of both the writing center's "multi-bordered, multi-positioned status at your institution" and "broad disciplinary and institutional changes." They urge WCAs to "think both locally and globally" and to "take significant risks." They prompt us to consider the allies with whom we can collaborate to "effect institutional change and to better the situation of [our] programs" (36-37). A multi-bordered writing center model with both a local and global mission, the MWC is one such product of collaborative risk-taking. I want to suggest that other writing centers engage with the movement in US higher education toward internationalizing the curriculum and educational experience, a trend that has the potential to influence an ever-growing number of students to enroll in FL courses and study abroad in immersion contexts. By sending tethers across multiple borders, writing centers can consolidate their hard-won legitimacy.

Still, I acknowledge that the MWC model may not be transferable to every college and university, just as not every writing center assists with speaking or with multimodal assignments. While certain unique institutional configurations and politics make some writing center models more feasible than others, the MWC is potentially transferable to any academic institution whose core values include internationalization. To conclude, I offer writing centers interested in exploring collaborative opportunities with FL colleagues four pieces of concrete, logistical advice.

1. *Strongly consider adopting the MWC model if your institution has a strong commitment to internationalization.*

> To quote Benedicte de Montlaur, "The future in America, and everywhere, is multilingual. And so is the present." In a *New York Times* editorial, de Montlaur, cultural counselor of the French Embassy in the US, describes a "nationwide" move toward "holistic language education" vis a vis "grass-roots initiatives to provide foreign language learning" at every level of the education system. In higher education, she mentions two particularly innovative, internationalized programs: a graduate program at Georgia Tech that combines foreign language and cultural studies and an undergraduate program at the University of Rhode Island in which students earn dual degrees in foreign language and engineering—in both cases to prepare students for careers in the global arena. In institutions like these with innovative visions of internationalized curricula, writing centers would gain considerably from tethering themselves to nationally-recognized programs.

2. *Breach the silos and form communities of practice.*

> I will not belabor this point since the importance of WCAs engaging in interdisciplinary and inter-departmental collaboration has been a theme in this chapter. I recognize, though, that silos continue to exist on college and university campuses. Sometimes they serve as mark-

ers of identity and affiliation, and they enable programs to safeguard territory and resources. Other times they keep faculty and administrators from developing the collaborative partnerships that produce innovative educational experiences. Clearly, at the University of Rhode Island, for one example, engineering and FL faculty breached the silos to innovate and, as a result, created a unique and distinctive internationalized engineering program.

3. *Start small, assess your progress, and use the assessment results to strengthen* successful collaborations.

Given the small, often collegial community and high degree of interdisciplinarity at liberal arts colleges, I was able to collaborate with seven FL departments in planning the MWC. Then in the second year of operation, three other FL departments joined in after hearing about the benefits of having trained writing tutors support FL learning. In a larger school with more silos, a writing center director and one or more interested faculty members could pilot a tutoring program for FL writers. To grow the program, it would be important to collect usage data as well as student and faculty feedback surveys. Both quantitative and qualitative data would be useful in conversations with other interested faculty and administrators who make budget decisions. Though a pilot program might be small, it could be strategically designed with a purpose—that is, with an eventual proposal for a larger program as the end game.

4. *Understand the values and practices of your collaborators—foreign language faculty.*

For an MWC to be both successful and sustainable, WCAs need to step across the multi-borders of their writing centers and find allies committed to improving their students' literacy skills. To build alliances that breed innovation, they need to understand the culture of their FL colleagues' discourse community.

This is the subject of the next and final chapter.

6 Developing an MWC with Foreign Language Faculty

As part of the collaborative community that is essential to sustaining an MWC, WCAs and FL faculty reciprocally share knowledge, solve problems, and synthesize best practices from their respective fields as together they learn to improve student learning. Not only must WCAs communicate writing center work to FL colleagues, but they must also understand the culture of FL academics. The heart of this chapter is an analysis of six interviews with FL faculty whose students regularly use the MWC. These six instructors are full-time—one full professor, three associate professors, one senior lecturer, and one lecturer—and they teach Arabic, German, Italian, Japanese, Russian, and Spanish. Three are international faculty who teach in their first language, and three are US citizens who teach in their additional language. All found unexpected community in the MWC, one remarking that she views the MWC as "a community resource for instructors and writers working together." In approaching conversations with colleagues in the foreign languages, WCAs can start with this chapter in which instructors talk about how the MWC not only enabled them to use writing to enhance their students' language acquisition (writing to learn the language) and write for different communicative purposes (learning to write in the language), but the MWC also helped faculty become better teachers of writing.

THE COMMUNICATIVE APPROACH

To understand the pedagogies and practices of FL academics, WCAs need to be aware of the communicative approach to FL instruction and how it inflects FL writing tutor training. A major paradigm shift in FL instruction, the move from Audiolingual Methodology (ALM) to Communicative Language Teaching, occurred at about the same time as the writing process movement in composition. In the early twentieth century, FL instructors imparted "a great deal of information about the language but did not have an expectation of language use" (*21st Century Skills*). Prior to the 1970s, FL instruction relied on the "grammar and text-translation metho[d]" central to the study of classical Greek and Latin texts. As the need to recruit and develop speakers of foreign languages arose during World War II, military schools developed an oral approach known as Audiolingual Methodology (ALM) (Savignon, "Communicative Competence" 2). Instructors would drill students in linguistic patterns by prompting them with a model sentence that the students would alter in some way. For example, the drill would begin with a sentence like "I eat," and students would have to substitute different present tense verbs (e.g., sleep, read, work) or transform the verb tense (e.g., ate, have eaten, will eat) (Lee and Van Patten 7). Both the grammar-translation and ALM methods stressed "pattern practice and error avoidance"—the former through reading and translating texts and the latter through listening to native speakers and repeating grammatical patterns (Savignon, "Communicative Competence" 1-2; Savignon, "Communicative Language" 125). Practitioners reasoned that language learning happened as students formed habits by mimicking the instructor; at the same time, error correction assured that students did not form bad habits (Lee and Van Patten 7-8). However, the strict focus on grammar prevented students from "say[ing] anything original that might lead them to produce an utterance with errors in it" (Lee and Van Patten 8). ALM restricted authentic communication and produced instructors (not to mention students) who were unable to "understand and speak the language" (Savignon, "Communicative Competence" 2). An MWC that supported ALM assignments would, no doubt, be a "Center as Storehouse," as famously described by Andrea Lunsford. Tutors would disburse "skills and strategies to individual learners" who focused on correcting their errors and replicating pattern sentences for ALM assignments (3-4).

However, in the 1970s, FL scholars began to express increasing dissatisfaction with their students' inability to communicate. They developed a new pedagogy called Communicative Language Teaching (CLT) that sought to address the limitations of ALM. WCAs who wish to expand their writing centers to include FL writing tutoring need to understand this important paradigm shift and the implications for

FL writing tutoring. Foreign language instructors who adopt CLT approaches teach "languages so that students use them to communicate with native speakers of the language" (*21st Century Skills*). To re-focus FL instruction on communication, CLT practitioners stress "communicative competence" (a term used by the sociolinguist Dell Hymes) in the four skills: listening, speaking, reading, and writing (Savignon, "Communicative Competence" 4). Communicative competence places the making of meaning above the mastery of grammatical forms, stresses the importance of sociocultural understanding, and advocates using language for different purposes (Savignon, "Linguistic" 6). CLT does not dispense with grammar instruction; instead, grammatical competence is built "not by stating a rule but by using a rule" as CLT integrates "form-focused exercises and meaning-focused experience" (Savignon, "Linguistic" 7, 9). Students' meaning-focused experiences take into account social and cultural contexts of language use: "social conventions . . . appropriateness of content, nonverbal language, and tone" as well as "cultural knowledge" and "cultural sensitivity" (Savignon, "Linguistic" 10). Meaning-focused experiences engage students in using "language for a variety of purposes," like writing an email (interpersonal), composing an academic essay (presentational), or analyzing a film (interpretive) (ACTFL). These three modes of communication—interpersonal, presentational, and interpretive—frame the proficiency benchmarks and performance indicators of the American Council of the Teaching of Foreign Languages (ACTFL), the national organization of language educators and administrators in the US. As will become evident in the interviews discussed below, the ACTFL guidelines inform the way FL instructors think about the four skills, including writing, in their courses.

WCAs can appreciate this paradigm shift in FL learning as it parallels the changes in writing instruction that occurred also in the 1970s. At the time, compositionists took issue with traditional pedagogies that emphasized the grammatical correctness of a written "product" (Clark 5). Just as CLT practitioners began to place the onus on students "to interpret, express, and negotiate meaning," compositionist/rhetoricians emphasized the writer, the writing process, and the making of meaning in the composition classroom (Lee and Van Patten 18; Savignon, "Communicative Language" 124, 127; Clark 6). English-language writing centers evolved to assist writers with the meaning-making process as they wrote for different purposes, and writing tutors became indispensable in offering the guidance and feedback writers needed to navigate the writing process. Similarly, the MWC model supports the development of writers in a way that meshes with CLT and the ACTFL guidelines. The MWC is a place where writers negotiate meaning with tutors, use grammar to communicate effectively, practice writing for different purposes, receive immediate feedback, and explore the social and cultural contexts of language use with peers who have more knowledge of the target culture(s).

FOREIGN LANGUAGE FACULTY AS WRITING INSTRUCTORS

The FL instructors I interviewed see the four skills—speaking, listening, reading, and writing—as interrelated, and they design courses in which they teach them all. Yet during their graduate training, most received very little, if any, instruction in how to teach writing or how to write in the target language. Their situation is not at all unusual given that writing studies, as discussed in chapter one, arose as a discipline in North America, and in other parts of the world, "the teaching of academic writing is not done in a systematic or institutionalized manner" (Canagarajah, *Geopolitics* 44). Not surprisingly, several of the interviewees received their training from experts in linguistics who tended to focus on oral language acquisition. Nasrin, the Arabic instructor, was certified in Teaching English as a Foreign Language, a linguistics-based program taught by two US academics in Tunisia. Her colleague in Italian, Piero, completed a graduate course in Teaching Italian as a Foreign Language that focused solely on "grammar and oral communication." As a graduate student of comparative literature, Felicia took a professional seminar on how to teach Spanish, but it was "geared towards graduate students in linguistics or perhaps people who were going to be working with language acquisition." When asked about training in second language writing, she said there was "virtually none" (although she did take a course that prepared her to teach first-year English composition). When Erik was in graduate school studying Japanese literature, he knew that most academic jobs would require him to teach Japanese language, and so he sought to develop that "skill set." He took "a course offered by one of the instructors who was a specialist in Japanese language pedagogy." Yet, as Erik recalled, "it was definitely more speaking-oriented."

Other instructors reported that their formative training experiences happened in the classroom during their first teaching jobs. Klara studied German literature at a US institution where she taught language courses as a graduate student. She took a training course that "focused on communicative language learning, and it was really focused on speaking in the classroom." She admits: "I don't remember it as very impressive . . . I did learn more while I was doing the teaching." As an undergraduate exchange student in the US, Piero had a "curricular internship" in which he taught an Italian course with a senior professor who mentored him. Lisette recounts how, as a graduate student in Russia, she had little classroom-based training: "I was thrown into it as a second-year graduate student. I was on fellowship my first year, and the second year they said: 'You are teaching Russian 101 as a TA.' And I was just thrown in. No training."

Despite not being formally trained to teach second/foreign language writing, all the interviewees incorporate writing, albeit in different ways and for different reasons, into their courses. To prompt discussion, I asked them to talk about how they balanced instruction in speaking and writing in the FL classroom. Lisette stated categorically, "it would be a very inauthentic experience to teach a language at all to adults without incorporating writing." Other instructors evoked the ACTFL guidelines in their responses. Nasrin stated that writing "is one of the main language skills. But it's not just writing, it's speaking, listening, reading, and writing. I think none of them are more or less important than the other." Similarly, in talking about the practice among the Japanese language instructors of having students write skits, Erik explained: "We do a lot of writing for oral performance in some way because we believe that's a useful skill to develop multiple areas of reading, writing, listening and speaking, the four ACTFL areas." Although my logical starting point for the MWC was the English writing center model with its strong emphasis on writing, my vision morphed as the FL instructors enabled me to re-imagine a writing center that would support second language writing in the context of CLT and the ACTFL guidelines.

WRITING TO IMPROVE SPEAKING

When asked why writing is an important part of the curriculum, the instructors talked about both "writing-to-learn approaches" in which writing is a "vehicle for language practice" and means to "proficient communicative abilities," and "learning-to-write approaches" in which students "become skilled writers" in the language (Reichelt et al. 28-29). WCAs are familiar and comfortable with developing writing skills; however, using writing to practice grammatical structures and syntactical patterns, to say the least, could be problematic for a community that believes the writing center is not a grammar fix-it shop. Yet, as I examined in chapter two, second language writers, unlike most first language writers who find their way to a writing center, are acquiring the language as they learn to write. For low-proficiency adult learners, who are already literate in a language, writing is an important tool for learning. Piero, for example, observed: "Actually teaching writing or helping a student write better is going to improve their oral abilities." He reasons that students speak "under pressure," but "when you write, you actually have time to put things in order, collect your ideas, find synonyms, enrich that vocabulary and that eventually is going to show after a little bit when they speak." Klara also made a similar case when she asserted that speaking "should be complemented with writing because it's one way for students to practice the language on their own when they don't have a speaking partner or someone who could engage with them." Writing is a means to learning the language because, as Klara pointed out, it is "a more reflective way of using the language." She continued, "in writing you have more time to find the right words and construct the grammar." The MWC fosters the connection between writing and speaking because the FL writing tutor becomes the "speaking partner," to use Klara's term, who helps writers negotiate vocabulary choices, parse grammar, and work through ideas and their arrangement.

Once students use writing to slow down and reflect on their language choices, these instructors hope that the students will then transfer their insights from the written to the oral realm. Piero, Lisette, and Klara describe very different ways that they use writing to help students learn the language, but all share the goal of wanting students to transfer the insights gleaned from writing to speaking. Piero believes that the knowledge writers acquire from writing the language "eventually is going to show when they speak." Illustrating the potential transfer of learning from written to oral language, Piero talked about how he uses writing to reinforce correct pronunciation:

There are specific sounds that especially English-speaking students may guess how to spell, but they will get the spelling wrong. So the *gn* sound, like gnocchi, they wouldn't know that it actually is a *g* and an *n*, so they need to know that whenever they see a *g* and an *n*, it is the *gn* sound. Or *sc* is not a hard sound . . . , so they need to make that kind of distinction. I do use the writing component a lot from week one, for example, in Italian 101. [Some letter combinations are] not just something that you can imitate or emulate. You can do that up to a certain point. If you just listen and repeat and everything is oral, I don't think it's going to stick. We could even discuss if a student is more of a visual learner or not, so my answer is actually influenced by the fact that I am a visual learner so I need to see words. I need to see the writing in order to help me produce and pronounce. And I have seen that in my students.

Alternatively, Lisette uses writing to help students move from simple to complex sentences, specifically "sentences that are connected by a phrase, a word in Russian which is basically the equivalent of 'that' or 'which,' but it's more complicated in Russian. The goal is to move them from the simple sentence 'I have a mother' to 'I have a mother that or who . . . .'" Like Piero, Lisette talked about writing as a tool for reflection, revision, and, ultimately, transfer. She reasoned, "I try to move them to those complex sentences not only orally but also in written genres. It's often easier for them to do it first in the written form because they can take the time to think about it, and they can revise." Whereas Piero wants writing to lead to better pronunciation and Lisette wants it to lead to more complex sentences, Klara constructs writing assignments that solidify difficult grammatical concepts. As a CLT practitioner she emphasizes "comprehension and making one's self understood" in speaking; writing, then, is the mode through which she expects a higher level of grammatical correctness. At the same time, grammatical correctness is not all she expects from writing assignments. Frustrated with assignments that prompted rote and predictable answers, Klara devised a prompt that would allow students to practice the subjunctive tense but also engage in expressive writing.

I've been trying to come up with a good assignment for the subjunctive—"If I were ___, I would do this and that." After first trying "if you win a million dollars, what would you do," everyone wrote the same: "Oh, I would buy a big house and a big car and donate a little to charity." I actually now have come up with an assignment that I feel works much better: "If you could live in a different time period and different place, where would you live, who would you be, what would your life be like?" And I've gotten really good responses from that. I mean from living as a cave person or in the Middle Ages or in the future, so it gives them some imaginative room.

Klara's assignment combines writing-to-learn-the-language and learning-to-write-in-the- language approaches because it forces students to use the subjunctive as they craft a creative and expressive essay. The essay assignment challenges them not just to master a grammatical form but also to communicate meaning. Like Piero and Lisette, Klara hopes her students' written mastery of the subjunctive will transfer to their speaking: "I'd like them to try to get it right or to work on the specific grammar issues that will ultimately also feed into their speaking."

While these three instructors use writing in different ways to make students slow down and think about their language use, they all anticipate that practicing the language in writing will transfer to performing the language when speaking. However, as the research on transfer shows, transfer does not occur automatically. This is where the FL writing tutors can help. Sometimes "context dependence" thwarts transfer when students may not know how to perform orally the skills they mastered in writing. In other cases, students may understand how to use a grammatical pattern but not why (Ambrose et al. 108-109). Tutors can "increase[e] the chances of transfer of learning" through "the practice of mindfulness or meta-cognition." Anne Beaufort describes metacognition as "vigilant attentiveness to a series of high-level questions as one is in the process of writing" (152). Thus, the Italian writing tutor working with one of Piero's students could prompt transfer by asking them to think about Italian spelling in relation to pronunciation. The tutor might ask the writer to brainstorm a list of words with consonant clusters unique to Italian (e.g., gnocchi, agnello, bagno, etc.), thereby raising awareness of the visualized consonant cluster in other familiar words. The tutor then could help writers transfer that awareness to speaking by doing some pronunciation practice. The Russian writing tutor working with Lisette's student might challenge them "to generalize to larger principles" (Ambrose et al. 118). For example, the tutor could ask the writer to articulate why they would need complex sentences in their oral repertoire, and what they could and could not communicate without knowledge of complex sentence structures. The German writing tutor might ask a student to "discuss conditions of applicability"—that is, the other topics or messages that would require the subjunctive (Ambrose et al. 117). In using these techniques, the FL writing tutors could elicit the transfer of knowledge from writing to speaking contexts.

WRITING TO COMMUNICATE MEANING

Besides using writing to support language acquisition and cultivate better speaking skills, FL instructors assign writing for a variety of other communicative purposes. The instructors interviewed talked about the communicative purposes of writing, making both implicit and explicit reference to the ACTFL "World Readiness Standards for Learning Languages," particularly the first two goal areas: communication and culture. The communication goal—that language learners should be able to communicate "in a variety of situations and for multiple purposes"—has three standards:

- Interpersonal Communication: Learners interact and negotiate meaning in spoken, signed, or written conversations to share information, reactions, feelings, and opinions.
- Interpretive Communication: Learners understand, interpret, and analyze what is heard, read, or viewed on a variety of topics.
- Presentational Communication: Learners present information, concepts, and ideas to inform, explain, persuade, and narrate on a variety of topics using appropriate media and adapting to various audiences of listeners, readers, or viewers. ("World")

The culture goal—that language learners should be able to "interact with culture competence and understanding"—has two standards:

- Relating Cultural Practices to Perspectives: Learners use the language to investigate, explain, and reflect on the relationship between the practices and perspectives of the cultures studied.

- Relating Cultural Products to Perspectives: Learners use the language to investigate, explain, and reflect on the relationship between the products and perspectives of the cultures studied. ("World")

The communication standard speaks to the purposes of writing assignments, and the culture standard addresses content. The standards also provide language that WCAs can use in staff training to describe the kinds of writing assignments FL writers are likely to bring to the MWC. Interpersonal, presentational, and interpretive assignments are not unusual in writing centers. However, WCAs would need to work with their staffs to support the cultural competence goals of assignments. Foreign language writing tutors would need to be trained to help writers understand intercultural audiences and communicate effectively across cultures in different genres (as discussed in chapter four).

The FL instructors' writing-to-communicate-meaning assignments fall into the categories of interpersonal, presentational, and interpretive. Erik, for example, favors presentational writing assignments as he imagines his students engaging with Japanese people in the business world. One of his assignments prompts writers to explain aspects of US culture to a non-US audience. Acknowledging that "writing is important," he observed that "99 percent of our students probably will never be in a situation where they have to do much writing in Japanese, no matter how far along they go." In designing advanced writing assignments, he aims to be practical as, he says, "it might be more important to stress presentation skills in business situations," to teach students to "read and understand something versus being able to write in a sophisticated scholarly way." As an example, he described an audio-visual digital project in which students write "for oral performance" by introducing "Carlisle [the town in Pennsylvania where Dickinson College is located] to visiting Japanese speakers." He prompts his students to draft a script that both introduces a local business and explains "how to get to these places, what's interesting about them, prices, hours." He brings an intercultural component to the assignment by directing students to provide "a short description in English and Japanese" to "visiting Japanese students." When the projects are completed, Erik makes them "publicly available on the web and so when [Japanese exchange] students come I can direct them to this website." In this complex assignment, students not only practice the Japanese language, but they must also grasp the intercultural rhetorical context, communicate in writing to an intercultural audience, create meaningful content, organize the information in a multimedia presentation, and provide the narration.

Through interpersonal writing assignments, FL instructors task students with employing intercultural rhetoric as they communicate in genres and to audiences from the target cultures. Erik, for example, assigns emails and letters—genres that involve "communicating among friends or students." He describes one such assignment on "formal letter writing conventions." He gives the students "a nice type of stationery and they'd be writing vertically, and we haven't required them to write vertically before. So what does it mean to write vertically and what are some of the letter writing conventions?" Besides learning new cultural conventions, the assignment also stresses writing process and organizational skills.

> We have them imagine that they're in Tokyo or someplace and writing to a teacher. So [they might write]: "I'm in Tokyo. Tokyo's cold. I went to see the temple yesterday. I'm working really hard in my Japanese classes. Is Carlisle cold?" There wasn't really a logic, so you can still teach organization and logic. Even in a letter writing format, you can't just stick unconnected sentences together.

Similarly, Lisette stresses "communication in many different ways," including writing, with her Russian language students. Also very practical in her approach, Lisette surmises that her students are more likely to communicate in Russian via "social media, which is almost all written communication. They're typing, they're commenting, and if they want to have authentic relationships with their Russian peers, then they need to know how to write and put sentences together. Social media writing looks very different than essay writing, of course, but it's still an important kind of writing." Specifically, she asks students to write "fictional email, or write fictional comments to a picture or Instagram post"—assignments that would require them to imagine a Russian audience. The purpose of those assignments, she explains, is to put students "in scenarios that they might find themselves in later on and hopefully their in-class writing is preparing them for doing it authentically later." While these genres are familiar, WCAs would need to train their FL writing tutors to talk to writers about negotiating authentic scenarios in which they must address different cultural audiences: Japanese exchange students who have just arrived in the US or Russian colleagues in emails or on social media.

Whereas Russian and Japanese instructors tend to work with more true beginners up through the intermediate level, few of whom become very advanced in four years, Spanish instructors have more students who are bilinguals, heritage speakers, or intermediate-level from high school and so positioned to make greater gains in proficiency than most true beginners. This may account for why Felicia discusses the interpretive writing assignments she and her colleagues give to their advanced students. Felicia reported on the evolution of her department's curriculum from assigning very little writing to introductory students to assigning writing at every level of the curriculum. The change occurred because her colleagues realized that students were not prepared for advanced writing assignments, that they "need some sort of ramp up." They came to this conclusion while designing "a coordinated curriculum" with "agreed on learning goals," which arose from "very deliberate discussions about the four skills: speaking, listening, reading, writing." Much like her colleagues, Felicia's introductory writing assignments reflect two key student learning goals: to practice "grammatical structures" and meaningful communication. The genres through which students practice those structures are interpersonal and presentational: "It can be description; it can be a funny dialogue; a skit. It's really anything in which they are getting practice using the language in a meaningful context." Felicia's advanced students, however, engage in "really disciplined textual analysis because I think that, that requires a kind of mental acuity and sharpness that is not necessarily required in other kinds of writing." Her preference for textual analysis arises from a core belief: "L2 writing skills develop your brain in ways that are valuable in itself," requiring "some mental acuity or flexibility." Like her literary scholar counterparts in the English department, Felicia wants her students to write with "clarity of thought just as it is in English." In fact, her writing-related learning outcomes are in line with traditional English writing goals: "to organize your thoughts and say something cogent where one idea relates to the next" and to articulate "your argument and how do you support it, how do you connect those ideas all together."

Another group of assignments these instructors described are closely aligned with the ACTFL culture standard and the CLT aim of exploring the social and cultural aspects of the language. For example, Erik gives advanced students the assignment to "present something that they're interested in about Japan." They must research Japanese culture, write a script, make an oral presentation, and then rewrite the script as a "more formal paper." Erik has them "working in the writing stage and also the speaking stage in all of these kinds of assignments." Similarly, Nasrin likened her writing assignments across the curriculum to "concentric circles" that "expand." The students begin with the self and move outward from "the personal to the family, to your group of friends, your college and workspace, to your society, to your country, and then you go on and so on." Once the students reach the outer circles, they write about the target culture: "it could be literary analysis; it could be political if we're talking about what's happening with Iran or what's happening with the Middle East." As Nasrin sums up, in these assignments, writers develop cultural competency as they "start to focus more on the other culture and interaction with the other culture."

Writing in a Culture

Interestingly, while CLT pedagogy and the ACTFL standards include cultural knowledge and intercultural sensitivity as essential skills for communicatively competent writers, intercultural rhetorical forms and conventions receive little attention in the ACTFL standards and tend not to be taught, at least not directly, in FL classrooms (with the exception of French). During the interviews the instructors were asked about written genres and conventions as well as writing instruction and standards in the target cultures, specifically in the universities where their students study abroad. Klara, Piero, Nasrin are international faculty who attended university in their native countries, and Lisette both participated in multi-year study abroad and worked abroad in Russia. Erik observed Japanese classrooms as a scholar conducting research in Japan, and Felicia directed a study abroad program in Spain for several years. All have knowledge of the study abroad programs in which their students enroll. With the notable exception of the French instructors who hail from an academic writing tradition with established genres and expectations (see chapter four), the interviewees reported that their assignments are in the US style—an approach that would be consistent with the culturally generic ACTFL categories of interpersonal, presentational, and interpretive.

Confirming the lack of writing instruction in most institutions of higher education outside the US, the six instructors stated that writing outside the US tends to be assigned and not taught. As noted in an earlier chapter, while the Bologna Reform has resulted in instructors assigning more writing in European universities, the interviewees indicated that writing was still more prevalent in US than other systems of higher education. Klara attributed the lack of writing instruction in German universities to "German Romantic history." In Romanticism, Klara explained, "it wasn't really considered that you could teach writing; it was kind of either you knew it or you didn't." Referring to an institution in Spain, Felicia stated: "Writing is not taught; students rarely get feedback on their writing." And Erik reported that the Japanese exchange students he met "really haven't had much writing instruction [in Japan]. So the native Japanese students who are coming here haven't had a lot of writing instruction throughout their education actually." Yet all the faculty indicated that instructors abroad still privilege certain genres and conventions, and so they have expectations—albeit unarticulated ones—regarding writing.

Some of the instructors pointed out that in countries outside of the US, writing may play a very small part, if any, in undergraduate education. Russian institutions, for one, prefer oral over written exams because of "the problem of plagiarism." Lisette explained that "plagiarism is so rampant that the traditional way of giving the exams has been oral. . . . Students are given a list of forty possible topics and then you show up, draw a card, and give a speech on that topic." She describes a writing culture in which "the Russian internet is full of websites to download papers on any topic, and even in the subway, you'll see people holding up cards that say 'Will Write Paper on Any Topic.' There's a whole industry of plagiarism." When writing is assigned, students may be mystified by the expectations and the directive feedback. According to Piero, in Italy "most of the exams are oral. They're literally called interrogations with the professors, and they usually are about one-hour conversations on the content." This preference for oral over written assessment is rooted in a tradition but one that is changing since the Bologna Reform. In Italy, some instructors assign a *tesina* or little thesis at the end of a course as well as a longer thesis as a requirement for the bachelor's degree. Piero explained the writing process revolves around regular meetings with a thesis advisor who reads a few pages at a time and offers feedback in person or via email. Piero's own experience of receiving feedback was formalist, authoritarian, and directive. He stated, "I feel in many cases the purpose of the feedback is to basically apply or respect or follow some sort of guidelines" of which he was unaware. This resulted in a trial-and-error approach: Piero submitted drafts only to be told "the footnote should be one-and-a-half centimeters from the bottom, and you should start with different numbers here, and, also, this is not the way you quote a book. . . ." When the feedback focused more on content, Piero "wouldn't say it's feedback; it's rather a correction. . . . They may give you like option A or option B, but it's clear that the professor would prefer option A, so you go with option A. . . . I don't want to say it's not constructive feedback because it is constructive feedback, and you learn something in that moment, but it's heavily guided in one direction."

No doubt, given the paucity of academic writing assignments and the lack of writing instruction, several instructors claimed, at first, that there were no standards. Klara described German academic writing as "more American style" in comparison to the "French," who "are very different in that respect. So Germany doesn't have the same kind of spelled out standards on how to write a paper." Similarly, Piero asserted, "Now there is not really guidelines. We don't really use MLA or Chicago. We don't really do that. Each professor apparently has his or her own way to do footnotes or in-text quotations." However, when pressed, all the instructors identified cultural differences in organizational patterns, sentence structure, the ethos of academic writers, and the aesthetics of writing.

1. Unlike US academic discourse, world academic discourses may not be linear and thesis-driven.

    - Arabic: "When you approach the topic you want, you start off with a lot of overviews, a lot of generalizations, and then you get to the point. It's just not like English."
    - German: "You can just work with a research question. You don't have to propose an answer to the question. I guess in that sense maybe that's more like the French, that you pose a question or a problem and then use the paper to propose different kinds of answers with the support of the material that you're working with."

- Russian: "Russian research papers don't have the linear structure that we often expect in a scholarly or research paper in the American context. . . . In the Russian research paper, you have your thesis, you have ideas, lines of inquiry, and there are supports for the thesis in the body, but the goal of the very end of the final paragraphs is to open it up to as many possible avenues for further research as possible. And it can even be poetic at times. . . . I've always considered it to show the author's breadth of potential analysis, sort of like I can't deal with all of this in this paper but look where this idea could go. And that just is very different in that not only do you not have the linear structure, you have these theses blooming out, but then the end just blows it up to all kinds of potential lines of inquiry."
- Italian: "The structure that I'm familiar with that I have seen, that I have done and that I see now, usually it's divided in three parts and the first part is descriptive, in the second part you have the case study or the subject matter that you're going to be dealing with, and then in the third part the analysis. In the descriptive section, you're basically describing what you know and what people know and what is known about the subject. The case-study is a text that you need to analyze or maybe a project that you're doing or a survey that you did. And then in the third part, you come up with your conclusions."
- Japanese: "One of the typical Japanese presentations would be to provide the audience with a lot of primary source material. In other words in my field [literary studies], it would be quotes from long passages from works and maybe magazine covers or advertisements that would be next to where the very works first appeared and maybe quotes from letters. . . . And what the audience would get in that case were just the primary materials in these sometimes big packets and the speaker would go through them."
- Spanish: "It's still quite common that students have one comprehensive exam at the end of the semester based on a reading list, and they somehow have to do some sort of summary. In a lot of cases, it might be an analytical summary, sort of a mix of summary and analysis, but it's

largely a regurgitation of what you read and what were the important points from your reading."

2. World academic discourses offer alternatives to the typical US ethos of the assertive yet impersonal and dispassionate scholar.

- German: "Traditionally in German academic writing, the writer would take his or her own voice out as much as possible. . . .You work with your sources and have them speak to each other."
- Russian: "In American writing, we are often taught not to use the I, and we tend to do a lot of hedging: 'one would argue that,' 'one might say that.' There's no room for hedging in Russian academic writing. The writer takes a very strong position, and Russian grammar allows for that, without necessarily using the I, which is interesting. The authorial position can be very strong in Russian academic writing, to the point that there's an entire tradition of name-calling in Soviet-era academic papers, of saying that 'my opponent or the other side is just wrong or they're ignorant,' and it's not seen as being an offensive scholarly move; in US academic writing you just couldn't do that."

3. Some world academic discourse cultures value sentence length and complexity beyond the norm of US academic writing.

- Arabic: "In Arabic you can write a full page with one sentence. . . . Punctuation was added much later; it was a much later development in the language."
- Italian: "If you're a good writer, you're going to write long sentences and long paragraphs that are complex."

4. Some world academic cultures embrace the aesthetic dimension of writing instruction.

- Japanese: "We don't really teach handwriting [to Japanese language learners in the US], and, yes, we expect students to be able to. We ask students to handwrite things because, in part, we think it's really important for learning the characters, so we have them handwrite a lot. But we don't teach them your handwriting is messy, fix it, and that's something that would be a much bigger part of their instruction in Japan."

Perhaps because writing standards are not explicitly stated in cultures that do not offer writing instruction, some instructors may not always have the language to talk about cultural differences in academic discourse. At the same time, intercultural rhetoric is an important dimension of cultural competence and essential to the skill set of FL writing tutors. To quote Lisette, "knowing writing genres and knowing about cultural writing differences is an important part of building cultural knowledge." Thus, even though Lisette does not always have a class proficient enough or likely ever to write a Russian-style research paper, she teaches them about the genre to "maximize intercultural appreciation and understanding"—something FL writing tutors in the MWC can also do. Japanese writing tutors, for example, can discuss why Japanese professors put such a strong emphasis on handwriting. Arabic writing tutors can examine how Arabic writers construct their indirect style of organization. More generally, all FL writing tutors can help writers construct the appropriate voice or ethos. In this way, FL writing tutors, given their language proficiency and interest in writing, can reinforce intercultural competence in all its complexity: cultural knowledge, sensitivity, and rhetoric.

The MWC as Change Agent

Up until this point, I have been looking at the work of FL writing tutors through the lenses of the ACTFL standards and CLT pedagogy to explain how the MWC enriches FL learning. As Erik commented, "I don't think I've ever thought of the MWC as remedial. I think it's something that can help all writers improve. . . . The most successful students use it the best, use it the most because they want to do better and it's a resource that works for them." My argument has been that WCAs who wish to build an MWC must have a solid grasp of the pedagogical values, standards, and best practices of their FL colleagues. Needless to say, this goes both ways: FL instructors would also benefit from learning about the values, standards, and best practices of WCAs. In this final section, I will explore how Dickinson's MWC has functioned as a change agent for FL faculty development. As the MWC took on the characteristics of a learning community, FL instructors began to develop and revise new writing pedagogies as they learned from writing program administrators, guest speakers, FL writing tutors, and each other.

The MWC directly and indirectly provides ongoing professional development in teaching writing to FL instructors. The interviewees specifically recalled formative experiences like the discussions in the MWC advisory committee meetings and writing program-sponsored guest speakers in second language acquisition. More generally, they credited the MWC with their acquiring new pedagogical tools. Klara said that the MWC helped her "reflect much more on how to teach writing." For example, she learned to curb her impulse "to comment or correct every little mistake" and to re-focus on "the main issues and also on the issues that were requested in the assignment." The MWC introduced her to "the whole idea of scaffolding," which she explained as "writing assignments and making them relate in one way or another to one or another but also to make them relate better to other things that are happening in the class." Like Klara, Lisette also changed the way she designed assignments: "the MWC allows me to assign more complex writing" and "more essays" in general because the students "can handle more because they have that support." Felicia explained how the MWC enabled her to develop the process approach to writing: "because of that support, there's more emphasis on revision as a process—that [revision] is not just revising grammar and scratching out adjectives that we consider incorrect. It's reformulating your ideas, going back to the drawing board to come up with a better support for this part of your argument or ditching that part of your argument because it's just not working." Given Felicia's view of writing as developing "mental acuity and flexibility," she appreciates that the "writing center gives me the backup for the support for that message [about revision] and for a lot of the legwork in doing that work."

Piero credited the MWC with his re-vision of his entire course, which he described in terms of backward design: he "started from the end, meaning the product." He explained, "So I started by working on the rubrics, and then the rubrics taught me how to be a better grader, and then it was still not enough. That also taught me how to fix my assignments and guide the students in order to arrive at the end point. And then eventually I incorporated elements in class." He attributed this insight to the MWC because "without the MWC, without the conversations with the tutors, without the training, without conversation with you [the WCA], I would never have thought about a proper way to grade, a proper way to write an assignment, and how to do that in class. I mean there was a system in place, and so I was able to apply the system to my teaching. So it was a direct result of me collaborating with the writing center." As a direct result of MWC interventions, Piero asks his "students to pay more attention now not only to form but also content, even in 101." Echoing the language of the MWC, he stated, "I do have more of a holistic approach when I explain to them how they should structure and write, even in 101." His holism takes him beyond "grammar" to "talking about introduction and completion and order for a 101 little composition." In addition, he changed his assignments so that now they are "longer" because he "added specific questions." Finally, despite coming from a writing culture in which he received formalist, authoritarian feedback, he gives "the students more guidance, and I give students instructions or suggestions on the grammar level, on the content level, and the overall form of the essay."

Having "pretty dramatically" changed how he taught writing as a result of the MWC, Erik articulated his insights into how new pedagogies can maximize student potential. Before the MWC, Erik would instruct students to write ten sentences about their families, and he would grade them solely on grammatical accuracy—not surprising given his early training that focused on speaking and grammar. The MWC, which he calls a "real catalyst," made him "realize that teaching writing was important" when "all of a sudden I was seeing the possibilities." The MWC in combination with a colleague's report from an ACTFL conference, made him aware of his students' "growth potential" and how his teaching methods could maximize that potential. First, he developed a "more sophisticated four-part rubric" which added "organization, complexity, and depth" to grammatical accuracy. Next, the writing center made him "think about teaching writing and that le[d] to peer review" in the classroom," and so he began to "require revision." He connected "having the Multilingual Writing Center" to the fact that his "expectations have gone up . . . for students because . . . they have this resource."

WCAs and FL faculty can easily find common ground when it comes to the goal of maximizing student learning. As the writing program and FL instructors work to expand that common ground and plan an MWC, both groups must agree to a relationship based on reciprocal learning and collaborative engagement. The MWC flourishes in the interstices between the disciplines. On the one hand, WCAs will need to work within the parameters of CLT and the ACTFL standards. They will need to embrace a holistic and non-hierarchical philosophy in which grammar is neither a less important nor a lower-order concern. They will need to train their tutors to be intercultural agents whose role will shift along the vertical language curriculum—in one session assisting beginner students as they write to bolster oral skills, and in another session supporting advanced students as they write to engage in complex interpersonal, presentational, or interpretive written communications. On the other hand, FL instructors can turn to WCAs when they have questions about how to teach writing—an essential element of language learning that they may not have been trained to teach. A successful MWC, then, promises to maximize the potential of FL learners, teachers, and tutors.

Appendix A: The Arc of a Tutoring Session

This exercise provides writing tutors with an overview of a session. You can have tutors practice these steps with each other and/or discuss the rationale for each step.

Before the session, read the appointment form on WCONLINE.

- o Why is it important to know what the writer will bring to the session and what the writer wants to work on?
- o Why is it important to know how long after the scheduled session the assignment is due?
- o Why is it important to know the writer's goals for learning the target language?

Greet the writer.

- o Is this the writer's first time being tutored?
- o Does the writer know how a session works? (If no, take a moment to explain the roles of the tutor and the writer in the session.)

Build rapport.

- o Does the writer seem nervous or unconfident? (You will need to emphasize positive learning environment for anxious writers.)
- o Does the writer like studying foreign language? Is the class going well?
- o Is the writer planning to pursue the language beyond the requirement?

- o Does the writer wish to study abroad in the target language?
- o What does the writer like most/least about writing in the language?

Let the writer set the agenda.

- o What does the writer want to work on?
- o What is the assignment? (Ask the writer to show you the assignment.)
- o When is the assignment due?

Read the essay.

- o The writer may choose to read the essay or may prefer that you read it.
- o Invite the writer to interrupt you when they want to fix something.

Engage strategically in conversation.

- o Use directive tutoring techniques as appropriate.
- o Ask nondirective, open-ended, probing questions. For example, how does your second paragraph relate to your thesis? How do these two sentences connect?
- o Help writers retrieve information they have learned. For example, what do you remember about how to use the subjunctive?
- o Prompt writers to elaborate on the reasoning behind their discursive moves. For example, can you talk me through your organization of this essay or paragraph?
- o Explain concepts that the writers cannot articulate, using simple language, analogies, and visual metaphors when you can.

Get the writer to write during the session.

- o Invite the writer to pick up the pen.
- o Walk away from the table if the writer needs time to write, review professor comments, and/or make revisions.

Bring closure to the session.

Appendix A 149

- Briefly summarize what you discussed during the session.
- What do you plan to do next before the paper is due?

Write your session log.

- What did the writer bring to the session, and how long did they have to work on it?
- What did the writer work on during the session? (Thesis, organization, logic, meaning, analysis, word choice, grammar, etc.)
- Did you or the writer notice any specific patterns of error?
- What writing techniques did you show the writer? (Reverse outlining, clustering, highlighting in multi-colored markers to parse a paragraph, noticing/hypothesis testing, thinking in the language, etc.)
- What specific concepts does the writer continue to struggle with? How did you discuss these issues? Did you recommend a follow-up visit to the professor?
- Did the writer articulate a revision plan?

Appendix B: Directive and Nondirective Tutoring Techniques

Writing tutors must learn to use directive and nondirective questioning techniques. With practice and training, writing tutors can learn to employ both kinds of questions strategically and with the goal of supporting the agency of writers, their ownership of their writing, and their learning goals.

Non-directive tutoring involves asking open-ended questions of the writer so that the writer can generate content, organize thoughts, make logical connections, address an audience, find a focus, proofread errors, etc. A nondirective tutor is a guide who helps a writer see their writing in a different way and then make strategic choices about content, form, and rhetorical situation.

Directive tutoring involves explaining writing concepts, grammar, and/or usage rules when a writer clearly lacks the knowledge to participate in nondirective interactions. A directive tutor is a coach who models a skill that the writer is expected to learn and emulate.

EXERCISE I: POSING NONDIRECTIVE AND DIRECTIVE QUESTIONS

- What is wrong with each statement below?
- How would you reword each one to make it nondirective?
- How would you reword each one to make it constructive and reflective of a positive learning environment?

1. You need to change your thesis because it does not connect to anything you wrote in the body.

2. Your evidence is weak and would not be convincing to anyone who does not already agree with you.
3. I cannot follow your logic or train of thought in this paragraph.
4. This sentence makes no sense.

EXERCISE II: STRATEGIZING WHEN TO BE DIRECTIVE AND NONDIRECTIVE

For each real-life scenario shared by a FL writing tutor, discuss how the writing tutor could employ directive and/or nondirective techniques.

Scenario A

An intermediate-level writer brought in a draft that barely answered the assignment prompt. After reading through the prompt, I realized she had completely misunderstood it. I set the draft aside and started re-reading the prompt with the writer, but she was not grasping the concept or tying it back to class material.

Scenario B

All of my sessions have been quite similar. When I ask writers what they want to work on, they say "grammar," and then they seem to assume that I am a human dictionary or grammar book. In some cases, they expect me to correct their essays for them.

Appendix C: Tutoring for Language Acquisition

Drawing on Second Language Acquisition research, these techniques are essential tools for an FL writing tutor:

1. *Noticing*: To acquire language, learners must notice the gap between actual and intended meaning. When writers produce language, FL writing tutors can help them to identify what they are unable to do, making the writers aware of their gaps in learning.
2. *Hypothesis Testing*: To acquire language, learners use trial and error to test how the language works. Their own "internal feedback" or "instructor feedback" triggers hypothesis testing. In addition, FL writing tutor feedback can initiate hypothesis testing as well as prompt writers to "compare [instructor] feedback to what they actually wrote" (Manchon 48).
3. *Metalinguistic Awareness*: To acquire language, learners must become aware of the forms of language. When writers seek to master a new skill, like verb tense or transitions, FL writing tutors can heighten their awareness of how they are shaping language by asking them to reflect on the "forms, rules, and form-function relationship" of language (Manchon 48).
4. *Negotiated Interaction:* To acquire language, learners must interact with writers of the target language. Negotiated interaction begins with noticing—that is, the writer and tutor realize that they have "different understandings and, through negotiation, arrive at a mutual one" (Williams, "Undergraduate" 83).

Scenario A

Can you identify where the tutor uses any of these approaches?

Even if a writer is not coming to me to practice holistic tutoring, I force them to. I tell them, "I just helped you understand the preterit form of the past tense. When we are reading through this, I want you to tell me which word to you is the preterit or where you should use the preterit." The writer is seeing their paper. They're not just waiting for me to tell them to do the correction. They're making the correction because I showed them already how to do it and how to change it from present or from future tense into preterit. Then it's their turn to make the corrections. I tell them: "This is what you just told me in English. Is that what you're trying to say?" Usually, they tell me it is not what they are trying to say. I then ask them, "What's wrong there? Is the context okay?" And then they tell me that the tense is wrong. I ask them, "Are you trying to say that this happened or that it is happening? What tense do you use? Did it happen continuously, or did it happen one time?" Imperfect or preterit? I tell them what they're telling me in their native language so they see, and then ask them what is wrong. That's a logical approach. They tell me this is wrong, and they fix it themselves.

Scenario B

Can you identify where the tutor uses any of these approaches?

I had a tutee who brought in *explication de texte* that she had to write on the movie *La Reine Margo*. She came in and she told me that she had a very good understanding of how to organize the paper.

She had to write an *explication de texte*: you have to put the summary of the text first, and then you analyze it. She jumped right into analyzing the text, and then towards the end she summarized. This was her first draft, so she was just trying to get words on paper. I explained to her that her summary is good for the most part and suggested she put it in the beginning so that the reader who hasn't seen the movie or read the book will know what she's talking about before she goes into the in-depth analysis about it. She said, "That makes sense, of course, let's do that."

After we fiddled around with the different paragraphs, making sure that the summary was first, I said: "So now you have to see that your transition sentences don't really work anymore, do they?" And she said, "Oh, I guess not." I replied, "Let's look at these sentences on a closer level and see what we can to do to change the words, change the syntax, to make sure that your paragraphs (I hate using this word because I think writing center tutors use this word way too much)—flow—that they move together and make sense." She agreed, and I continued: "You mention this character in the last sentence of this summary, do you talk about him in the first, in your next paragraph?" She admitted, "No, I really don't." So I asked, "Who do you talk about in this paragraph?" She responded, "Oh, *La Reine Margot*." I then prompted her to work out a transition sentence that involves her at the end of the first paragraph so the reader knows what to expect. We went word-by-word to figure out what would work best.

She wrote, "*Margot à créer une révolution*"—Margot created a revolution. I asked, "do you really want to use the word *creer*, to create? Do you think that's the best word to use?" She admitted "that's just the word I know." I said, "Let's get the dictionary, or let's get the thesaurus and look at different words. Give me English words that you think you want to use, and let's try to find the best translation." She ended up choosing *participer* which means "to participate in." She chose that word because *La Reine Margot* didn't necessarily make a revolution; she was a part of the revolution. Then we found a transition. Then I said, "now what does this paragraph say?" After that, we continued the whole cycle. What is the message? How do you move to the next message? What is the transition? I showed her how to move from organization to content to the word level in her choice of transition sentences.

Scenario C

What role is the tutor being forced to play? How are the writers shaping the role of the tutor? How might this tutor use the techniques above to reconstruct a more effective role?

One tutor described their most difficult session: "Many of my sessions have been quite similar. When I ask the writers what they want to work on, they say 'grammar,' and then they seem to assume that I am a human dictionary or grammar book who will correct their essays for them."

Scenario D

How might a writing tutor employ negotiated interaction in discussing this essay with the writer?

Essay

In today's world the religons are extraordinarily different. All over the world religons look funny to some people because they are so different.

People believe in a number of different things on Earth. For example, in Christianity we think it's normal to go to church and shout sometimes. If you took someone from Hinduism to a church and they saw someone shouting they would think it's crazy. Just like if we go to India and see thousands of people in front of a building throwing rocks. We would think that's crazy too. If you're used to it you think it's normal if you're not you think it's crazy.

In conclusion, it's all in what you believe. That's the reason the religons today are so different.[26]

Appendix D: Google Translate Exercise

This exercise helps tutors explore the limitations of Google Translate and analyze the features of a piece of writing that has been Google translated. You can choose your own sample of student writing to submit to Google Translate and compare the Google Translate output for different levels of writing.

- Can you summarize the gist of the Google translated paragraph?
- What is problematic about this translation? How would you pinpoint the sources of the problem? Is it grammar, word choice, sentence structure? Make a thorough list of the problems.
- Where would you start with the writer? How would you practice "informed flexibility"?

English Original

In Pat Barker's 1994 novel *The Eye in the Door*, Lieutenant Billy Prior has recently returned to London from the front lines of France during World War I. Declared unfit for duty and sent home because of "asthma"—one of the physical excuses used to send mentally damaged soldiers back to England—Billy knows that it is the subconscious wounds more deeply entrenched that keep him out of the front lines. In a society that casts censure and blame on any young man back on the Homefront with no visible wounds, Billy attempts and eventually fails to hide his profound mental injuries from both the public and those closer to him: his girlfriend Sarah and his psychologist, Dr. Rivers. He suffers from "shell-shock," later to be known as PTSD, in which his own consciousness fights against him, reminding him constantly of the war in both his waking and sleeping hours through the use of an "eye in the door"; a symbol that confronts him both literally in the door of a women's prison, and figuratively in the sleeping state of his own mind. It is particularly in sleep that Billy's nightmares and loss of reality plague him through acute sensory imagery exacerbated by his own vision and interpretation of "the eye," which alters his awareness of consciousness and creates a sense of duality within both his nightmares and himself.[27]

Arabic

عاد اللفتنانت بيلي ، Pat Barker 1994 The Eye in the Door في رواية بريور حديثًا إلى لندن من الخطوط الأمامية لفرنسا خلال الحرب العالمية الأولى. تم الإعلان عن عدم ملاءمته للواجب وإرساله إلى المنزل بسبب "الربو "- وهو أحد الأعذار الجسدية المستخدمة لإرسال الجنود المصابين بضرار عقلية مرة أخرى إلى إنجلترا - بيلي يعلم أن هذه الجروح اللاشعور أكثر رسوحا التي تبقيه خارج الخطوط الأمامية Homefront. في مجتمع يلقي باللوم ويلقى اللوم على أي شاب يعود على فشل في نهاية المطاف لإخفاء إصاباته العقلية Billy بدون جروح واضحة ، يحاول العميقة من الجمهور وأولئك الأقرب إليه: صديقته سارة وطبيبه النفسي ، د. الأنهار. وهو يعاني من "صدمة الصدمة "، التي عُرفت فيما بعد باسم "اضطراب ما بعد الصدمة" PTSD ، مذكرأه باستمرار بالحرب في ساعات حيث يحارب وعيه ضده ، اليقظة والنوم من خلال استخدام "العين في الباب "؛ رمزا يواجهه حرفيا في باب سجن النساء ، وبشكل مجازي في حالة النوم الخاصة بعقله. في النوم على وجه الخصوص فإن كوابيس بيلي وفقدانه للواقع يزعجه من خلال الصور الحسية الحادة التي تتفاقم بسبب رؤيته وتفسيره "للعين "، الذي يغير من وعيه بالوعي ويخلق شعوراً بالازدواجية داخل كوابيسه

Chinese

在帕特巴克 1994 年的小說"門之眼"中，比利·普雷斯中尉最近在第一次世界大戰期間從法國的前線返回倫敦。宣布不適合執勤並因"哮喘"而被送回家 - 這是以前的身體藉口之一將精神受損的士兵送回英格蘭 - 比利知道潛意識的傷口更加根深蒂固，讓他不在前線。在一個對任何回到 Homefront 並且沒有明顯傷痕的年輕人施加責難和責備的社會中，Billy 試圖並且最終未能掩蓋他對公眾和離他更近的人的深刻精神傷害：他的女朋友 Sarah 和他的心理學家 Dr 河流他遭受了"貝殼衝擊"，後來被稱為創傷後應激障礙，他自己的意識與他作鬥爭，通過使用"門眼"，在他的醒著和睡眠時間裡不斷提醒他戰爭;一個像徵，無論是在女子監獄的門口，還是在他自己心靈的睡眠狀態下，都面臨著他的面孔。特別是在睡夢中，比利的噩夢和現實的失落通過他自己的視覺和對"眼睛"的解釋而加劇了他的急性感官形象，這改變了他的意識意識，並在他的噩夢和他自己內部創造了二元感。

French

Dans l'ouvrage de Pat Barker paru en 1994 dans The Eye in the Door, le lieutenant Billy Prior est récemment rentré à Londres des premières lignes de la France pendant la Première Guerre mondiale. Déclaré inapte au service et renvoyé chez lui à cause de «l'asthme» - l'une des excuses physiques renvoyez des soldats endommagés mentalement en Angleterre - Billy sait que ce sont les blessures subconscientes plus profondément enracinées qui le maintiennent à l'écart des lignes de front. Dans une société qui blâme et blâme tout jeune homme sur le Homefront sans aucune blessure visible, Billy tente de dissimuler ses blessures mentales profondes à la fois au public et à ses proches: sa petite amie Sarah et son psychologue, Dr Rivières. Il souffre d'un «choc d'obus», plus tard connu sous le nom de SSPT, dans lequel sa propre conscience se bat contre lui, lui rappelant constamment la guerre à ses heures de veille et de sommeil grâce à l'utilisation d'un «œil à la porte»; un symbole qui le confronte à la fois littéralement à la porte d'une prison pour femmes et au figuré dans son état de sommeil. C'est surtout dans le sommeil que les cauchemars et la perte de réalité de Billy le tourmentent à travers une imagerie sensorielle aiguë exacerbée par sa propre vision et interprétation de «l'œil», ce qui modifie sa conscience de conscience et crée un sentiment de dualité à la fois dans ses cauchemars et dans lui-même.

German

In Pat Barkers Roman The Eye in the Door von 1994 ist Lieutenant Billy Prior kürzlich während des Ersten Weltkrieges von den Fronten Frankreichs nach London zurückgekehrt. Er wurde wegen „Asthma" für untauglich erklärt und nach Hause geschickt - eine der körperlichen Ausreden schickt psychisch geschädigte Soldaten zurück nach England - Billy weiß, dass es die unterbewussten Wunden sind, die tiefer eingegraben sind, die ihn von der Front fernhalten. In einer Gesellschaft, die jeden jungen Mann an der Homefront tadelt und beschuldigt, ohne sichtbare Wunden zu haben, versucht Billy und scheitert schließlich daran, seine tiefgründigen psychischen Verletzungen sowohl vor der Öffentlichkeit als auch vor ihm zu verbergen: seine Freundin Sarah und sein Psychologe Dr Flüsse. Er leidet unter dem „Schalenschock", der später als PTSD bekannt wird, in dem sein eigenes Bewusstsein gegen ihn kämpft und ihn sowohl in seinen Wach- als auch in seinen Schlafstunden durch den Einsatz eines „Auges in der Tür" ständig an den Krieg erinnert; ein Symbol, das ihm buchstäblich in der Tür eines Frauengefängnisses und bildlich im Schlafzustand seines eigenen Geistes gegenübersteht. Es ist vor allem im Schlaf, dass Billys Alpträume und der Verlust der Realität ihn durch eine akute Sinneswahrnehmung plagen, die durch seine eigene Vision und Interpretation des „Auges" verschlimmert wird, was sein Bewusstseinsbewusstsein verändert und ein Gefühl der Dualität sowohl in seinen Albträumen als auch in sich selbst erzeugt.

Hebrew

ברומן של פאט בארקר מ- 1994 "העין בדלת", סגן בילי פריור חזר לאחרונה ללונדון מקווי החזית של צרפת במלחמת העולם הראשונה. הכריז כי אינו ראוי לתפקיד ושולח הביתה בגלל "אסתמה" - אחד התירוצים הפיזיים ששימשו לשלוח חיילים שניזוקו נפשית בחזרה לאנגליה - בילי יודע שהפצעים התת-מודעים מעוגנים עמוק יותר, שמרחיקים אותו מהקווים הקדמיים. בחברה שמטילה גינוי ואשמה על כל גבר צעיר שחוזר על העורף בלי פצעים גלויים, בילי מנסה, ובסופו של דבר לא מצליח להסתיר את הפגיעות הנפשיות העמוקות שלו הן מהציבור והן מקרוב אליו: חברתו שרה והפסיכולוגית שלו, ד"ר נהרות. הוא סובל מ"הלם קרב", שנודע מאוחר יותר בשם PTSD, שבו התודעה שלו נאבקת בו, מזכירה לו כל הזמן את המלחמה, הן בשעות הערות והן בשינה, באמצעות "עין בדלת "; סמל העומד מולו, פשוטו כמשמעו, בפתח בית-סוהר לנשים, ובאופן משכנע במצב השינה של מוחו. בייחוד בשינה, סיוטיו של בילי ואובדן המציאות מטרידים אותו באמצעות דימויים חושיים חריפים המחריפים בחזונו ובפרשנותו ל"עין ", שמשנה את מודעותו לתודעה ויוצרת תחושה של דואליות בתוך הסיוטים שלו ושל עצמו.

ITALIAN

Nel romanzo di Pat Barker del 1994, The Eye in the Door, il tenente Billy Prior è recentemente tornato a Londra dalle prime linee della Francia durante la prima guerra mondiale. Dichiarato non idoneo al dovere e rimandato a casa a causa di "asma" - una delle scuse fisiche usate per mandare soldati mentalmente danneggiati in Inghilterra - Billy sa che sono le ferite subconsce più profondamente radicate che lo tengono fuori dalle prime linee. In una società che lancia una censura e incolpa di qualsiasi giovane sul Homefront senza ferite visibili, Billy tenta e alla fine non riesce a nascondere le sue profonde ferite mentali sia dal pubblico sia da quelli più vicini a lui: la sua ragazza Sarah e il suo psicologo, Dr Fiumi Soffre di "shock shell", in seguito noto come PTSD, in cui la sua stessa coscienza combatte contro di lui, ricordandogli costantemente della guerra sia nella sua veglia che nelle ore di sonno attraverso l'uso di un "occhio nella porta"; un simbolo che lo confronta sia letteralmente nella porta di una prigione femminile, sia in senso figurato nello stato di sonno della propria mente. È soprattutto nel sonno che gli incubi e la perdita della realtà di Billy lo affliggono attraverso acute immagini sensoriali esacerbate dalla sua stessa visione e interpretazione di "l'occhio", che altera la sua consapevolezza della coscienza e crea un senso di dualità all'interno dei suoi incubi e di se stesso.

Japanese

パット・バーカーの 1994 年小説「The Eye in the Door」では、第 1 次世界大戦中、フランスの最前線からロンドンに戻った。精神的に傷ついた兵士をイングランドに戻してください - ビリーは、彼が最前線から守ることがより深く根深い潜在的な傷であることを知っています。家の中で目に見えない傷のない若い男に責任を負わせ、責任を負わせる社会の中で、ビリーは、公衆と彼の近くの人たちから深い精神的傷害を隠そうとしません。彼のガールフレンドのサラと彼の心理学者、川。彼は後に PTSD と呼ばれる"シェルショック"に苦しみ、自分の意識が彼と戦い、"目の中の目"を使って起きている時間と眠っている時間の両方で常に戦争を思い起こさせる。彼は女性の刑務所のドアの中に文字どおり直面しているシンボルであり、比喩的には彼自身の心の眠っている状態です。ビリーの悪夢や現実の喪失は、自分のビジョンと意識の解釈を悪化させた急性の感覚的なイメージを通して彼を苦しめ、特に意識を変え、悪夢と自分の両面で二重性を生み出す。

Portuguese

No romance The Eye in the Door de 1994, de Pat Barker, o tenente Billy Prior retornou recentemente a Londres das linhas de frente da França durante a Primeira Guerra Mundial. Declarou-se inapto para o dever e mandou para casa por causa da "asma" - uma das desculpas físicas usadas para Mande soldados mentalmente feridos de volta para a Inglaterra - Billy sabe que são os ferimentos subconscientes mais profundamente entrincheirados que o mantêm fora das linhas de frente. Em uma sociedade que critica e culpava qualquer jovem do Lar sem ferimentos visíveis, Billy tenta e eventualmente não consegue esconder seus profundos ferimentos mentais tanto do público quanto daqueles que estão mais próximos dele: sua namorada Sarah e seu psicólogo, Dr. Rios. Ele sofre de "choque de cascas," mais tarde conhecido como TEPT, no qual sua própria consciência luta contra ele, lembrando-o constantemente da guerra tanto em suas horas de vigília quanto de sono através do uso de um "olho na porta"; um símbolo que o confronta literalmente na porta da prisão de uma mulher, e figurativamente no estado de sono de sua própria mente. É particularmente durante o sono que os pesadelos e a perda de realidade de Billy o atormentam através de imagens sensoriais agudas exacerbadas por sua própria visão e interpretação do "olho," que altera sua consciência da consciência e cria um senso de dualidade tanto em seus pesadelos quanto em si mesmo.

Russian

В романе Пэт Баркера «Глаз в дверях» лейтенант Билли Прай недавно вернулся в Лондон из-под линии фронта во время Первой мировой войны. Объявлено непригодным к ответственности и отправлено домой из-за «астмы» - одного из физических оправданий, отправить умственно поврежденных солдат обратно в Англию - Билли знает, что это подсознательные раны, более глубоко укоренившиеся, которые удерживают его от линии фронта. В обществе, которое бросает порицание и обвиняет любого молодого человека в Homefront без видимых ран, Билли пытается и в конце концов не скрывает своих глубоких умственных травм как от общественности, так и от тех, кто ближе к нему: его подруга Сара и его психолог, доктор Реки. Он страдает от «раковинного шока», позже известного как ПТСР, в котором его собственное сознание борется против него, постоянно напоминая ему о войне как в его бодрствовании, так и во время сна через использование «глаза в дверь»; символ, который противостоит ему как буквально в дверях женской тюрьмы, так и фигурально в спящем состоянии его собственного разума. Особенно во сне, что кошмары Билли и потеря реальности поражают его через острые сенсорные образы, усугубляемые его собственным видением и интерпретацией «глаза», что изменяет его осознание сознания и создает -увство двойственности как в его

Spanish

En la novela de Pat Barker, 1994, El ojo en la puerta, el teniente Billy Prior regresó recientemente a Londres desde el frente de Francia durante la Primera Guerra Mundial. Se declaró no apto para el servicio y fue enviado a casa debido al "asma", una de las excusas físicas utilizadas para enviar soldados mentalmente dañados de vuelta a Inglaterra. Billy sabe que son las heridas subconscientes más profundamente arraigadas las que lo mantienen fuera de las líneas del frente. En una sociedad que impone censura y culpa a cualquier joven que regresa a Homefront sin heridas visibles, Billy intenta, y eventualmente falla en ocultar sus profundas lesiones mentales, tanto al público como a las personas más cercanas a él: su novia Sarah y su psicólogo, el Dr. Ríos. Sufre de "shock", más tarde conocido como PTSD, en el que su propia conciencia lucha contra él, recordándole constantemente la guerra en sus horas de vigilia y sueño mediante el uso de un "ojo en la puerta"; un símbolo que lo enfrenta, literalmente, en la puerta de una prisión para mujeres, y figurativamente en el estado de sueño de su propia mente. Es particularmente en el sueño que las pesadillas y la pérdida de la realidad de Billy lo aquejan a través de imágenes sensoriales agudas exacerbadas por su propia visión e interpretación de "el ojo", que altera su conciencia de conciencia y crea un sentido de dualidad tanto en sus pesadillas como en él mismo.

Appendix E: Creating a Positive Learning Environment by Sharing Second Language Learning Experiences

If you are a FL writing tutor, then you have experienced learning a second language—whether you are a domestic student who has achieved proficiency through coursework and immersion experiences, a bilingual student whose home and school languages are different, or an international student studying in a foreign country.

As we read in chapter three, your attitude toward the writers with whom you work can contribute to or undermine a positive learning environment. For this exercise, think about when you learned a new language:

- What did you find most difficult?
- What linguistic hurdles did you encounter?
- What made you almost give up?
- How did you surmount those hurdles? Personal resilience? A good teacher? Something else?
- What did you find most rewarding?
- What made you persist in your language learning?

Write a brief narrative that you would share with an anxious FL writer whom you encountered in the MWC.

Share your responses with each other and talk about the benefits or problems of sharing the various narratives with struggling writers.

Appendix F: Practicing Intercultural Competence in a Writing Center Session

Exercise I

In this scenario, the tutor is a US student whose first language is English, and the writer is an exchange student from France. The writer is learning about federalism in her political science course, and the instructor has asked the students to pick a policy issue and discuss whether that issue should be the purview of state or national government. The writer chose to focus on protections for the LGBTQ community in light of the fourteenth amendment, which forbids states from restricting the basic rights of citizens.

TUTOR: You want to think of your paper as kind of like a tunnel. You start with the idea of federalism and the main issues, and then you solely talk about LGBTQ rights and the Fourteenth Amendment. But then in your conclusion, broaden that and look at the issue from a more global perspective. Like what influence would this have on the country?

WRITER: Okay. At the end of the conclusion, does it have to be an open . . . I don't know how to explain this. I know in French, we have to do this. It's like to be open—like a reflection to think about something.

TUTOR: It can be. I don't think it *has* to be, but it definitely *can* be.

WRITER: Okay.

TUTOR: What were you thinking?

WRITER: I'm not sure yet. So I mean the—the structure of the essay in French is so different, so that's why we don't do essays. We do like, it's like a question. Then we say yes, but no, but yes, but no, but yes. But in the US you have to be sure what you say, and it's just like *ugh*!

TUTOR: I think you're right that the conclusion is a place where you *can* kind of go back and forth, and you can kind of talk about the other side of the issue. I think in the paper, we really argue one side, but the conclusion is a place where you could ask questions about the other side.[28]

- How would you describe the writer's "writing culture shock"?
- What critical difference(s) does the writer articulate between US and French cultures?
- What information about the writing culture might the tutor be missing?
- How might the tutor explain the difference and frame the writer's options for revision?

Exercise II

How does academic writing differ across cultures? Do college instructors from different cultures have differing definitions of "good" writing? For this exercise, FL writing tutors who have studied abroad as visiting or domestic students will need to have a writing assignment that they wrote in the foreign language.

- Considering both the writing process and product, what do you think the instructor for whom you wrote this essay considers good writing? Do you think the instructor's definition of good writing is consistent with other instructors at the university where you wrote the essay? You should consider the purposes and audiences of writing, conventions (i.e., thesis, hedging, etc.), organization, sentence construction, the rules for incorporating outside sources, appropriate tone, the role of the writer in the essay, among others.
- How might your insights about intercultural rhetoric inform your tutoring practice?

Appendix G: What Would You Do? Holistic Tutoring Scenarios

You can use these scenarios gathered directly from FL writing tutors to anticipate tricky sessions and troubleshoot effective strategies.

How might these tutors use holistic tutoring techniques to help these writers?

SENTENCE-LEVEL TROUBLES

1. Frequently, I work with writers who come in with a first draft that includes the professors' editorial comments. It is clear that the writer did not attempt to correct any errors on their own before their appointment with me. It is so frustrating that they bring the draft to me before they even review it themselves. What should I do the next time this happens?
2. A writer from an intermediate-level class brought in a four-page paper, and her main concern was grammar. The student refused to read her paper aloud. Her grammar mistakes frequently impeded meaning so that I could not understand her ideas. Every time I asked her a nondirective question regarding a grammar error, she could not recall the rule, and she would say "I don't know." It was hard for me not to point out the mistakes every time she said "I don't know." How could I make her engage with me in working on her own essay?
3. Sometimes the language learners who are beginners don't know enough about grammar or sentence structure to write out their thoughts in a complex sentence, so I encourage them to write shorter sentences and use the simpler sentence structure that they know. When they do this, their meaning inevitably shifts. Should I have come up with some other way to help them so that their original meaning is not compromised?

Appendix G 169

ESSAY-LEVEL TROUBLES

1. An intermediate-level writer brought in a draft that barely answered the assignment prompt. After reading through the prompt, I realized she had completely misunderstood it. I set the draft aside and started re-reading the prompt with the writer, but she was not grasping the concept or tying it back to class material. What more could I have done?
2. I had a difficult session with a writer who wrote a very sparse essay. He did not describe his topic in much detail, and he did not try to extend or develop any points. He also used the exact same syntactical pattern over and over again. How could I have helped him develop his ideas and incorporate different syntactical patterns?
3. A writer came to the MWC with a plan to work on so many things at the same time. Of course, there were the usual grammar errors, but this writer also had problems with idea development and essay structure, even in English. I also noticed that he had written part of his essay in English and used an online translator because the translations were very bad. Where do I start with a writer like this?
4. A writer was told to write a thesis-driven essay, but he just kept repeating the thesis over and over again without any analysis. How do I move the writer forward without just giving him my ideas?
5. I worked with a writer who brought in a final draft that was, literally, a mess. The essay was due in one hour, and so the writer was extremely anxious and rushed. I read the essay and quickly realized that the writers should not submit it. I admitted to the writer that the essay read like he had written it without thinking too much. I told him that if I were him, I would start from scratch. The writer insisted that he had to meet the deadline and was unwilling to ask for an extension. As a result, I spent twenty-five minutes explaining how the writer might link his ideas together to make the train of thought more logically connected. Did I do the right thing?

Foreign Language Anxiety

1. I met with a writer who obviously did not want to be in the MWC. He was very discouraged with his essay. When I asked him to clarify a phrase or reword a sentence, he would shut down. He told me he regretted taking the language and that he did not care about it. I decided to adjust my attitude to make him feel more comfortable and less intimidated. I told him, "Yeah, I know, this language is ridiculous." I did not like having to do that, but his attitude did seem to improve. I would rather have encouraged him and tried to improve his relationship with the language rather than confirm his apathy. But he did open up and offer more input by the end. What was the right thing to do?
2. A writer came to a session, and he looked so nervous. I found out he was an intermediate-level student, but it was his first time in the MWC. As we talked, it became clear to me that he was so afraid of being judged. How could I have reassured him?

Appendix H: Holly and Leila: A Problem-Based Learning Exercise

Since problem-based learning is a student-centered technique, prior to a large group discussion, small groups of tutors should read the transcript one section at a time and then pause to discuss the questions that appear at each section break.

Leila is an exchange student from France who also tutors a foreign language (though not French). This is her first visit to the MWC. She is working with Holly, an English writing tutor. As a first-time exchange student, Leila is nervous about the content of her essay and her command of English. Holly greets Leila at the door.

HOLLY: So what are we working on today?

LEILA: I have this assignment. I am supposed to write about how the resistance against European colonization and religion play in the development of Creole culture. These are my outlines and ideas. And this is my first draft. It's almost finished. I have just to finish this part and make a conclusion. So I wanted just some help with subtle proofreading.

HOLLY: Great. What I typically like to do is to read the paper out loud just to catch things that we don't necessarily see if we're not . . . if you're reading it silently. Would you like to read it or would you like me to read it?

LEILA: I guess we can do it bit by bit.

HOLLY: All right. That works. We can stop anytime. Feel free to make notes to yourself, change anything you want to, anything you notice along the way, and I'll just be jotting some things down. Don't take it personally. Don't worry about it.

LEILA: No problem. On the contrary, I need this.

HOLLY: *(laughs)* Yeah. Okay.

LEILA: Okay so . . . *(starts to read her essay aloud)* "In the Caribbean, resistance was a survival mechanism for the Africans enslaved. It took several forms, but the goal was the same: finding a way to survive in a hostile environment while remembering their own identity. However, resistance did not ignore the context of European power, so people adapted. Creolization is a manifestation of these two clashing cultures, European and African and the making of the new. On one side, slaves and African descents resisted to not fully accept European culture, and on the other side, they had to adapt in order to survive. By adapting I mean adopting the European cultural norms, whether it would be language, religion, propriety, or history. Among the development of Creole culture, I will focus on religion as one of the manifestations of both resistance and adaptation. Then I will explain how language was a way of resisting to it, and finally I will discuss how music is an example of adjustment and struggle against the European regimen."

HOLLY: How do you feel about that? Do you want to take a look at that piece or do you want to move on and come back or do the whole thing?

LEILA: We can start with that piece.

HOLLY: Okay. Did you notice anything in particular while you were reading it just now that you wanted to adapt or change or that you had questions about?

LEILA: Um . . . I don't know. I guess maybe just, uh, here, like when I read it, it was like more fluent to say "and on the other side."

HOLLY: That's true. That's true. Also, in English we typically say "on one hand," and "on the other hand." That's just the expression.

LEILA: Oh, okay.

Questions

1. Did Holly and Leila set an agenda for the session?
2. How would you describe Holly's version of the reading-out-loud technique?
3. What are the benefits and limitations of her technique in this particular instance?
4. How else could she have started the session?

Holly notices something unusual and switches gears to talk about the cultural aspects of writing.

HOLLY: The other thing that I noticed . . . I know like each language and each culture sort of has its own way of writing, so it depends in American universities. Different professors want different things. Have you written a paper for this professor before?

LEILA: No, it's the first one.

HOLLY: Okay. Can I see your prompt and see if there is any indication of what she wants?

LEILA: *(Digs around in her folder and pulls out the assignment prompt.)*

HOLLY: *(Reads the prompt.)* Title, thesis statement, examples. Okay. All right. You have a very French way of writing, like this is your direction. And usually that's fine.

LEILA: Yeah. *(She laughs.)*

HOLLY: It should be fine. But some professors are particular about either giving this very direct roadmap or not. Did your professor say anything about how she wants that formatted?

LEILA: No.

HOLLY: All right. Then you're probably fine.

LEILA: Okay.

HOLLY: It's just a thing to pay attention to because some professors care a lot and some really don't. You should be fine. *(She pauses and thinks.)* One thing, though, we do typically try to avoid the first person in an academic paper. Do you think there's a way that you could adapt, just edit a tiny bit, these few sentences to take out the first-person references?

LEILA: I can change it and put it in the passive voice here. I mean *(starts rewriting and composing aloud).* . . . Among the development of culture, a focus on religion can be made as well as the manifestation of both resistance and . . .

HOLLY: We try to avoid passive voice too. That's the challenge. But let's look at it.

LEILA: Okay. *(She laughs. Then she thinks for a moment.)* So can I say "we"?

HOLLY: Let's look at it and see what we can do. *(She reads the draft.)* I would suggest just saying . . . the thing about a thesis statement is that you're trying to make a strong point. You just want to say, "Here's the truth."

LEILA: Okay. So this may be more my statement. My thesis. *(She reads the thesis.)* "On one side, slaves and African descents resisted to not fully accept European culture, and on the other side, they had to adapt in order to survive. By adapting I mean adopting the European cultural norms, whether it would be language, religion, propriety, or history." And this is the way I organize. *(She reads what Holly has called the roadmap.)* "Among the development of Creole culture, I will focus on religion as one of the manifestations of both resistance and adaptation. Then I will explain how language was a way of resisting to it, and finally I will discuss how music is an example of adjustment and struggle against the European regimen."

HOLLY: Yeah. All right. Let's see. *(She reads.)* "Those of African descent or people of African descent. . . ." What we probably would say—descent as a noun is just like a thing that goes down, not a descendant.

LEILA: Okay.

HOLLY: *(Reads the introduction paragraph to herself.)* You're focusing on religion as a manifestation, language, and music. Then I think you're right. The sentence about how they adapted through religion, language, and music might be your thesis. So you can make those three pieces of it very clear without saying I'm going to do this, and then I'm going to do this, and then I'm going to do this. Does that make sense?

LEILA: Yeah.

HOLLY: So do you want to go ahead and try to write a new thesis statement now? You can just talk at me if you want to and I'll jot it down, or you can write if that's easier. Since those are going to be three short sentences, do you think you could combine them as one?

LEILA: Yeah.

HOLLY: Religion, language, and music are all examples of adjustment and struggle or manifestations of resistance. Your points are clear, but just make them into one sentence.

LEILA: Yeah, I can do that. Yeah, definitely.

HOLLY: Beautiful. Awesome. See? It was so close. It was already almost there.

LEILA: Thank you!

Questions

1. How well did Holly explain the notion of cultural rhetoric to Leila?
2. How well did she explain US academic conventions?
3. How else might she have approached this conversation?

Holly continues the discussion of the introductory paragraph.

HOLLY: All right. And then the only other thing I noticed in this paragraph, and it's a tiny little nitpicky thing, and it's just because English is different from French: adjectives always come before nouns. "Enslaved Africans." But, yeah. That's just a little thing. And we might come across that again. That's a really easy mistake to make because you're just thinking in French in your head and I get that. Not a problem.

LEILA: Usually, I don't know if I have to put "not to" or "to not."

HOLLY: Typically, we would try "not to." "To not" results in splitting an infinitive. You use the infinitive of the verb "to accept." *(She reads part of a sentence from the introduction.)* ". . . slaves and African descents resisted to not fully accept European culture. . . ." Typically, we would try not to split that infinitive. So "on one hand, slaves and people of African descent . . ."

LEILA: *(Finishes the sentence)* ". . . resisted not to fully accept . . ."

HOLLY: Because "fully" is still splitting the infinitive. You would say "not to accept European culture fully."

LEILA: Okay. *(She writes down the correction.)* So "not to accept European culture" fully?

HOLLY: Yep. Nice catch. Do you feel comfortable with this paragraph?

LEILA: Yeah.

HOLLY: All right. Let's move on.

Questions

1. Does this exchange exemplify holistic tutoring?
2. Would holistic tutoring have been possible or even desirable in this instance?

Leila starts reading the next paragraph.

LEILA: Okay. European presence in the Caribbean can be described as destructive, brainwashing, and horrible for all non-Europeans. This presence was that cruel because it was global. It conquered everything and everybody from the bodies to the minds to the beliefs. Catholicism was the way of saving slaves from damnation. It was a way also to maintain order in the plantation, as Catholicism teach a certain obedience to the master. Of the different forms of power, colonial or independent, have feared the non-established religions. In Haiti, even when the new leader came in power, after the revolution and the institution of an independent country, voodoo was forbidden. He issued a decree and considered the person practicing it as full of bad intentions. But people resisted, as voodoo still exists today. In the Dominican Republic, the enslaved Africans being hammered by Catholicism and having no way to avoid it, disguised a deity in Catholic saints. In these two examples, people decided not to follow the rules of the master. The fact that non-White people did not accept what they were told to do enhanced beliefs and ways of understanding life to an actual pride in the Caribbean . . . *(She breaks off.)* This sentence is hard!

HOLLY: Yes.

LEILA: *(Continues reading to the end of the paragraph.)* These rituals would not be found elsewhere and would not be relevant either. Though it is in Haiti and in the Dominican Republic that people need these aspects of the Caribbean culture to remember the past in order to improve their future.

HOLLY: Okay. What is it about that sentence that you want to change?

LEILA: I guess I have to formulate it—maybe to split it up in two sentences—because it's really long, and it's not clear what I mean.

HOLLY: Yeah, it sounded like you were having trouble just getting through it.

LEILA: Yeah. It's like the fact that people did not accept what they were told to do so this is what they were told to do. Maybe I could find a way to just make it smaller. *(She reads aloud the problematic part.)* Enhanced beliefs and ways of understanding life to an actual pride in the Caribbean. Maybe "beliefs and way of understanding life" can be also reduced.

HOLLY: What do you mean by an actual pride in the Caribbean?

LEILA: People are proud of the voodoo and the religions they have—like, really proud.

HOLLY: So are you trying to say that they took what they were told, and it grew into this pride? That this pride came out of the resistance? Is that what you're saying?

LEILA: Yeah.

HOLLY: I think it might be this word "enhanced" that's giving us some challenges also. It sounds like the pride is a result of the resistance, and the colonization and attempted oppression are growing out of it. "Enhanced" doesn't have that connotation of transition or causation to enhance something. "Enhance" means to make it better or make it more, you know? So I think—I don't know. How could you make it really clear where this pride is coming from? Do you know what I mean?

LEILA: Yeah, I'm not sure I have the answer. I'm not sure I'm a hundred percent sure where this pride is coming from. What I see is that people in the Caribbean are proud of having resisted and having signs of manifestations of the old culture when they were enslaved.

HOLLY: Okay. Yeah. That makes sense. I just want you to connect everything you're saying. It is all here in this paragraph. It's just this piece about the pride doesn't feel like it's connected back to what you were saying earlier. Does that make sense?

LEILA: Yeah.

HOLLY: I think like this sentence is part of the problem also: "These rituals will not be found elsewhere and will not be relevant either." The rest of this paragraph is really strong by the way. You make a really good point, and you say it really clearly, but it doesn't lead into this sentence at the end of the paragraph.

LEILA: Okay.

HOLLY: You just need something to tie them together. How are they tied together? This really strong evidence and information about what happened during colonization—how is it related to the pride in Haiti today and the unique rituals that don't exist anywhere else?

LEILA: I guess it's like that today because the whole Caribbean culture led the slaves to rebel against the masters, and so I guess also they are proud about it and about the voodoo and the deities because it's a way of remembering how they felt against masters, against Europeans, against colonization.

HOLLY: *(Takes notes.)* Okay. (Continues to write.) Okay. It's like that today because the whole of Caribbean culture was one of the ways that led to rebellion against slave masters. It's a way of remembering how they felt against colonization. All right. So you have all this stuff about colonization and why religion was so important in colonization. Then people resisted because even though their own spiritual beliefs, their cultural/spiritual beliefs, were outlawed, those beliefs continued to exist. They disguised their deities in Catholic saints. Great, all of those things are connected to this. People decided not to follow the rules of the master, awesome, yes. Here the fact that non-white people did not accept what they were told to do enhanced beliefs and ways of understanding life to an actual pride in the Caribbean. Okay. You're looking for a new way to say what they were told to do. What does that describe? How would you describe all these things put together that they were told to do with one noun?

LEILA: Hmm. *(Thinks.)* It's rules, but not only the rules.

HOLLY: Oppression?

LEILA: Yeah, oppression.

HOLLY: Is that what you're trying to? Yeah, that's what it sounds like to me.

LEILA: Yeah, yeah.

HOLLY: So the fact that non-white people did not accept oppression maybe encouraged the beliefs and ways of understanding life to become actual pride? Because that's what you're saying here: that all these things led to rebellion. And today it exists because that's how they remember their own culture. Which you do say in that last sentence. It's just this one that is a little bit tricky and hard to understand. Do you want to keep working on this bit? Or do you want to come back to it on your own time?

LEILA: Yeah, I can come back to it.

HOLLY: Okay. Keep thinking about it and see what you come up with. That's fine.

LEILA: Maybe I will just erase it and find another.

HOLLY: That's fine.

Questions

1. Where do Holly and Leila negotiate meaning in this part of the conversation?
2. Does Holly tutor holistically?
3. How else might Holly have handled the negotiation of meaning?

LEILA: *(She starts reading the next paragraph.)* "In French Caribbeans, another way of controlling the enslaved was in the unique language. By doing so, the slave masters could easily understand what were saying the slaves and they would be able to prevent any revolt. Though the enslaved, and later the colonized have created their own language, the creole, they adapted themselves to the master's language so that they could be able to understand whatever he would say, but they disguised their language too. Mixing French and English words with words coming from their African languages and adapting an African syntax, they created a new way to communicate. Until the 1990s, the French creole was considered a language that was to be taught in school and resisted to represent French hegemony, and, as a result, creole is now taught in primary schools. Children are not taught anymore that their ancestors were kings but Africans, Arabs, Asians and Europeans."

HOLLY: Beautiful. That was really strong. That's one of your major strengths, I think, in this whole paper, is like making your point. And you make it and that's awesome.

LEILA: Really? Great. I had the impression that I was just, I was thinking obvious things. And I thought I should go further. But I don't know how to do it.

HOLLY: Maybe it is obvious to you because you've been studying these things and reading about them. I only know this sort of minimally. I've studied colonization, but I haven't done it in detail, and so I haven't thought about language, like Creole as a way of resisting. That's not a thing I ever thought of. So that's really awesome. Um *(sighs)* if it seems obvious to you, I think that says something powerful about how well you know your subject matter.

LEILA: Okay.

Question

1. What do you think about the way Holly addressed Leila's concern that her points are too obvious?

HOLLY: How do you feel about that paragraph? Are there things you want to change? Questions you have? Issues you have?

LEILA: For me it's okay. Yeah.

HOLLY: There are a couple of little, nit-picky grammary things I found. In English we don't put "the" before a language. So it's just Creole not "the" Creole. And also the name of a language is always capitalized. So you're going to want a capital C there.

LEILA: Yeah.

HOLLY: Also, it's just French Caribbean. One unit, no plural.

LEILA: Okay.

HOLLY: And then my other question; you obviously have this in your thesis. You're going to talk about religion and then language and then music. So we know you're moving on to language, but it would be nice to have just a sentence or two here to connect the ideas. Have something of a transition. You have "another way," so that's a start. But maybe if you had a sentence at the end of this paragraph to show how religion and language might be connected, or how it was important to have multilateral resistance or something like that. Does that make sense?

LEILA: Yeah.

HOLLY: Just a little brief transition to tie your ideas together is always helpful. All right. Do you want to move on?

LEILA: Yeah.

HOLLY: It looks like we just have a little bit left.

LEILA: Yeah. "Music as language is a way to communicate during often long and painful centuries of slavery. Music was a voice to spread the news, a catalyzer of emotions, and a unifier."

HOLLY: Okay. That's very short. Here you have a really obvious connection to what you talked about. You don't have to worry about a transition because you're saying they're all tied together, uniting religion and language through music. Great. I'd love it if you could develop how those things happened.

LEILA: Yeah. I had problems with my computer, and it was midnight . . . .

HOLLY: Oh, yeah. I get ya. Yup, that happens. When is this due?

LEILA: Two hours.

HOLLY: Okay. *(Laughs)*

LEILA: Yeah. *(Laughs)*

HOLLY: In that case, do you just want to stop here and take some time? You can use the rest of this time to develop this paragraph. Or do you want to brainstorm now how you're going to develop that paragraph? I can help you if you want to or you can do it on your own. It's up to you.

LEILA: Hmmmm. Yeah I can start it. I have already some kind of brainstorm. I guess I can write. And then I will have to make a conclusion, right?

HOLLY: Yes. Yes.

LEILA: Okay. This is going to be a hard part.

HOLLY: Your conclusion—if it helps to think about it this way—should answer "so what?" Why did you spend all this time telling us this stuff? Why should we care? That's what your conclusion should answer; tell us why these things are important. It might help to tie it into other things you've talked about in class, like why it's related to why you're taking the class in the first place or why you were interested in reading about this, studying about this in the first place. That kind of thing. Or it might be relevant to something that's happening in society today. Tell your reader why we should care—if that helps your conclusion at all.

LEILA: *(Writing and composing aloud)* Okay. So here, I can say that music was like a mix of African rhythm and European melodies at the beginning. I guess it were like two different currents of music—the music that they used to enter the European space. By being musicians, a lot of people just had the possibility to insert themselves and access to better places—just after the end of slavery. And on the other side, there was the music like the work songs and the ceremonial songs, which were really more rooted in African religion and related to religion and ceremonies and a critique of society.

HOLLY: *(Listening)* Mmm hmm. Mmm hmm.

LEILA: So music was playing to religion on one side and to language too because there was singing in Creole.

HOLLY: Awesome. Did creolization, did the language develop more through the music?

LEILA: Yeah.

HOLLY: Yeah? Awesome, very cool. Uh do you think that you have enough ideas?

LEILA: Yeah.

HOLLY: And you have them in order to develop them?

LEILA: Yeah, yeah.

HOLLY: All right, how do you feel about the whole thing?

LEILA: I'm okay.

HOLLY: Do you have any other questions or issues, things you're worried about?

LEILA: No, I guess I'm, I'm going to be attentive to the "I," the adjectives, and the structure of the sentences. Short sentences, effective and not long—you know like how we really like in French.

HOLLY: Yeah.

LEILA: Even in French I have difficulties to make actual sentences, but . . .

HOLLY: Yeah, a good rule of thumb is if that if a sentence takes up more than three lines, it's probably too long. Even that is pretty long depending on what you're talking about. I think for the most part you get your ideas across really clearly. I'm really impressed. It's hard. It can be really hard to express yourself clearly in a foreign language, so I'm really impressed.

LEILA: Thank you.

HOLLY: I think you know what you still need to be working on. Do you feel like you are confident that in the next hour you can finish it up?

LEILA: Yeah.

HOLLY: Awesome.

LEILA: Yeah, definitely. I have my conclusions.

HOLLY: Perfect. All right you can go ahead and take my notes if they will be helpful to you at all.

LEILA: Thank you.

HOLLY: You're very welcome.

Questions

1. How well did Holly help Leila achieve her goals for the session?
2. How effective is Holly in getting Leila to articulate a revision plan?

Appendix I: One-Day Tutor Training Agenda and Monthly Staff Training Schedule

8:30-9:00 Breakfast and Introductions

9:00-10:00 Tutoring Basics

- Why Foreign Language Faculty Assign Writing
- Holistic Tutoring
- Directive and Non-Directive Tutoring
- *Practice: Directive and Non-Directive Tutoring Techniques* (Appendix B)
- The Arc of a Tutoring Session (Appendix A)

10:00-11:00 Helping Writers Acquire the Language

- Noticing, Hypothesis Testing, Metalinguistic Awareness
- *Practice: How to Use Those Moves* (Appendix C)
- Negotiated Interaction
- *Practice: Negotiating Meaning with a Writer* (Appendix C)

11:00-11:15 Break

11:15-12:00 Working with Writers Who Translate

- Online Translators
- *Practice: Google Translate: Friend or Foe?* (Appendix D)
- The Role of Translation in the Writing Process

12:00-1:00 Lunch

1:00-2:00 Helping Writers Develop and Organize Ideas

- A Panel with Experienced MWC Tutors

2:15-2:45 MWC Scheduling, Policies, and Procedures

2:45-4:30 Working with Specific Foreign Languages

- You will break into ten groups based on language and work with your faculty mentor from the foreign language department.

Monthly Staff Meetings

- Creating a Supportive Learning Environment (Appendix E)
- Culture and Writing (Appendix F)
- Joint Meeting with English Writing Tutors (Appendix G or H)
- Advanced Holistic Writing Tutoring Techniques
- What Professors Need to Know

(Foreign language professors who are interested in tutors' insights about how students learn to write in a foreign language attend the meeting and pose questions/offer advice.)

Notes

CHAPTER ONE

1. Until recently, the IWCA directory listed the contact information for member writing centers from sixty-six countries. The directory included centers that identified with the philosophy and principles of the IWCA. The IWCA Directory disappeared for awhile and no longer exists on the IWCA website. Recently, it has reappeared at a new site maintained by The Writing Center at St. Cloud State University in collaboration with the IWCA.

2. Many MWC-like arrangements exist with varying degrees of formality. As mentioned in the Introduction, the National Census of Writing reports that 141 writing centers offer support for languages other than English (Gladstein).

3 In Austria, Alpen-Adria University offers German, Czech, Italian, and Slovenian. In Kuwait, American University offers Arabic, English, French, Italian, and Spanish. In Sweden, Chalmers University of Technology offers Arabic, Bosnian, Chinese, English, and Swedish. In Switzerland, Franklin University offers English, French, German, and Italian.

4. Afghanistan: American University. Algeria: Mostagem University. Azerbaijan: ADA University. Bahrain: University of Bahrain. Quebec, Canada: Bishop's University, Dawson College, Vanier College. Chile: Pontificia Universidad Catolica de Chile, Universidad de Magallanes. China: Hong Kong Polytechnic University, University of Macau. Egypt: American University in Cairo. France: American University in Paris. Germany: Leuphana Universitat Luneberg, Ludwig Maximillian Universitat—Munich, Universitat of Education—Ludwigsburg, Universitat Tubingen. Greece: Hellenic American University, American College of Thessaloniki. Hungary: Central European University. India: Asoka University. Iraq: American University of Iraq. Italy: John Cabot University. Japan: Kanda University of International Studies, Osaka Jogakuin College, Rikkyo University, Teachers College Tokyo, Temple University Tokyo. Kazakhstan: Nazarbayeu University. Kyrgyzstan: American University of Central Asia. Lebanon: Lebanese American University. Mongolia: Mongolia International University. Netherlands:

Radboud University. Norway: University of Tromso, University of Bergen. Poland: University of Lodz, University of Silesia. Qatar: College of the Atlantic, Northwestern University in Qatar, Texas A & M University at Qatar, Virginia Commonwealth University Qatar. Saudi Arabia: King Saud University, Princess Nora bint Abdulrahman University for Women. South Korea: Catholic University of Korea, Ewha Woman's University, Gwangju Institute of Science and Technology, Hanyang University, Kyungbook International University. Sweden: Stockholm University, Umea University. Turkey:Bilkent University, Bogazici University, Istanbul Sehir University, Kadir Has University, Middle East Technical University. Ukraine: National University of Kyiv-Mohyla Academy.

5. Canada: Concordia University. China: Chinese University of Hong Kong. Estonia: University of Tartu. Germany: Ruprecht-Karls Universitat Heidelberg, Techincal Universitat of Darmstadt. Japan: Ritsumeikan Asian Pacific University, Waseda University. Lebanon: American University of Beirut. Netherlands: Mastricht University, University of Twente. Qatar: Qatar University. Sweden: Linkoping University, Lund University, Malmo University, Sodertorn University, Uppsala University.

6. Austria: FH Wien University of Applied Sciences. Chile: University of Tarapaca. Colombia: Pontificia Universidad, Universidad Javeriana, Universidad Santiago de Cali. Denmark: Aarhus University. Germany: European University Viadrina, Friedrich Schiller University Jena, HTWG Konstanz, Johannes Gutenberg Universitat Mainz, Katholische Stiftungsfachhochschule, Ruhr University Bochum, Universitat Bayreuth,Universitaet Hamburg, University of Education—Freiburg, Universitat Konstanz. Iceland: University of Iceland. Romania: West University of Timişoara. Saudi Arabia: University of Nizwa.

7. My examination of sixteen German writing center websites revealed that 25 percent (or four) were English-only and thirteen percent (or two) were German and English.

Chapter Two

8. Higher order concerns (HOCs) are the global issues that writers grapple with as they construct meaning: thesis, focus, idea development, organization, logical connections, voice, audience, tone. Lower order concerns (LOCs) are the sentence-level issues that writers attend to once meaning is in place: usage, syntax, word choice, punctuation, spelling.

9. When students fill out the appointment form, they can choose as many as apply: finding a topic; prewriting and planning; developing an idea; deepening analysis; using evidence strategically to support claims; creating a thesis; organizing an essay; making logical connections; maintaining a focus; building paragraphs; writing to an audience; using transitions; writ-

ing effective sentences; researching a topic; citing sources correctly; and editing for grammar mistakes.

10. These percentages are based on the following sample sizes: total English sessions with writers who are self-reported native English speakers, N = 1954; total English sessions with writers who are self-reported nonnative English speakers, N = 1397; total sessions with FL writers, N=1784.

11. In spring 2015, semi-structured interviews were conducted with eight tutors: two from Spanish and one each from Italian, Hebrew, French, Russian, Arabic, and Chinese. The tutors represented seven of the ten foreign languages for which the MWC provides writing tutoring. The interviewees were both self-reported native and nonnative speakers of the target languages; they include domestic and international, bilingual and heritage speakers. All have lived abroad and studied a second language.

Language and tutoring backgrounds of interviewed tutors

Language(s) Tutored	Tutoring Experience (# of semesters)	Language Level	Native (NS) or Nonnative Speaker (NNS)	Study Abroad
Spanish and English	3	Major	NNS of Spanish	Ecuador (one semester) Argentina (one semester)
French and English	3	Major	NNS of French	Toulouse (one semester)
Chinese (Mandarin)	2		NS/Matriculated International	United States
Arabic	4	300-level (one short of minor)	NNS	Oman (summer)
Russian	2	Minor	NNS	Moscow (summer)
Spanish	2		NS/Immigrant (in US since age 13)	
Hebrew	2	Placed out of Hebrew	K-12 Hebrew school (half day in English and half day in Hebrew)	Israel (half-year in high school; multiple month-long visits to Israel)
Italian	2	Major	NNS	Genoa (summer) Bologna (semester)

Eleven tutors were invited to participate in the study; eight volunteered. The interviews, which took place in my office, were scheduled for an hour but most ended before an hour. All tutors signed an informed consent form. The interviews began with several quick demographic questions (compiled in above table). There were four themes underlying the interview questions: the definition of holistic tutoring, personal examples of it, insights into what makes holistic tutoring difficult or easy, and ideas about how WCAs can best support tutors. The interviews were audio-taped using a Livescribe pen and transcribed by the researcher who omitted vocal fillers like "um" and "ah."

12. Translated from French by Julien Herpers.

13. Translated from Korean by Diane Lee.

Chapter Four

14. Perhaps the most well-known is the DIE Exercise: describe, interpret, evaluate a "person/place/thing/idea/event/behavior" (Williams, "Examining" 149). The LENS heuristic reimagines DIE in four steps: "look objectively," "evaluate assumptions," "note other ways of interpreting," and "substantiate with local people" (Williams, "Examining" 157).

15. Harbord describes a similar genre in pre-1989 Soviet Union universities known as the "referat," which he describes as a "summative literature review."

16. Thanks to Federico Corradini, Renato de Medeiros, Gaston Dorigutti, Maksim Gaetskii, and Manuela Hernandez Perez, and Eléa Kayiranga Lionnet for their insights, and to Manuela for the apt phrase "humble perspective."

Chapter Five

17. For other narratives of humble origins, see Abels, Broussard, Miller, and Puma.

18. North then goes on to state more determinedly, "I want a situation in which we are *not* required to sustain some delicate but carefully distanced relationship between classroom teachers and the writing center, not least because the classroom teachers are directly involved with, and therefore invested in the functioning of, that center" (16). Although a less distant relationship with classroom teachers could result in "stormy politics and raised voices," he believes it will "generate as many new tensions as new opportunities" (16).

19. The ethnographic tour occurred during my first year at Dickinson when I visited thirty different departments.

20. This phrase was found on the Dickinson College website in 2010 but has since been revised.

21. This language can be found in Dickinson's "Strategic Plan III"; it is part of Strategic Goal D under the subheading "The Dickinson Student Experience."

22. In "Choosing Beans Wisely," published in the *Writing Lab Newsletter* in 2001, Lerner points out that his 1997 study was "flawed, both statistically and logically" (1).

23. The MWC has since abandoned the HOC and LOC terminology. Instead, we talk about writing versus language acquisition skills or global versus sentence-level revision. In chapter two in which I discuss holistic tutoring practices, I explain why thinking of writing concerns in hierarchical terms can be problematic in second language writing contexts.

24. When recruiting, the advisory committee does make an effort to identify international students, heritage speakers, and gifted language students in the first year so as to invite them into English tutor-training course. As a result, there are several tutors on staff who work with writers in more than one language.

25. My colleague Lucile Duperron, Associate Professor of French and Francophone Studies, developed the satellite writing center at the Dickinson Center in Toulouse for students who attended the Université de *Toulouse*.

Appendices

26. The essay used in this exercise comes from "Teacher Evaluation Essay Five Qualities Of An Effective Chinese Writing Competition Singapore Gradede." Oracleboss, 20 Nov. 2018, http://www.oracleboss.com/chinese-essay-writing/teacher-evaluation-essay-five-qualities-of-an-effective-chinese-writing-competition-singapore-gradede/. 28 February 2019.

27. Thanks to Audrey Schlimm for allowing me to use this passage from her undergraduate essay "Sensation and the Subconscious within a Nightmare in *The Eye in the Door.*"

28. The excerpt comes from a writing center session that was recorded and transcribed by Elizabeth Pineo and Sagun Sharma.

Works Cited

21st Century Skills World Languages. Partnership for 21st Century Learning, 2011 http://www.p21.org/component/content/article/1994. Accessed 10 July 2018.

Abels, Kimberly Town. "The Writing Center at the University of North Carolina at Chapel Hill: A Site and Story Under Construction." *The Writing Center Director's Resource Book,* edited by Christina Murphy and Byron L. Stay, Lawrence Erlbaum, 2006, pp. 393-02.

"About." *Dickinson College,* 14 Mar. 2017. http://www.dickinson.edu/about/.

"Academic Writing Center." *Pontificia Universidad Catolica de Chile,* english.uc.cl/Servicios/asesorias.html. Accessed 26 October 2016.

"Academic Writing Center." *Universidad de Magallanes,* www.umag.cl/awc/. Accessed 26 October 2016.

Aiken, Milam, and Shilpa Balan. "An Analysis of Google Translate Accuracy." *Translation Journal,* vol. 16, 2011, translationjournal.net/journal/56google.htm.

Ambrose, Susan A., et al. *How Learning Works: Seven Research-Based Principles for Smart Teaching,* Jossey-Bass, 2010.

American Council for the Teaching of Foreign Languages. ACTFL, https://www.actfl.org/. Accessed 10 July 2018.

"The Ascent of Global Learning." NAFSA, https://www.nafsa.org/professional-resources/publications/ascent-global-learning

Atkinson, Dwight. "Second Language Writing and Culture." *Handbook of Second and Foreign Language Writing,* edited by Rosa M. Manchon and Paul Kei Matsuda, Walter de Gruyter, 2016, pp. 545-65.

Barr, Jason J. "Developing a Positive Classroom Climate." *Idea,* no. 61, 2016, 1-9.

Bartholomae, David. "The Study of Error." *College Composition and Communication,* vol. 31, no 3, 1980, pp. 253-69.

Bazerman, Charles, et al., editors. *Genre in a Changing World.* Parlor and the WAC Clearinghouse, 2009.

—, editors. *International Advances in Writing Research: Cultures, Places, Measures.* Parlor and the WAC Clearinghouse, 2012.

—, editors. *Traditions of Writing Research.* Routledge, 2010.

Bean, Janet, et al. "Should We Invite Students to Write in Home Languages: Complicating the Yes/No Debate." *Second-Language Writing in the Composition Classroom*, edited by Paul Kei Matsuda, et al., Bedford/St. Martin's, 2006, pp. 225-39.

Beaufort, Anne. *College Writing and Beyond*. Utah State University Press, 2007.

Ben-Ghiat, Ruth. "Gutting US Foreign Language Education Will Cost Us for Generations." *CNN Opinion,* 29 Jan. 2019, https://www.cnn.com/2019/01/29/opinions/duke-professor-mla-report-foreign-language-departments-ben-ghiat/index.html.

Blau, Susan, and John Hall. "Guilt-Free Tutoring: Rethinking How We Tutor Non-Native-English-Speaking Students." *Writing Center Journal,* vol. 23, 2002, pp. 23-44.

Boquet, Elizabeth. "Tug-of-War: Snapshots of Life in the Center." *Stories from the Center: Connecting Narrative and Theory in the Writing Center,* edited by Lynn Craigue et al., NCTE, 2000, pp. 17-30.

Brauer, Gerd. "Academic Literacy Development." *Writing Programs Worldwide: Profiles of Academic Writing in Many Places,* edited by Chris Thaiss, et al., Parlor and the WAC Clearinghouse, 2012, pp. 467-84.

Bromley, Pam. "Re: Writing in Various Languages." WCENTER, 12 Aug. 2016, wcenter@lyris.ttu.edu. Accessed 27 July 2018.

Broussard, William. "Collaborative Work, Competitive Students, Counternarrative: A Tale from Out of (the Academy's) Bounds." *Writing Lab Newsletter,* vol. 28, no.1, 2003, pp. 1-5.

Bruce, Shanti, and Ben Rafoth. *ESL Writers: A Guide for Writing Center Tutors.* Boynton/Cook, 2004.

—. *Tutoring Second Language Writers*, Utah State University Press, 2016.

Canagarajah, A. Suresh. A Geopolitics of Academic Writing. U of Pittsburgh P, 2002.

—. "Translingual Writing and Teacher Development in Composition." *College English*, vol. 78, no. 3, Jan. 2016, pp. 265-73.

Capossela, Toni Lee. *The Harcourt Brace Guide to Peer Tutoring*. Harcourt Brace, 1998.

Carino, Peter, and Doug Enders. "Does Frequency of Visits to the Writing Center Increase Student Satisfaction? A Statistical Correlation Study—or Story." *Writing Center Journal*, vol. 22, no.1, 2001, pp. 1-5.

Carlino, Paula. "Who Takes Care of Writing in Latin American and Spanish Universities?" *Writing Programs Worldwide: Profiles of Academic Writing in Many Places,* edited by Chris Thaiss, et al., Parlor and the WAC Clearinghouse, 2012, pp. 485-98.

Castelvecchi, Davide. "Deep Learning Boosts Google Translate Tool." *Nature,* vol. 27, September 2016, http://www.nature.com/news/deep-learning-boosts-google-translate-tool-1.20696.

"Center for Academic Writing." *Central European University*, caw.ceu.edu/. Accessed 26 October 2016.

"Center for Teaching and Learning English Writing Lab." *Hanyang University*, hanyangowl.org/. Accessed 26 October 2016

Chitez, Madalina, and Otto Kruse. "Writing Cultures and Genres in European Higher Education." *University Writing: Selves and Texts in Academic Societies,* edited by
Montserrat Castello and Christiane Donahue, Brill, 2012, pp. 153-75.

Cimasko, Tony, and Melinda Reichelt, editors. *Foreign Language Writing Instruction: Principles and Practices.* Parlor, 2011.

Clark, Irene L. "Process." *Concepts in Composition: Theory and Practice in the Teaching of Writing,* edited by Irene L. Clark, Erlbaum, 2003, pp. 1-70.

Cohen, Andrew D., and Amanda Brooks-Carson. "Research on Direct versus Translated Writing: Students' Strategies and Their Results." *The Modern Language Journal,* vol. 85, no. 2, 2001, 169-88.

"Commission on Language Learning." *American Academy of Arts and Sciences,* www.amacad.org/content.aspx?d=21896. Accessed 2 November 2016.

Connor, Ulla. "Mapping Multidimensional Aspects of Research: Reaching to Intercultural Rhetoric." *Contrastive Rhetoric: Cross-Cultural Aspects of Second Language Writing* edited by William V. Rozycki, et al., Cambridge University Press, 1996, pp. 299-15.

Daly, Herman E. "Globalization Versus Internationalization—Some Implications." *Ecological Economics*, vol. 31, 1999, pp. 31-37.

Davis, Sarah. "Something from Nothing." *Writing Lab Newsletter,* vol. 25, no. 6, 2001, pp. 14-16.

de Montlaur, Benedicte. "Do You Speak My Language? You Should." *New York Times,* 26 Mar. 2019, www.nytimes.com/2019/03/26/opinion/learn-foreign-language.html. Accessed 28 Mar. 2019.

Deardorff, Darla K. "Assessing Intercultural Competence." *New Directions for Institutional Research,* vol. 49, 2011, pp. 65-79

Devlin, Kat. "Learning a Foreign Language a 'Must' in Europe, Not So in America." *Pew Research Center,* http://www.pewresearch.org/fact-tank/2015/07/13/learning-a-foreign-language-a-must-in-europe-not-so-in-america/. Accessed 23 May 2018.

Dickson, Marcia. "Directing without Power: Adventures in Constructing a Model of Feminist Writing Program Administration." *Writing Ourselves into the Story: Unheard Voices from Composition Studies,* edited by Sheryl I. Fontaine and Susan Hunter, Southern Illinois University Press 1993, pp. 140-53.

Dinitz, Sue, and Jean Kiedaisch. "Creating Theory: Moving Tutors to the Center." *The Writing Center Journal,* vol. 23, no. 2, 2003, pp. 63-76.

"Diversity Initiative." *About IWCA/ Position Statements*, International Writing Center Association, 20 Nov. 2006, writingcenters.org/wp-content/uploads/2008/06/iwca_diversity_initiative1.pdf.

Donahue, Christiane. "'Internationalization' and Composition Studies: Reorienting the Discourse." *College Composition and Communication*, vol. 61, no. 2, 2009, pp. 212-43.

—. "The Lycee-to-University Progression in French Students' Development as Writers." *Writing and Learning in Cross-National Perspective*, edited by David Foster and David R. Russell, NCTE, 2002, pp. 134-91.

Dryer, Dylan B. "Appraising Translingualism." *College English*, vol. 78, no. 3, January 2016, pp. 274-83.

Dysthe, Olga. "How a Reform Affects Writing in Higher Education." *Studies in Higher Education*, vol. 32, no. 2, 2007, pp. 237-52.

Ede, Lisa, and Andrea Lunsford. "Some Millennial Thoughts about the Future of Writing Centers." *The Writing Center Journal*, vol. 20, no. 2, 2000, 33-38.

Eyler, Joshua R. *How Humans Learn: The Science and Stories behind Effective College Teaching.* West Virginia University Press, 2018.

"Fact Sheets on the European Union." *European Parliament*, www.europarl.europa.eu/atyourservice/en/displayFtu.html?ftuId=FTU_5.13.6.html. Accessed 2 November 2016.

Farkas, Carol-Ann. "'Idle Assumptions are the Devil's Plaything': The Writing Center, the First-Year Faculty, and the Reality Check." *Writing Lab Newsletter*, vol. 30, no.7, 2006, pp. 1-5.

"Foreign Language Writing Tutoring." *Dickinson College*, http://www.dickinson.edu/info/20158/writing_program/794/multilingual_writing_center. Accessed 14 Mar. 2017.

Foster, David. "Making the Transition to University: Student Writers in Germany." *Writing and Learning in Cross-National Perspective*, edited by David Foster and David R. Russell, NCTE, 2002, pp. 192-41.

Friedlander, Alexander. "Composing in English: Effects of a First Language on Writing in English as a Second Language." *Second Language Writing: Research Insights for the Classroom*, edited by Barbara Kroll, Cambridge University Press, 1997, pp. 109-25.

Frisby, Brandi N., and Matthew M. Martin. "Instructor-Student and Student-Student Rapport in the Classroom." *Communication Education*, vol. 59, no. 2, 2010, pp. 146-64.

Ganobscik-Williams, Lisa. "Reflecting on What Can be Gained from Comparing Models of Academic Writing Provision." *Writing Programs Worldwide: Profiles of Academic Writing in Many Places,"* edited by Chris Thaiss, et al., Parlor and the WAC Clearinghous, 2012, pp. 499-12.

Gardiner, Ann. "Resources for Language Tutors." WCENTER, 20 Oct. 2015, wcenter@lyris.ttu.edu. Accessed 27 July 2018.

Geller, Anne Ellen, et al. *The Everyday Writing Center: A Community of Practice.* Utah State University Press, 2007.

Gevers, Jeroen. "Translingualism Revisited: Language Dfference and Hybridity in L2 Writing." *Journal of Second Language Writing,* vol. 40, 2018, pp. 73-83.

Gillespie, Paula, and Neal Lerner. *The Longman Guide to Peer Tutoring.* 2nd ed., Pearson, 2008.

Gkonou, Christina. "Anxiety over EFL Speaking and Writing: A View from Language Classrooms." *Studies in Second Language Learning and Teaching,* vol. 1, no. 2, 2011, pp. 267-81.

Gladstein, Jill, and Brandon Fralix. *National Census of Writing,* 2019, https://writingcensus.swarthmore.edu/.

"Global Study and Engagement." *Dickinson College,* http://www.dickinson.edu/global. Accessed 6 August 2018.

Goldberg, David, Dennis Looney, and Natalia Lusin. "Enrollments in Languages Other than English in United States Institutions of Higher Education." *Modern Language Association,* www.mla.org/pdf/2013_enrollment_survey.pdf. Accessed 26 October 2016.

Google Translate. Google, translate.google.com/. Accessed 14 July 2017.

Groves, Michael, and Klaus Mundt. "Friend or Foe? Google Translate in Language for Academic Purposes." *English for Specific Purposes,* vol. 37, 2015, pp. 112-21.

Guerra, Juan C. "Cultivating a Rhetorical Sensibility in the Translingual Writing Classroom." *College English,* vol. 78, no. 3, January 2016, pp. 228-33.

Gunner, Jeanne. "Decentering the WPA." *WPA: Writing Program Administration,* vol. 18, no.1/2, 1994, pp. 8-15.

Harbord, John. "Writing in Central and Eastern Europe: Stakeholder and Directions in Initiating Change." *Across the Disciplines: A Journal of Language, Learning, and Academic Writing,* vol. 7, April 2010, wac.colostate.edu/atd/articles/harbord2010.cfm.

Hess, J. Daniel. *The Whole World Guide to Culture Learning.* Intercultural Press, 1994.

Higgins, Christina. "'Ownership' of English in the Outer Circle: An Alternative to the NS-NNS Dichotomy." *TESOL Quarterly,* vol. 37, no. 4, 2003, 615-44.

Holley, Lynn C., and Sue Steiner. "Safe Space: Student Perspectives on Classroom Environment." *Journal of Social Work Education,* vol. 41, no. 1, 2005, pp. 49-64.

Horner, Bruce, et al. "Language Difference in Writing: Toward a Translingual Approach." *College English,* vol. 73, no.3, 2011, pp. 303-21.

Horwitz, Elaine K., et al. "Foreign Language Classroom Anxiety." *Modern Language Journal,* vol. 70, no. 2, 1986, pp.125-32.

Howard, Jeremy. "The Wonderful and Terrifying Implications of Computers that Can Learn." *TED*, Nov. 2014, www.ted.com/talks/jeremy_howard_the_wonderful_and_terrifying_implications_of_computers_that_can_learn.

Huhtala, Anne, and Hanna Lehti-Eklund. "Writing a New Self in the Third Place: Language Students and Identity Formation." *Pedagogy, Culture and Society*, vol. 18, no. 3, 2010, pp. 273-88.

"International Exchanges on the Study of Writing." *WAC Clearinghouse*, https://wac.colostate.edu/books/international/. Accessed 7 December 2018.

"International Writing Center." Kyungbook National University, iwc.knu.ac.kr/. Accessed 26 October 2016.

"ISAWR Mission Statement." International Society for the Advancement of Writing Research, isawr.org/mission-statement/. Accessed 6 March 2020.

Jonassen, David H., and Woei Hung. "All Problems Are not Equal: Implications for Problem-Based Learning." *Interdisciplinary Journal of Problem-Based Learning*, vol. 2, 2008, pp. 6-28.

Kaplan, Robert. "Cultural Thought Patterns in Intercultural Education." *Language Learning*, vol. 16, 1966, pp. 1-20.

—. "What in the World Is Contrastive Rhetoric?" *Contrastive Rhetoric Revisited and Redefined*, edited by Clayann Gilliam Panetta, Erlbaum, 2001, pp. vii-xix.

Kirkpatrick, Andy. "Linguistic Imperialism? English as a Global Language." *Handbook of Language and Communication: Diversity and Change*, edited by Marlis Hellinger and Anne Pauwels, DeGruyter, 2008, pp. 333-64.

Knutson, Elizabeth. "Thinking in English, Writing in French." *The French Review*, vol. 80, no. 1, 2006, pp. 88-109.

Kobayashi, Hiroe, and Carol Rinnert. "Effects of First Language on Second Language Writing: Translation versus Direct Composition." *Language Learning*, vol. 42, no. 2, 1992, pp. 183-215.

Kossman, Barbara. "Computers and the Perception of the Writing Center." *Writing Lab Newsletter*, vol. 25, no. 5, 2001, pp. 1-3.

Kramsch, Claire. "The Privilege of the Nonnative Speaker." *PMLA*, vol. 112, no.3, May 1997, pp. 359-69.

Krashen, Stephen. *Principles and Practice in Second Language Acquisition*. Pergamon, 1982.

Krepels, Alexandra Rowe. "An Overview of Second Language Writing Process Research." *Second Language Writing: Research Insights for the Classroom*, edited by Barbara Kroll, Cambridge University Press, 1997, pp. 37-56.

Lape, Noreen. "Going Global, Becoming Translingual: The Development of a Multilingual Writing Center." *Writing Lab Newsletter*, vol. 38, no. 3-4, 2013, pp. 1-6.

—. "Training Tutors in Emotional Intelligence: Toward a Pedagogy of Empathy." *Writing Lab Newsletter*, vol. 33, no. 2, 2008, pp. 1-6.

Le, Quoc V., and Mike Schuster. "A Neural Network for Machine Translation, at Production Scale." *Google Research Blog*, 27 Sept. 2016, research.googleblog.com/2016/09/a-neural-network-for-machine.html.

Lee, James F., and Bill Van Patten. *Making Communicative Language Teaching Happen*. McGraw-Hill, 1995.

Leki, Ilona. "Learning to Write in a Second Language: Multilingual Graduates and Undergraduates Expanding Genre Repertoires." *Learning-to-Write and Writing-to-Learn in an Additional Language*, edited by Rosa Manchon, John Benjamins, 2011, pp. 85-109.

—. "Techniques for Reducing Second Language Writing Anxiety." *Affect in Foreign Language and Second Language Learning*, edited by Dolly Jesusita Young, McGraw Hill, 1998, pp. 64-88.

Lerner, Neal. "Choosing Beans Wisely." *Writing Lab Newsletter*, vol. 26, no. 1, 2001, pp. 1-4.

—. "Counting Beans and Making Beans Count." *Writing Lab Newsletter*, vol. 22, no.1, 1997, pp. 1-4.

—. "Of Numbers and Stories: Quanitative and Qualitative Assessment Research in the Writing Center." *Building Writing Center Assessment that Matter*, edited by Ellen Schendel and William J. Macauley, Jr., Utah State University Press, 2012, pp.106-114.

"Letter from Members of the House of Representatives." *American Academy of Arts and Sciences*, 21 Nov. 2014, www.amacad.org/multimedia/pdfs/AAASHouseLetter.pcf.

"Letter from US Senators." *American Academy of Arts and Sciences*, 20 Nov. 2014, www.amacad.org/multimedia/pdfs/AAASSenateLetter.pdf.

Li, Xiao Ming. *"Good Writing" in Cross-Cultural Context*. SUNY University Press, 1996.

Liebman, JoAnne. "Contrastive Rhetoric: Students as Ethnographers." *Journal of Basic Writing*, vol. 7, no. 2, 1988, pp. 6-27.

Long, Michael H. "The Role of the Linguistic Environment in Second Language Acquisition." *Handbook of Second Language Acquisition*, edited by W. C. Ritchie and T. K. Bhatia, vol. 2, Academic, 1996, pp. 413-68.

Lovejoy, Kim Brian, et al. "Linguistic Diversity as Resource." *Pedagogy: Critical Approaches to Teaching Literature, Language, Composition, and Culture*, vol. 18, no. 2, 2018, pp. 317-43.

Lu, Min-Zhan, and Bruce Horner. "Introduction: Translingual Work." *College English*, vol. 78, no. 3, January 2016, pp. 207-18.

Lunsford, Andrea. "Collaboration, Control, and the Idea of a Writing Center." *The Writing Center Journal*, vol. 12, no.1, 1991, pp. 3-10.

Lusin, Natalia. "The MLA Survey of Postsecondary Entrance and Degree Requirements for Languages Other Than English, 2009-10." *Modern Language Association, Mar. 2012, www.mla.org/content/download/3316/81618/requirements_survey_200910.pdf.

Macauley, William J., Jr. "Connecting Writing Center Assessment to Your Institution's Mission." *Building Writing Center Assessments that Matter*, edited by Ellen Schendel and William J. Macauley, Jr., Utah State University Press, 2012, pp. 57-81.

MacIntyre, Peter D. and Robert C. Gardner. "Methods and Results in the Study of Anxiety and Language Learning: A Review of the Literature." *Language Learning*, vol. 41, no.1, 1991, pp. 85-117.

Mackiewicz, Jo, and Isabelle Thompson. "Motivational Scaffolding, Politeness, and Writing Center Tutoring." *Writing Center Journal*, vol. 33, no. 1, 2013, pp. 38-73.

Manchon, Rosa M. "The Language Learning Potential of Writing in Foreign Language Contexts: Lessons from Research." *Foreign Language Writing Instruction: Principles and Practices*, edited by Tony Cimasko and Melinda Reichelt, Parlor, 2011, pp. 44-64.

—, editor. *Learning-to-Write and Writing-to-Learn in an Additional Language*. John Benjamins Publishing, 2011.

Manchon, Rosa M., and Paul Kei Matsuda, editors. *Handbook of Second and Foreign Language Writing*. Walter de Gruyter, 2016.

Matsuda, Paul Kei. "The Lure of Translingual Writing." *PMLA*, vol. 129, no. 3, 2014, pp. 478-83.

—. "Teaching Composition in the Multilingual World: Second Language Writing in Composition Studies." *Exploring Composition Studies: Sites, Issues, and Perspectives*, edited by Kelly Ritter and Paul Kei Matsuda, Utah State University Press, 2012, pp. 36-51.

Matsuda, Paul Kei, and Dwight Atkinson. "A Conversation on Contrastive Rhetoric." *Contrastive Rhetoric: Cross-Cultural Aspects of Second Language Writing*, edited by William V. Rozycki, et al., Cambridge University Press, 1996, pp. 277-298.

Miller, William V. "Now and Later at Ball State." *Writing Lab Newsletter*, vol. 6., no. 6, 1982, pp. 1-2.

Naydan, Liliana M. "Generation 1.5 Writing Center Practice: Problems with Multilingualism and Possibilities via Hybridity." *Praxis: A Writing Center Journal*, vol. 13, no. 2, 2016, www.praxisuwc.com/naydan-132, pp. 28-35.

North, Stephen. "The Idea of a Writing Center." *College English*, vol. 46, no. 5, 1984, pp. 443-46.

—. "Revisiting the 'Idea of a Writing Center.'" *The Writing Center Journal*, vol. 15, no.1, 1994, pp. 7-19.

"Number of International Students in the United States Reaches New High of 1.09 Million." *IIE: The Power of International Education*, 13 Nov.

2018, https://www.iie.org/Why-IIE/Announcements/2018/11/2018-11-13-Number-of-International-Students-Reaches-New-High.

O'Donnell, Mary E. "Policies and Practices in Foreign Language Writing at the College Level: Survey Results and Implications." *Foreign Language Annals,* vol. 40, no. 4, 2007, pp. 650-71.

"Open Doors: Fast Facts." *IIE: The Power of International Education,* https://www.iie.org/Research-and-Insights/Open-Doors/Fact-Sheets-and-Infographics/Fast-Facts. Accessed 1 August 2019.

Ortega, Lourdes. "Reflections on the Learning-to-Write and Writing-to-Learn Dimensions of Second Language Writing.' *Learning-to-Write and Writing-to-Learn in an Additional Language,* edited by Rosa Manchon, John Benjamins Publishing, 2011, pp. 237-50.

Oxford, Rebecca L. "Anxious Language Learners Can Change Their Minds: Ideas and Strategies from Traditional Psychology and Positive Psychology." *New Insights into Language Anxiety: Theory, Research, and Educational Implications,* edited by Christina Gkonou, et al., Multilingual Matters, 2017, pp. 177-97.

Phillipson, Robert. *Linguistic Imperialism Continued.* Routledge, 2009.

"Position Statement on Racism, Anti-Immigration, and Linguistic Intolerance." *About IWCA/Position Statements,* International Writing Center Association, 9 Nov. 2010, http://writingcenters.org/wp-content/uploads/2008/06/Arizona_Statement_final1.pdf.

Powers, Judith K. "Rethinking Writing Center Conferencing Strategies for the ESL Writer." *The Writing Center Journal,* vol. 13, no. 2, 1993, pp. 39-47.

Poziwilko, Linda. "Writing Centers, Retention, and the Institution: A Fortuitous Nexus." *Writing Lab Newsletter,* vol. 22, no. 2, 1997, pp. 1-4.

Puma, Vincent D. "The Write Staff: Identifying and Training Tutor-Candidates." *Writing Lab Newsletter,* vol. 14, no. 2, 1989, pp. 1-4.

"Quick Facts." *Dickinson College,* http://www.dickinson.edu/info/20048/history_of_the_college/1909/quick_facts. Accessed 6 August 2018.

Rafoth, Ben. *Multilingual Writers and Writing Centers.* Utah State University Press, 2015.

Reichelt, Melinda. "Defining 'Good Writing': A Cross-Cultural Perspective." *Composition Studies,* vol. 31, no.1, 1999, pp. 99-126.

—. "L2 Writing in Languages Other than English." *Handbook on Second and Foreign Language Writing,* edited by Paul Kei Matsuda. Walter de Gruyter, 2016, pp. 181-200.

—. "Toward a More Comprehensive View of L2 Writing: Foreign Language Writing in the US" *Journal of Second Language Writing,* vol. 8, 1999, pp. 181-204.

—, et al. "Key Issues in Foreign Language Writing." *Foreign Language Annals,* vol. 45, 2012, pp. 22-41.

Reynolds, Dudley W. *One on One with Second Language Writers: A Guide for Writing Tutors, Teachers, and Consultants.* U of Michigan P, 2009.

Ritter, Jennifer. "Recent Development in Assisting ESL Writers." *A Tutor's Guide: Helping Writers One to One,* edited by Ben Rafoth, Boynton/Cook Publishers, 2000, pp. 102-10.

Rubio-Alcala, Fernando D. "The Links between Self-Esteem and Language Anxiety and Implications for the Classroom." *New Insights into Language Anxiety: Theory, Research, and Educational Implications,* edited by Christina Gkonou, Mark Daubney, and Jean-Marc DeWaele, Multilingual Matters, 2017, pp. 198-223.

Russell, David R., and David Foster. "Rearticulating Articulation." *Writing and Learning in Cross-National Perspective,* edited by David Foster and David R. Russell. NCTE, 2002, pp. 1-47.

Ryan, Leigh, and Lisa Zimmerelli. *The Bedford Guide for Writing Tutors.* Bedford/St. Martins, 2010.

Sasaki, Miyuki. "L2 Writers in Study-Abroad Contexts." *Handbook of Second and Foreign Language Writing,* edited by Rosa M. Manchon and Paul Kei Matsuda, Walter de Gruyter, 2016, pp. 161-80.

Savignon, Sandra J. "Communicative Competence." *The TESOL Encyclopedia of English Language Teaching,* edited by John I. Liontas, Wiley, 2018, pp. 1-7.

—. "Communicative Language Teaching." *Routledge Encyclopedia of Language Teaching and Learning,* edited by Michael Byram, Routledge, 2000, pp. 124-29.

—. "Communicative Language Teaching: Linguistic Theory and Classroom Practice." *Interpreting Communicative Language Teaching: Contexts and Concerns in Teacher Education,* edited by Sandra J. Savignon, Yale University Press, 2002, pp. 1-27.

Schmidt, Richard W. "The Role of Consciousness in Second Language Learning." *Applied Linguistics,* vol. 11, no. 2, pp. 129-58.

Schreiber, Brooke Ricker, and Missy Watson. "Translingualism [does not equal] Code-Meshing: A Response to Gevers' 'Translingualism Revisited.'" *Journal of Second Language Writing,* vol. 42, 2018, pp. 94-97.

Schultz, Jean Marie. "Foreign Language Writing in the Era of Globalization." *Foreign Language Writing Instruction,* edited by Tony Cimasko and Melinda Reichelt, Parlor, 2011, pp. 65-82.

Schuster, Mike, Melvin Johnson, and Nikhil Thorat. "Zero-Shot Translation with Google's Multilingual Neural Machine Translation System." *Google Research Blog,* 22 November 2016, research.googleblog.com/2016/11/zero-shot-translation-with-googles.html. 2016.

Scott, Virginia Mitchell. *Rethinking Foreign Language Writing.* Heinle and Heinle, 1996.

Severino, Carol. "The 'Doodles' in Context: Clarifying Claims about Contrastive Rhetoric." *The Writing Center Journal*, vol. 14, no.1, 1993, pp. 44-61.

—. "'Multilingualizing' Composition: A Diary Self-Study of Learning Spanish and Chinese." *Composition Studies*, vol. 45, no. 2, 2017, pp. 12-31.

—. "The Sociopolitical Implications of Response to Second Language and Second Dialect Writing." *Journal of Second Language Writing*, vol. 2, no. 3, 1993: 181-201.

—. "The Writing Center as Site for Cross-Language Research." *Writing Center Journal*, vol. 15, no. 1, 1994, pp. 51-61.

Severino, Carol, and Jane Cogie. "Writing Centers and Second and Foreign Language Writers." *Handbook on Second and Foreign Language Writing*, edited by Paul Kei Matsuda. Walter de Gruyter, 2016, pp. 453-472.

Shapiro, Shawna, et al. "Teaching for Agency: From Appreciating Linguistic Diversity to Empowering Student Writers." *Composition Studies*, vol. 44, no. 1, 2016, pp. 31-52.

Spack, Ruth. "The Acquisition of Academic Literacy in a Second Language: A Longitudinal Case Study, Updated." *Crossing the Curriculum: Multilingual Learners in College Classrooms*, edited by Vivian Zamel and Ruth Spack, Routledge, 2004, pp. 19-39.

"Strategic Plan III." *Dickinson College*, 14 Mar. 2017, http://www.dickinson.edu/info/20084/institutional_research/1901/student_experience

"Students' Right to Their Own Language." *Conference on College Composition and Communication*, http://www.ncte.org/library/NCTEFiles/Groups/CCCC/NewSRTOL.pdf

Swain, Merrill, and Sharon Lapkin. "Problems in Output and the Cognitive Processes They Generate: A Step Towards Second Language Learning." *Applied Linguistics*, no. 16, vol. 3, 1995, pp. 371-91.

Thaiss, Christopher. *International WAC/WID Mapping Project*. http://mappingproject.ucdavis.edu/homepage. Accessed 28 January 2017.

—, et al. editors. *Writing Programs Worldwide: Profiles of Academic Writing in Many Places*. Parlor and the WAC Clearinghouse, 2012.

"The Writing Center Directory." *The Writing Center at St. Cloud State University*, https://web.stcloudstate.edu/writeplace/wcd/index.html. Accessed 26 February 2020.

Thompson, Isabelle, and Jo Mackiewicz. "Questioning in the Writing Center." *Writing Center Journal*, vol. 33, no. 2, 2014, pp. 37-70.

Thorp, Holden, and Buck Goldstein. "How to Create a Problem-Solving Institution." *The Chronicle of Higher Education*, 29 Aug. 2010, http://www.chronicle.com/article/How-to-Create-a/124153/?sid=cr.

Tierney, William G. *The Impact of Culture on Organizational Decision Making*. Stylus, 2008.

Trimbur, John. "Translingualism and Close Reading." *College English*, vol. 78, no. 3, Jan. 2016, pp. 219-27.

"University of Helsinki Language Policy." *University of Helsinki*, www.ub.edu/slc/socio/Policy_Helsinki.pdf. Accessed 1 November 2016.

Van Patten, Bill, and William R. Glass. "Grammar Learning as a Source of Language Anxiety: A Discussion." *Affect in Foreign Language and Second Language Learning*, edited by Dolly Jesusita Young, McGraw Hill, 1998, pp. 89-105.

van Weijen, Daphne, et al. "L1 Use during L2 Writing: An Empirical Study of a Complex Phenomenon." *Journal of Second Language Writing*, vol. 18, 2009, pp. 235-50.

Webb, Nathan G., and Laura Obrycki Barrett. "Student View of Instructor-Student Rapport in the Classroom." *Journal of the Scholarship of Teaching and Learning*, vol. 14, no. 2, 2014, pp. 15-28.

Wenger, Etienne, Richard McDermott, and William M. Snyder. *Cultivating Communities of Practice*. Harvard Business School, 2002.

White, Kelsey D., and Emily Heidrich. "Our Policies, Their Text: German Language Students' Strategies with and Beliefs about Web-Based Machine Translation." *Die Unterrichtspraxis*, vol. 46, no. 2, 2013, pp. 230-50.

Wildavsky, Ben. *The Great Brain Race: How Global Universities are Reshaping the World*. Princeton University Press, 2012.

Williams, Jessica. "Undergraduate Second Language Writers in the Writing Center." *Journal of Basic Writing*, vol. 21, 2002, pp. 73-91.

Williams, Tracy Rundstrom. "Examining Your LENS: A Tool for Interpreting Cultural Differences." *Frontiers: The Interdisciplinary Journal of Study Abroad*, 2009, pp. 289-306.

Woodall, Billy R. "Language-Switching: Using the First Language while Writing in a Second Language." *Journal of Second Language Writing*, vol. 11, 2002, pp. 7-28.

World Readiness Standards for Learning Languages. ACTFL, https://www.actfl.org/sites/default/files/publications/standards/World-ReadinessStandardsforLearningLanguages.pdf. Accessed 19 July 2018.

Writing Across Borders. Directed by Wayne Robertson. Oregon State University Center for Writing and Learning and Writing Intensive Curriculum Program, 2005.

"Writing Center Directory." *International Writing Centers Association*, web.stcloudstate.edu/writeplace/wcd/index.html. Accessed 26 October 2016.

"Writing Center for Academic English." *Leuphana University*, www.leuphana.de/zemos/writing- center.html. Accessed 26 October 2016.

Wu, Yonghui, et al. "Google's Neural Machine Translation System: Bridging the Gap between Human and Machine Translation." *Cornell University Library*, 8 Oct. 2016, arxiv.org/abs/1609.08144.

Yastibas, Gulsah Cinar, and Ahmet Erdost Yastibas. "The Effect of Peer Feedback on Writing Anxiety in Turkish EFL." *Procedia-Social and Behavioral Sciences,* vol. 199, 2015, pp. 530-38.

Young, Dolly Jesusita. "Creating a Low-Anxiety Classroom Environment: What Does Language Anxiety Research Suggest?" *Modern Language Journal*, vol. 75, no. 4, 1991, pp. 426-37.

Zamel, Vivian. "Responding to Student Writing." *TESOL Quarterly,* vol. 19, 1985, pp. 79-97.

About the Author

Noreen Groover Lape is Associate Provost of Academic Affairs and Director of the Writing Program/Norman M. Eberly Multilingual Writing Center at Dickinson College in Carlisle, Pennsylvania. Her work in the field of writing studies has appeared in journals such as *Writing Lab Newsletter, Composition Forum, WAC Journal*, and *Praxis: A Writing Center Journal*. "Going Global, Becoming Translingual: The Development of a Multilingual Writing Center," which first appeared in the *Writing Lab Newsletter*, was chosen for inclusion in *The Best of the Independent Rhetoric & Composition Journals 2014*. The Dickinson College Writing Program has won the Martinson Award of Excellence in Writing Program Administration (2016) from the Small Liberal Arts College-Writing Program Administrators consortium as well as the Writing Program Certificate of Excellence (2018) from the Conference on College Composition and Communication.

Photograph of the author by Carl Sander Socolow. Used by permission.

Index

academic culture, 28, 80 82, 86, 97, 121, 141
academic journals, 3
academic voice, 56, 81, 97, 104, 139, 141–142
academic writing, 10, 14, 18, 21, 44, 49, 51, 78, 82, 95–97, 118, 128, 137, 139, 141, 167
access, 16, 20, 23, 45, 73, 104, 183
acculturation, 83–84, 89–91
administration, 103, 106
administrators, x, 4, 11, 16, 29, 85, 100–101, 103, 107, 109, 124, 127, 143
Affective Filter Hypothesis, 71
African (region), 81, 172, 174, 176, 180, 183
African American, 44
algorithms, 48–50, 54, 56
algorithms, phrase-based, 48–50
Ambrose, Susan A., 61, 132–133
American Council for the Teaching of Foreign Languages (ACTFL), 127–129, 133, 136–138, 142, 144–145
anglicisms, 45–46
anxiety, 7, 11, 24, 54, 60, 62–67, 73, 75
appointments, 8, 42, 71, 111, 119, 122
Arabic language, vii, 16, 69–72, 105, 112, 114, 125, 128, 139, 141–142, 157, 187, 189
Argentina, 16, 25, 30, 159

argument, xii, 10, 32, 39, 42, 44, 46, 84, 89–90, 95, 101, 109, 111, 136, 142–143
assessment, 11, 83, 87, 108, 110–111, 124, 138
assignments, 8, 25, 42–43, 47, 54, 57, 63, 78–81, 85–88, 92–93, 95, 115–116, 123, 126, 131, 132, 134–137, 139, 143–144, 147–148, 151, 167, 169, 171, 173
assimilationist approaches, 90–91
Atkinson, Dwight, 80
audience, xii, 27–28, 45, 50, 52–53, 58, 96, 98–99, 111, 135–136, 140, 150, 167, 188
Audiolingual Methodology, 125–126

Bartholomae, David, 29, 46, 55
Bazerman, Charles, 18–19
Bean, Janet 57–58
bilingual, ix, x, 23, 28, 49, 105, 165, 189
Blau, Susan, 34
Bologna Declaration, 83–84, 122, 138, 189
Boquet, Elizabeth, 5, 103
Brauer, Gerd, 84–85
Bromley, Pam, vii–viii
Brooks-Carson, Amanda, 46, 57

Canada, 16, 187–188

209

Canagarajah, A. Suresh, 18, 21, 28, 32, 128
Caribbean culture, 172, 176–179, 181
Carino, Peter, 108–109
Carlino, Paula, 19, 83
Chile, 20, 187–188
China, 16, 23, 87, 187–188
Chinese language, vii, 16, 48, 50, 58, 87–89, 93, 98, 105, 112, 114, 158, 187–189, 191
Cimasko, Tony, 4
Clark, Irene L., 127
classrooms, 12, 23–26, 36, 42, 65, 66, 69, 85–86, 88, 90, 95, 101, 119, 120, 127, 129, 137, 144, 190
code-meshing, 27, 29
Cogie, Jane, 9, 34–35
cognition, 39, 42, 57, 82
Cohen, Andrew D., 46, 57
collaborate, 101, 112, 122, 124
collaboration, x, 30, 66, 99, 102–103, 104, 107, 111, 112, 114, 115, 120, 123, 144, 187
collaborative projects, x, 85, 101, 103, 112, 122–125, 144
Communicative Language Teaching (CLT), 126–129, 131, 136–137, 142, 145
community, 4, 6, 10, 12, 15, 18, 21, 23, 33, 50, 52, 54, 98–99, 102, 107–108, 112, 120–122, 124–125, 130, 142, 166
competence, x, 8, 10, 23, 77–79, 91–92, 96–99, 126–127, 133–134, 142, 166
composition, 36–37, 55, 58, 81, 87, 126–128, 144
comprehensibility, 9, 51
computers, 47–48, 113, 182
confidence, 24–25, 61–62, 66, 72–73, 94–95, 184
Connor, Ulla, 89

contrastive rhetoric, 80
conventions, 8, 27, 37, 78–80, 86, 89–93, 96–99, 127, 135, 137–138, 167, 175
conversation, viii, 3, 12, 18, 23, 30–31, 35–36, 38, 41, 63, 79–80, 93–94, 97, 111, 148, 175, 180
courses, xi–xii, 12, 16, 20, 23, 25, 43, 44, 54, 58, 77, 80–82, 84–85, 93, 95, 100, 104–105, 109–111, 118–121, 123, 127–129, 135, 138, 143, 153, 166, 169, 191
Creole languages, 171–172, 174, 181, 183
cross-culturalism, 87, 92, 97
cross-disciplinarity, x, 107
culture, x, 6, 8–12, 14, 22–24, 28, 30–31, 32–33, 44–45–49, 50, 53, 64, 77–83, 85, 86–100, 102–107, 111–113, 118, 123–125, 127–128, 133–139, 142, 144, 167, 171–180
culture shock, 17, 87, 90, 95, 101, 107
curriculum, 4, 15, 101, 104, 122, 129, 136, 137, 145
customs, 49, 50

de Montlaur, Benedicte, 123
departments, 104, 107, 120–122, 136, 186
dialects, 21, 32
Dickinson College, x–xii, 15–16, 37, 40, 54, 58, 100, 105–106, 108, 109, 122, 134, 142, 190–191
dictionaries, 43–46, 48, 55, 70–71, 151, 154
directive tutoring, 9, 52, 118, 138–139, 148, 150–151
disciplines, 19, 21, 80, 85, 122

discourse, 13–14, 21, 33, 52, 80, 90–91, 98, 121, 124, 139
discourse community, 21, 52, 124
discussion, 7, 9–11, 39, 43, 46, 84, 92–93, 96, 118, 122, 129, 171, 175
diversity, 6, 24, 26, 29–33, 90, 96
dominant culture, 14, 16–18, 24, 28, 32, 78
Donahue, Christiane, 81, 95–96
drafts (working with), 7, 35, 38, 41–42, 45–46, 59, 71, 73, 75, 115, 119, 134, 151, 153, 168, 169, 171, 174
Dryer, Dylan B., 27–29
dysfunction, 64–65
Dysthe, Olga, 83

editing, 6–7, 37, 38, 42–43, 50–53, 120, 189
education, x, 12, 15–16, 19–20, 22–23, 32–33, 65, 80, 83–84, 90–91, 101, 105, 107, 114, 122–123, 138
emotions, 88, 182
empathy, 10, 67, 68, 75
Enders, Doug, 108–109
engagement, 19, 24, 42, 69, 72, 121, 144
English as a Foreign Language (EFL), 4, 36, 66, 99
English as a Second Language (ESL), 4, 34
English-centric writing centers, x, 4, 6, 11, 14–21, 27, 33–34, 38, 101, 111
English-only writing centers, 17, 20, 188
enrollment, 15, 23, 110, 113
error, ix, 6, 26, 29, 31, 35, 40, 49, 53–56, 63, 65, 67–69, 71, 75–76, 112, 119–120, 126, 139, 149–150, 152, 168–169

essays, 10, 19, 27, 35, 47, 57–59, 79, 87–88, 94, 97, 104, 112, 119, 120, 143, 151, 154, 167
ethnocentrism, 79, 91, 98–99
ethnography, 11, 102–107, 111, 121, 190
ethos, x, 27, 73, 95, 103, 139, 141–142
evaluation, 6, 81, 85–86, 107, 190–191
exercises, 6, 8–10, 35, 38, 68, 92–93, 127, 147, 156, 165, 167, 191

faculty, viii, ix–x, 3, 5, 11–13, 30, 83–85, 100–105, 107, 111–112, 114–115, 118–121, 124–125, 137–138, 142, 144, 186
faculty development, 12, 85, 142
feedback, 25, 63, 83, 128, 139, 144
first language (L1), 7, 21, 24, 34–38, 40, 45–47, 49, 54, 56–58, 59, 64, 125, 130, 166
five-paragraph essay, 87, 89, 95
flexibility, 35, 37, 45, 58, 136, 143, 156
fluency, 23, 41, 57, 58, 64, 66, 68, 76, 104–105, 112, 172
foreign language anxiety, 75
Foster, David, 82, 97
France, 16, 18, 23, 28, 81, 83–84, 93, 96–97, 121, 156, 158, 166, 171, 187
Friedlander, Alexander, 57–58
Frisby, Branci N., 65, 66

genres, 8, 27, 32, 37, 77, 79–82, 84, 87, 95–99, 104, 112, 116, 118, 131, 134–138, 142, 190
geopolitics, 18, 21, 128
German language, vii, viii, 16, 20, 25, 46–47, 52, 61, 84–85, 87, 96–98, 105, 112, 114, 116, 121,

125, 129, 133, 138–139, 141, 159, 187–188
Germany, 16, 23, 77, 84, 87, 139, 187, 188
Gevers, Jeroen, 26–27, 29
Gillespie, Paula, 12, 34
Gkonou, Christina, 64, 67
Gladstein, Jill, 187
globalization, xii, 3, 6, 14–16, 18, 21–22, 27, 85
goals, viii, x, 8, 12, 16, 23–24, 26–28, 33, 39, 45, 47, 52, 57, 65, 69, 75, 90–91, 102, 106–108, 112, 114, 130–131, 133–134, 136, 140, 144, 147, 150, 172, 184
Goldberg, David, 23
Goldstein, Buck, 101–102
Google Translate, 10, 47–56, 156, 185
government, 6, 20, 22, 81, 166
grammar, vii, 6, 12, 25, 30, 34–38, 40, 42, 50, 54–56, 61, 67–71, 115–116, 126–128, 130–132, 136, 141, 143–145, 149–151, 154, 156, 168–169, 189
Groves, Michael, 49, 50
Guerra, Juan C., 28–29, 162, 164
guides, 34, 62, 99, 104
Gunner, Jeanne, 103

habits, 40, 59, 103, 126
Haiti, 177, 179
Hall, John, 34
handwriting, 119, 141–142
Hanyang University, 20, 188
Harbord, John, 33, 190
Hebrew, vii, 16, 72–73, 105, 112–114, 160, 189
hedging, 141, 167
hegemony, 15, 21, 24, 32, 180
Heidrich, Emily, 47, 52
heritage speaker, xii, 13, 35, 60, 78, 145, 198, 200

Hess, J. Daniel, 78, 92
heuristics, 10, 37, 91–92, 104, 190
higher-order concerns (HOCs), vii–viii, 7, 34–35, 115–117, 188
holistic tutoring, 6–9, 11, 37–38, 40, 42–43, 45, 47, 51, 53, 59–61, 123, 144–145, 153, 168, 176, 190–191
Horwitz, Elaine K., 63, 64, 65
hybridity, 6, 28
hypothesis testing, 7, 9, 38, 40–41, 59, 149, 152

identities, 27, 80
idioms, 46, 55, 116
immersion, 23, 36, 58, 62, 91, 97, 99, 122, 123, 165
inclusion, 20, 22, 32, 38
Input Hypothesis, 48
institutions, x, 11–12, 14, 16, 18–19, 22–24, 32, 80, 83–85, 87, 100–109, 111–112, 120, 122–123, 129, 138, 177
instruction, 10, 12, 25, 36, 66, 77, 80, 84–85, 92, 121, 125–129, 137–139, 141–142
instructors, 25–26, 36–40, 42, 47, 51–53, 57, 64–68, 73, 75, 77, 83, 85–86, 88, 90–91, 98, 101, 115, 119, 125, 126–130, 132–139, 142–145, 152, 166–167
intercultural competence, ix–x, 8, 22–23, 77, 79–80, 91–92, 96–99, 134–135, 137, 142, 145, 167
interdisciplinarity, 16, 19, 123
International WAC/WID Mapping Project, 19
International Writing Center Association (IWCA), 16, 20–21, 32, 187
internationalization, 22, 123
interpersonal communication, 66, 127, 134–136, 138, 145

interviews, 5, 8, 12, 40, 68, 79, 103, 125, 127, 137, 189–190
Italian language, vii–viii, 16, 25, 59, 83–84, 88–89, 95, 105, 112, 114, 116, 121–122, 125, 128–129, 131–132, 140–141, 161, 187, 189
Italy, 16, 23, 83, 84, 88–89, 138, 187

Japan, 16, 23, 90, 99, 137–138, 142, 187–188
Japanese language, vii, 16, 49, 77, 80, 90–91, 105, 112, 114, 125, 128–129, 134–138, 140,–142, 162
journals, 20, 21, 85

Kaplan, Robert, 79–80
Kirkpatrick, Andy, 18, 28
Kobayashi, Hiroe, 57–58
Korea, 16, 20, 188
Korean language, vii, 20, 49, 51–53, 190
Kramsch, Claire, 24
Krashen, Stephen, 39, 62, 75
Kruse, Otto, 84
Kyungbook National University, 20, 188

language acquisition, viii, ix–x, 4, 7, 9, 34, 36–40, 42–43, 45, 56, 62, 66, 76, 89, 117–118, 125, 128, 133, 143, 191
language-learning, 28, 71, 90–91
Lape, Noreen, 51, 63
Latin, 44, 77, 83, 126
learning environment, xi, 5,–7, 20, 23–24, 53, 60–69, 71, 73–76, 95, 99, 119, 147, 150, 165, 172
learning-to-write, 26, 38, 43, 77, 130, 132
Leki, Ilona, 38, 65–66

Lerner, Neal, 12, 34, 107–109, 111, 191
Leuphana University, 20, 187
lingua franca, 6, 18, 20–22, 24–25, 28
linguistics, 5–6, 15, 22–24, 26–29, 31–33, 36, 37, 44, 48, 56, 62, 64, 71, 73, 89–91, 106, 118, 126, 128, 165
listening, 5, 12, 22, 126–129, 136
literacy, 14, 23–24, 32–33, 37, 76, 101, 106, 124, 130
literary analysis essays, 44, 87, 95, 136–137, 140
literature, viii, 3, 5, 77, 94, 96–97, 116, 128–129, 190
lower-order concerns (LOC), 7, 34–35, 41, 115–117, 188
Lunsford, Andrea, 111, 122, 126
Lusin, Natalia, 22

Macauley, William, 103–104, 106
Mackiewicz, Jo, 66–67, 75, 115
Manchon, Rosa M., 4, 25–26, 37–39, 42, 152
manuscripts, xii
marginalized students, 21, 32, 102, 111
Matsuda, Paul Kei, xii, 4, 27–29, 78, 80
meaning-making, 57, 68, 89, 127
memory, 57, 62
mentoring, 186
metacognitive reflection, 10, 41, 42
metalinguistic awareness, 7, 9, 38, 40, 41, 42, 59
Modern Language Association (MLA), 22, 23, 139
monolingualism, ix, 4, 6, 14–15, 21–22, 24, 26–27–29, 32–33, 81
motivation, 36, 61–62, 66, 68–69, 71–73, 99

multilingual neural machine translation (MNMT), 48–50, 53
multilingualism, vii, ix, xi, 3–5, 8, 10, 14–15, 17, 22,–29, 32–33, 48, 52–53, 105, 107, 123
Mundt, Klaus, 49, 50

National Census of Writing, 3, 108, 187
native English speakers, 22, 189
Naydan, Liliana M., 14–15, 21
negotiated interaction, 16, 19, 47, 51–52, 54–55, 68, 164
networking, 48, 54
neural networks, 48
nondirective tutoring, 9, 118, 148, 150–151, 168
nonnative English speaker, 4–5, 16, 18, 24, 28, 31, 189
nonnative speakers, 4–5, 16, 18, 24, 28, 31, 189
Norman M. Eberly Multilingual Writing Center, vii, 25
North, Stephen, 101
noticing, 16, 18, 47, 49–51, 55, 68, 158, 161
Noticing Hypothesis, 48

O'Donnell, Mary E., 25
oppression, 178–179
oral communication, ix, 64, 83–84, 86, 88, 95, 126, 128–131, 133, 134, 137–138, 145
Ortega, Lourdes, 25–26, 37
Output Hypothesis, 39

pedagogy, x, 3, 5–6, 8, 10, 12, 14–15, 24–27, 29, 30–31, 35–37, 42, 57–59, 62, 82–84, 86, 90–92, 99, 103–104, 114, 120, 125–128, 137, 142–144
performance, 9, 48, 57, 64, 85, 127, 129, 134
Peru, 85

placement test, 118
plagiarism, 138
Portuguese language, vii, 16, 74, 105, 112–114, 162
power structures, 5, 10, 13, 31, 33, 97, 102–103, 172, 177
prewriting, 46, 57, 188
problem-based learning, 11, 171
problem-solving strategies, 11, 39, 42–43
proficiency, x, 22, 33, 57, 82, 127, 130, 136, 142, 165
pronunciation, 130–132
proofreading, 6, 67, 74, 171

Qatar, 19, 20, 188
qualitative methods, 11, 103, 105, 107–108, 111, 124
quantitative methods, 11, 105, 107–109, 111, 124

Rafoth, Ben, xii, 4–5, 14–15, 35, 43, 45
rapport-building, 66, 67, 71
reading, ix, 11–12, 29, 34, 40, 46, 54, 59, 83, 86, 90, 93, 94, 97, 126–129, 136, 140–141, 151, 153, 169, 171–173, 176–177, 180–181, 183
Reichelt, Melinda, 4, 23, 25–26, 36–37, 57, 87, 88, 130
religion, 9, 49–50, 171–172, 174–175, 179, 181–183
retention, 65, 108–109
revision, xii, 9, 11, 25, 35, 37, 51–53, 89, 96, 99, 104–105, 131, 143–144, 149, 167, 184, 191
rhetoric, 8, 18, 62, 77, 79–80, 95, 97, 104, 135, 142, 167, 175
rhetoric and composition, 18
rhetorics, 3, 32–33, 99
Rinnert, Carol, 57–58
Ritter, Kelly, 42

Rubio-Alcala, Fernando D., 62–64
rubrics, 86, 116, 144
Russell, David, 82
Russia, 16, 129, 137
Russian language, vii, 16, 77, 79, 98, 105, 112, 114, 116, 125, 129, 131–132, 135–136, 138, 140–142, 163, 189

Savignon, Sandra J., 126–127
scaffolding, 66–67, 75, 143
scenarios, 68–69, 74, 93, 107, 151, 166
Schultz, Jean Marie, 21, 32
Schuster, MIke, 48–49
science, 10, 53, 90, 166
scripts, ix, 8, 134, 137
second language (L2), vii, x, 3–4, 7, 9–10, 24, 25, 27–29, 34–39, 42, 43, 45, 49, 54, 56–58, 61, 64–68, 71, 73, 80, 88, 90, 92–93, 98, 99, 104–106, 119, 128–130, 136, 143, 165, 189, 191
second language acquisition, viii, x, 3–4, 7, 9–10, 24–25, 27, 29, 34, 36–39, 45, 56, 61, 66, 68, 71, 88, 90, 93, 105–106, 128–130, 143, 152, 165, 189, 191
self-confidence, 62
self-perceptions, 63–64
sentence-level concerns, 6, 11, 35, 38, 41, 45, 51, 53, 115, 117–120, 188, 191
Severino, Carol, xii, 9, 27, 28, 34–35, 68, 90, 92
silo mentality, 100–105, 107, 111, 120–124
skills, xi, 7, 22–24, 36–38, 40, 56, 62, 72–73, 78, 82, 84, 99, 101, 106, 111–112, 117–118, 124, 126–130, 132, 133–137, 145, 191
Spain, 16, 23, 137–138

Spanish language, vii, ix, 16, 25–26, 30, 40–41, 44, 46, 49–50, 55, 59, 69, 83, 85, 93, 105, 112–114, 121–122, 125, 128, 136, 140, 164, 187, 189
speaking skills, 12, 19, 21–22, 28, 44, 69, 71, 79, 90, 106, 123, 127–133, 136–137, 144
spelling, 115, 131, 132, 188
stakeholders, 11, 102, 105, 107, 109, 114
standards, 10, 21, 31, 64, 89, 133–134, 137, 139, 142, 145
student-centered practices, 11, 15, 171
study abroad, 15–16, 19–20, 23, 78, 86–88, 92, 106, 121–123, 137, 148
Switzerland, viii, 48, 187

teaching, 12, 18–19, 21, 25, 27, 51–53, 65–66, 68, 84, 119, 128–130, 143–144
Test of English as a Foreign Language (TOEFL), 27
testing, 7, 9, 38, 40–41, 59, 149, 152
Thaiss, Chris, 19
thesis-driven arguments, 90, 139, 169
Thorp, Holden, 101–102
Tierney, William G., 102–104, 106
traditions, 87–88, 137, 138, 141
training, viii–xii, 3, 6, 7–9, 16, 25, 30–31, 34–35, 45, 52, 62, 68–69, 78, 81, 83, 93, 99–100, 105, 114–115, 117–119, 125, 128–129, 134, 143–144, 150
transfer, 39, 83, 123
translation, xii, 7, 10, 36, 38, 43–59, 72, 98, 103, 106, 108, 112, 116, 118, 126, 154, 155, 169

translingualism, ix, 6, 15, 26–32, 73
translingualist, 6, 27, 29
Trimbur, John, 6, 26–29
trust, 66, 72, 73, 120
tutor-training, 34, 62, 66, 117, 191

Universidad de Magallanes, 20, 187
usage, 27, 29, 38, 40, 45, 51, 53, 105, 108–109, 116, 124, 150, 188

value-added appeals, 11, 105–107, 109, 111
values, x, 15, 30–31, 36, 49–50, 92, 103, 106–107, 112, 115, 123–124, 142
Van Patten, Bill, 39, 64, 66, 68, 126–127
vocabulary, 25, 36–37, 44, 51, 57, 61, 64, 73, 130

WCENTER (mailing list), vii–viii
WCONLINE (software), 8, 108, 147
Wildavsky, Ben, 18, 19, 20
Williams, Jessica, 42

World Readiness Standards for Learning Languages, 77, 133
writing across the curriculum (WAC), 19
writing anxiety, 20, 69, 72, 74–75
writing center administrators, vii–x, 3–6, 9, 11–13, 31–32, 75, 89, 100–106, 108–109, 111–112, 114, 115, 119, 122–127, 130, 134–135, 142, 144–145, 190
writing centers, vii–viii, x, 3–6, 8, 12–21, 23, 27, 30, 32–34, 37, 51, 52, 84–85, 101–103, 109, 111, 121–124, 126–127, 134, 187; English-centric, x, 4, 6, 11, 14–21, 27, 33–34, 38, 101–111; English-only, 17, 20, 188
writing culture shock, 17, 87, 90, 91, 94–95, 99–100, 102–108, 176
writing prompts, 10, 12, 40, 86–87, 92, 99, 122, 129, 131–132, 151–152, 169, 173
writing studies, viii, x, 3, 6, 18, 38, 51, 66, 82, 128

Young, Dolly, 63–67

Zamel, Vivian, 34

www.ingramcontent.com/pod-product-compliance
Lightning Source LLC
Chambersburg PA
CBHW032213230426
43672CB00011B/2547